HOSTAGE TO MYSELF

DISCOVER HOW TO RESCUE YOURSELF FROM THE SELF-SABOTAGING BEHAVIOR THAT IS PREVENTING YOU FROM LIVING THE LIFE YOU DESERVE

J. PAUL NADEAU

Published by:

J. Paul Nadeau

Toronto, Canada

The information contained in this book is based upon the research and personal and professional experiences of the author. It is not intended as a substitute for consulting with a healthcare provider. Any attempt to diagnose and treat an illness should be done under the direction of a healthcare professional.

The author does not advocate the use of any particular protocol but believes the information in this book should be available to the public. The author is not responsible for any adverse effects or consequences resulting from the use of the suggestions discussed in this book. Should the reader have any questions concerning the appropriateness of any procedures mentioned, the author strongly suggests consulting a professional healthcare advisor.

Cover photo: Che Rosales
Bio photo: Jodi Thibodeau
Interior production: Gary A. Rosenberg • www.thebookcouple.com
Cover design: Brenda Adams and Joshua Jadon

Printed in the United States of America

10   9   8   7   6   5   4   3   2   1

To my wonderful daughters, Aimée and Cassie,
who have enriched my life in ways
I could never have imagined.

Contents

Acknowledgments

A very special thank-you to my brother and friend, Robaire Nadeau, whose constant encouragement and support reminded me of the importance of my mission and my vision. His wisdom and guidance always steered me in the right directions. Thank-you from the bottom of my heart Robaire; you are my rock.

To Sejal Barai, who encouraged me in my journey and provided much-appreciated support: an ear when I needed one, and words of wisdom which live in the pages of this book. You walk the walk and talk the talk.

To Farah Bhanji, whose personality and character are always refreshing reminders that in all things we must remain truly humble. Your thoughts, for which I am grateful, appear more than once in the pages of this book.

To Pat Sayer, who kept me thinking with his insight and many wise views.

To Heather Sessions and Mireille Awad-Arnberg, who supported me, encouraged me, and believed in me when I found myself in the eye of the storm.

To John Green, playwright and author, for his guidance and help.

To David Gilbert[1] for his contribution on Emotional Freedom Techniques (Appendix B)

To Carol Reyes, who reminded me of the importance of persistence —of knocking twice or even three times before a door is answered.

And a very special thank-you to everyone I've met and dealt with in my rich career whose stories inspired me and whose attitudes and actions helped put my guideposts to paper. It's because of you that this book has been written. Thank you and may God continue to bless you on your personal journeys. To everyone who encouraged me to write this book, I thank you. It's done. I'm proud to share it with you.

---

1. Appendix B: EFT—Emotional Freedom Techniques Practitioner

Preface

It's been said that it's not so much what happens to us that matters; it's how we respond to what happens that does.[2] In my years as a trained Investigator, Hostage Negotiator and International Peace Keeper, I was privileged to meet and observe people from all walks of life, each with unique stories, attitudes and experiences. I watched how an almost identical set of circumstances frequently affected individuals very differently, based upon—but not limited to, their backgrounds, their ability to process thoughts, and the value which they would attach to an event. I've witnessed very different responses from hostage victims who had experienced similar events; and I have marvelled at the choices they made because of those events.

While we are each endowed with a fundamental ability to choose our responses to whatever injustices, hardships and dilemmas come our way, factors such as fear can *and often do* eat at our confidence blocking our road to choice. The resulting indecision, if allowed to rule and dominate can quickly become a sad pattern perpetuating itself unconsciously—which in turn can easily become a syndrome. You won't even see it coming. This is the essence of being taken hostage by your *self*, whether external forces are the instigator or whether the cause lies entirely within your own personal perception. And this is the pivotal moment when choosing must occur— that is, the choice of reacting to continue the "powerless-seeming" state in which you find yourself, or to direct yourself to apply the

---

2. Epictetus, Greek Stoic philosopher, A.D. c. 55–135

un-hostaging principles set out in this book—to follow the guideposts I offer you and to exit the misery of hostage. Bear in mind that each adversity which takes you hostage can either defeat you or strengthen you, depending upon what you choose to do with it. Also bear in mind that choice—choosing—is an action. Action requires muscle. And change does not happen simply because we want it to. We must consciously exercise our minds to make it happen. We must choose the positive over the negative. The guideposts I have set out in this book will be there to lead you as you embrace this process of choosing and of change.

And in the process of guiding you out of a state of hostage, this book will challenge you to become more conscious of your thoughts with increasing regularity, of the emotions they are evoking *as* they enter your conscious mind, and of the technique of interrupting those thoughts and emotions which cause pain or simply do not serve you or your overall goals, be they personal or professional or both. To this end, each chapter begins with a story that introduces a principle. May you enjoy the stories and learn from the principles. That's what I'm after for you.

My Journey to Manhood

L̲ike many others, I was raised in an environment that required me to depend on myself at a very young age. My father was a violent alcoholic who often took out his rage on my mother, siblings and I. For as far back as I can remember, I felt defenseless to protect my family and myself from my father; and at the age of about seven, I decided that when I grew up I'd become a policeman so I could arrest men like my father. He never gave me the chance to arrest him however. He killed himself before I would ever join the police.

Without my father as a role model, I had to learn about growing into a man by examining and modeling the behavior of others. As is often the case with abused children (and before I eventually found my way into manhood), I frequently misbehaved in school and was appropriately labeled a trouble-maker. My delinquent classroom conduct assured me several regular strappings. My grades were so poor that I developed the belief that I couldn't retain a thing and that I wouldn't amount to anything either. That misguided way of thinking was reinforced in me by the very people who should have been building me up: my teachers.

I came to believe the bad boy image others had labeled me with and suffered the sting of many wooden rulers on the palms of my hands for my disruptive delinquent behavior. A consistent failure, I somehow managed to graduate from one grade to another. I suspect that I passed simply because my teachers didn't want me in their classes the following year. I often felt humiliated and inferior to my classmates and they came to know me as a disruptive, rebellious, troublemaking bad boy.

Remarkably, in grade 7, things took an unexpected and wonderful turn. One of my teachers, Mr. Coggins, was preparing our class for a test. In his "Let's go team!" speech to the classroom, he told everyone he expected them to pass—except for me. He singled me out by saying: *"I know everyone is going to pass this test—except for you, Nadeau. I already know you're going to fail."*

That was the pinch I needed to turn things around. I felt an overwhelming sense of shame and embarrassment; and for the first time I studied my heart out. I was motivated to prove Mr. Coggins wrong. The next day I wrote the test; and as was customary in his class, once the tests had been graded, he distributed the papers by first calling the person with the lowest grade to the front of the classroom, followed by the second lowest and so forth. I had always been the first to stand and collect my paper. I had become conditioned to believe that I was a failure and behaved accordingly. But on that day he didn't call my name first. Name after name, my classmates were summoned to the front of the classroom to collect their papers. I was the second last to be called. For me, that was a defining moment. For the first time ever, I discovered that I could do so much more than I had come to believe I could; and although my original motivation to succeed was misdirected, that was the day I began to believe in myself. My former thoughts and beliefs about my abilities and limitations had been expectantly captured, and I was no longer a hostage to them—**or to myself**. From that moment on, I applied myself and my life unfolded in ways I had once believed impossible. My quality of life changed drastically and wonderfully because I now attracted success by simply improving my thoughts, attitudes and actions. That new confidence led to an unbeatable attitude, and that attitude resulted in success with whatever challenges I chose to undertake.

I managed to "un-hostage" myself from the negative thoughts and beliefs that had once held me captive, and I eventually joined the police as I had promised myself years earlier. As an officer, I became a subject matter expert in many specialized areas of police work including the Sexual Assault and Child Abuse Unit, Hostage Negotiations, International Peacekeeping, Anti-Terrorism and Criminal Investigations. Each of those positions provided me with hundreds of opportunities to learn from experts how to help those who felt hopeless and in need. My work required me to study psychology and develop an understanding of human behavior necessary to recognize how people thought and behaved—both victims and perpetrators. I interacted and worked closely with dozens of highly skilled specialists from all walks of life including behavioral scientists, psychologists, criminologists and university professors. I developed the necessary acute listening and communication skills needed to deal with every situation and individual I encountered, and eventually I became more than a "protector" as I had first set out to become. Along the way I picked up valuable skills and discovered I could help broken, discouraged and damaged people.

The lives I helped along the way were a testament to my childhood dream to serve and protect others. And in the process I discovered that I too could crack and feel broken; but I also discovered how to repair *my* broken pieces. Human beings are not that different from one another after all. Perhaps we are far more alike than we are different. And it has been my experience that the key to healing lies in *our* ability to establish and nourish that interconnectedness.

In conclusion, it is my conviction that what I've discovered on my ongoing journey will be of help to you too.

Introduction

I. Rationale: Why a book on Hostaging?

Why a book on "hostaging" you might ask. With all the self-help books available on motivation and self-confidence out there, what makes this book different? The response to this lies not only in the "What," but in the "Who," and in the "How," as you will discover as you wind your way through the chapters.

The "What" That we all, as human beings, feel "hostaged" to the pressures of a world in dynamic change and need help and support in varying degrees to navigate this increasingly and often over-whelmingly complex contemporary world is a fact with which we are all too familiar, often leaving us with the feeling of a need for rescue. Support in this book comes from a series of guideposts that grew out of all the experience I lived during my career, and the stories I encountered of hostages who found their way to freedom.

The "Who" That we all—*all*—can find, in this book, with its guideposts, a beacon of light in the darkness of a world which, for all our best efforts, all-too-often scares us with its uncertain future (which one might say is the main hostage-taker of the moment). Accompanied by a host of hostage-taking fear factors from the cultural phenomenon of breakdowns in personal relationships to job insecurity to terrorism to global warming to those little voices in our heads that tell us we're not good enough, to name but a few—all of this can leave us feeling powerless against seeming absolute power.

The "How" That we all—not only **_can,_** but **_must,_** develop a capacity to *un-hostage* ourselves, given that we must navigate, loosely speaking, a hostage culture, a de facto consequence of the times in which we live—the speed of which does not allow us the luxury of infinite time to find solutions to our discomforts. An underlying sense of alienation and panic has become, not the unusual, but the norm, whether we are conscious of its effects or not.

And so, to answer the question "Why a book on 'becoming hostage'?" Because this book dares to forge ahead with hope in the form of the guideposts, tried and true, which can equip you with a personal sense of empowerment, whether your hostage challenge comes from outside yourself or within yourself—where you become your worst enemy; for hostage is hostage, whatever the cause of its existence, and must be met, not with fear, but with confidence:

> *"Hostage is a crucifying aloneness. It is a silent, screaming*
> *slide into the bowels of ultimate despair. Hostage is a man*
> *hanging by his fingernails over the edge of chaos, feeling*
> *his fingers slowly straightening. Hostage is the humiliating*
> *stripping away of every sense of fibre of body and mind*
> *and spirit that makes us what we are. Hostage is a mutant*
> *creation filled with fear, self-loathing, guilt and death wishing.*
> *But he is a man, a rare, unique and beautiful creation*
> *of which these things are no part."*
> —BRIAN KEENAN[3]

---

3. Brian Keenan is an Irish writer whose work includes the book *An Evil Cradling,* an account of the four-and-a-half years he spent as a hostage in Beirut, Lebanon (April 11, 1986 to August 24, 1990).

II. Why Me?

I hadn't planned to write this book. It was written after sharing a number of my law enforcement and International Peacekeeping stories with a myriad of people, many of whom enjoyed and appreciated hearing the discoveries I had made in helping victims and suspects alike over the years and suggested I put what I had experienced to paper. Upon much reflection, I found myself compelled to share, in this book, what I had discovered, so that it could bring hope and help to those who read it—to you, the reader.

My professional life as a Detective, Hostage Negotiator and International Peacekeeper has been dedicated to the service of others, and has allowed me to develop a keen understanding of what protects people from living without borders once adversity strikes. This, in turn, has given me rare and first-hand insight into human behavior— into how people may and do respond quite differently from one another when adversity strikes. I've seen a broad spectrum of reaction—from those who choose to respond negatively to those who choose to respond positively, the latter determined to beat their setbacks. And beat them, they did. What was it that led to such opposite reactions, I queried? And as I questioned and began to discover patterns, I began to document these reactions as guideposts in a diary, which led to the writing of this book.

I don't possess a degree in psychology or psychiatry. Rather, my knowledge of human behavior is founded in hundreds of first-hand encounters with victims (of abuse, neglect, substance misuse and hopelessness, among other undesirable and unfortunate human conditions), as well as with witnesses, innocent bystanders and criminal offenders. Most importantly, the combination of these encounters led me to discover certain fundamental principles that motivate an innate capacity for people to rescue *themselves* from a state of being held "hostage" as they tapped into their own latent motivation for survival and grabbed onto guidepost directions I held out to them; the result of which was that the cages and cells that once kept them hostages were blasted open, leading the way to freedom of choice and direction. I realized, firmly, in my role as catalyst, that anyone,

anyone, can be galvanized into action with the right stimulus. Furthermore, I realized that self-sabotage operates in much the same way for anyone who falls prey to its crippling effects. It is a learned behavior, and not one into which one is born. The pattern of hopelessness which it perpetuates is often difficult, once ingrained, to modify and extricate. But not impossible. That which we learn, we can unlearn; and as self-healing takes place, with the right stimulus and direction, the results are astonishing.

III. Goals

My goal in writing this book was/is: to help you identify the **cause(s)** which might lead you to hold yourself hostage or allow yourself to be held hostage (be it in a personal or professional relationship, a career, a thought or series of thoughts, or any of the many other life situations or circumstances which promote this syndrome); to identify the subsequent learned **behaviors** which accompany and perpetuate the hostage state; to recognize that the **pivotal moment** when self-sabotage occurs is when one or all of these three demons take hold of you, dominating your thoughts and shaping your subsequent actions, which in turn form the pattern of behavior of self-sabotage; and, to allow you to **un-hostage** yourself, to free yourself from negative thoughts and feelings of regret, blame, and worry. You have the power within yourself to take control of your life and your thoughts. I want you to remember that.

Now, the notion that you choose to allow a hostage-taking syndrome of negative thoughts, self-destructive actions, and the inevitable subsequent pattern of behavior, is met with disbelief and reluctance to accept by most victims of self-sabotage. It is nevertheless a choice, and one which can be *un*chosen once the key to your mindset has been turned and the door to understanding those choices has been opened. I view my role in the adjusting of your thinking process and the act of un-hostaging yourself as simply that of educator, facilitator or coach. In this book, I offer you not rules—for rules smack of the authoritative which, if broken, can create a sense of guilt—but rather, principles which act as guideposts derived from a set of critical life skills which are provided to encourage you, the reader, to reclaim power and control over yourself; over your thoughts, choices and actions. I say reclaim because your "power and control" is never truly taken from you. More often it is simply pushed into a dark room in your mind, waiting to be given permission to resurface. Only you can provide that permission. With determined application of these principles and faithful attention to—and application of—the guideposts, it will become second nature for you to perform the actions to un-hostage and reclaim your "self," and to let go and discard whatever does not serve your "self" and your best interests.

So, my ultimate goal is to share this process with you and to affirm, from first-hand experience (my own and that of the countless lives which have been positively impacted by adherence to the simple strategies laid out in this book), that a more confident, creative, hopeful *you* can resurface and leave the self-hostage experience behind permanently as you move forward with renewed purpose, passion and focus. And who, you might well ask, is included in the *you* for whom this book is intended?

IV. You, the Reader

When I began the process of thinking about writing a book about hostage-taking which would reference my long career experience, I knew it would prove to be an eye-opener to those interested in a career in law enforcement, investigations or security. However, I also knew that the concept and reality of hostage-taking was/is not limited to its traditional definition of one person or group physically taking someone helplessly hostage. I knew that we are quite capable of taking *ourselves* hostage in any number of ways, for any number of reasons, and with many manifestations, some recognizable, others less so. And while hostage-taking is an unfortunate fact of life with sped-up frequency in some regions of our current geo-political world, it is a pointless and unnecessary syndrome enacted by individuals who fall into the trap of self-sabotage for a plethora of reasons beyond the scope of this current work. And so, the book has evolved more as a direct conversation with you, the reader, from any and every walk of life.

The **you** is anyone and everyone who feels and realizes that his/her path forward, the quality of his/her life on a more or less daily routine, is cluttered with self-defeating patterns and thoughts which leaves them feeling that they are not in control of their choices, that they are indeed hostage to forces not only from without (i.e. circumstances) but from within—for the two become so inextricably intertwined as to become two halves of a whole, often leaving you struggling for oxygen, and for hope. May I assure you, dear reader, that we are ALL taken hostage by our thoughts at some point, sometimes repeatedly, despite who we are or what walk of life we have chosen. No one is exempt—not even the biggest and brightest of stars, of millionaires or billionaires, even of motivational speakers themselves. At some point, we are all capable of succumbing to the self-hostage phenomenon.

When I cast my mind back to my upbringing and my life overall, I recognize the times when I was hostage to factors which set me desperately searching for rescue. Rescue implied to me that an outside force, person or persons, would appear to help me out of my unhappy circumstances. But no one did appear. No rescue was at hand. I could have sat on the "rock" of my solitude until I was a very old man, awaiting some nameless, faceless rescue "party," like someone lost in the wilderness. But when I realized that the wilderness was the landscape of my own making—and *of my own mind*—I began to feel a strong impetus to take action to get out of the uncomfortable place in which I had somehow landed. That rescue, I eventually concluded, could only come from *within myself.*

And so began the gradual evolution of the strategies you will learn about in the pages of this book. And whenever I have felt discouraged or been knocked down, I have spiralled right back to the things I've written about in these pages: the strategies I learned growing up and learned more deeply in the trenches helping others; and strategies which have enabled me to adjust my life-navigation system when necessary for survival. These strategies are yours for the taking, and they will serve you for the rest of your life, whether you're a teenager having a tough time with bullying (moral, verbal or physical); a grad student trying to pay off seemingly insurmountable debt while simultaneously striving for career opportunity or even just a job; a struggling dreamer with goals you fear are unattainable; a professional trapped in an unrewarding career; a person "trapped" in a complex, perhaps stifling and unrewarding or even intolerable relationship; or really anyone who, for any number of reasons, has temporarily lost focus and hope, this book is for you.

V. Summary

In this book, you'll discover:

- ❖ The difference between being taken hostage by force and taking yourself hostage. The key concepts in both types share some psychological similarities; and understanding them will help you find the key to freedom;

- ❖ The importance of regular "self-examinations" as a step to positive and lasting change from within. Discovering what your weaknesses and strengths are by being brutally honest during self-examinations, which can lead to self-directed action and self-improvement;

- ❖ Who your "hostage-takers" are and how they can manipulate and control your beliefs and actions;

- ❖ How these hostage-takers become your captors and their effect on your internal monologues;

- ❖ The role your personal power and control plays in your life and how to reclaim it once it's been hidden from you;

- ❖ The importance of discovering the root cause of what contributed to your captivity and using that knowledge to help free yourself from whatever is keeping you captive;

- ❖ The steps to take to free yourself from your captive and sabotaged state;

◆ The Stockholm Syndrome and how it can brainwash your thoughts and take you hostage;

◆ Learned Helplessness (a condition that arises when someone is subjected to an abusive environment or toxic set of circumstances long enough that it feels normal and they simply give up and accept their fate); How to recognize if you're in such a place and how to get the hell out if you are; for, as the inimitable Winston Churchill so cleverly said: "If you find yourself going through hell, keep going."

◆ Making the right choices and decisions (based upon what you want and not on what someone else wants or expects from you) via a process of thoughtful planning when faced with adversity, and having the courage to make tough decisions, take action and readjust if things don't work out the first time. Just because you step off the path doesn't mean you have to keep off it;

◆ The vital importance of taking positive action to reach your goals. Simply thinking about doing something is not enough. Too many people settle because they're afraid of taking risks or of failing. "It's going to hurt" they tell themselves. That chatter inside your head can take you hostage. And *that* is what will really hurt. Some of the most successful people in this world failed numerous times before they succeeded. Directed and positive action will help you reach your dreams;

◆ EFT: The Emotional Freedom Technique as taught by David Gilbert and its numerous benefits to overcome fear and more;

◆ How some things in life are "Empty and Meaningless" and how you should keep them that way until you can attach the right meaning to them;

◆ The importance of Gratitude and Faith to living a happier life.

VI. In Conclusion

Finally, throughout these pages I'll be referring to self-defeating, intrusive and negative thoughts as "hostage-takers" and "zombies." I'll be discussing the importance of detecting who/what the offenders are, the methods they use to commit their "crimes" (their general Modus Operandi or M.O.), and how to effectively plan against their incursions.

In this book you will discover ways in which you can recognize signs of an impending offense or attack on your state of mind, and the methods to free yourself when you've been taken hostage by your thoughts. You'll become a cautious "thought detective" and enforce the principles which, through thinking and choosing, will protect you from becoming a victim of a hostage-taking.

Please note: These Key Terms which will weave themselves in and out of the narrative: ***Overgeneralization, Magnification, Labeling, Emotional Thinking and Blame***[4]—indicate practices which I will encourage you to systematically avoid and eventually extricate altogether from your thought processes. Instead, I will coach you to anticipate the arrival of those "criminals," fear and doubt; to truthfully, fully, and objectively assess your circumstances and your reaction(s) when adversity strikes; and, to galvanize your courage to activate your anti-hostage defense team, as you shift your thoughts into action to produce the results necessary to achieve your freedom, growth, and success.

And so begins the journey into your future, where power and control belong—not to the crippling forces of fear and doubt—but to you. Yes, to ***you***!

---

4. Cognitive distortions—Aaron Beck, David Burns: http://psychcentral.com/lib/15-common-cognitive-distortions/

Hostage

Hostage: There are several definitions for the word "hostage"; but the classically simple one is this: a person whose freedom and movements are being directly or indirectly controlled by someone other than themselves under a threat of physical harm and/or imminent death. This book, however, makes its foray into an extension of this definition to include the notion of taking one's *self* hostage. The hostage-taker is different in these two definitions: the first is from *an outside taker,* the second from *within yourself.*

This chapter demonstrates the difference between being hostaged by external forces and being hostaged by the internal self. On the one hand, someone taken hostage by another or others has no choice in the matter; whereas someone who hostages himself/herself may practice the right of choosing to not be a hostage—thus, the simple importance of choice. In the latter, you choose. It's that simple. Understanding this key principle will help you deal with those times you find yourself becoming your own hostage.

April 2005

It was five months into the mission. I couldn't believe I had made it to Jordan to serve as an International Peacekeeper during the Iraqi war. It was a decision that I had wrestled with because of the danger involved and the fact that I would be leaving my precious daughters for several months, knowing that I may never return alive. The thought of serving my country and making a difference, however small, outweighed my fears. There I was, doing something greater than myself. Their permission to let me go made it a bit easier.

This mission was Canada's way of not sending soldiers to the front lines during the Iraqi war. Instead, Canada had elected to deploy Peacekeepers to train Iraqi police cadets. Our mandate was to train three thousand cadets every eight weeks in matters of self-defense, weapons, survival, criminal investigations, human rights, democracy and procedures of arrest. Initially, I was in charge of the Criminal Investigations Division, teaching human rights and investigative techniques, and with two instructors assigned to my tutelage: Willie Burns, a wonderful Brit who fast became a true and lasting friend, and an Aussie, Jill Henry.

As the mission progressed I was selected to join the Advocacy and Counselling Branch, winning out over seventeen other international trainers who had also applied for that position. I really thought I had heard everything until I met these brave Iraqi men who dropped by my office for counselling and heard their stories, often sad, disturbing and heart-wrenching.

My partner was a Finnish officer by the name of Jarmo Uttalla. Jarmo stood a foot taller than I and was one of the kindest men I had ever met. We had immediately bonded, as is essential in the circumstance of fighting an enemy, and had become exceptionally effective partners. We watched each other's back vigilantly. For ours was an unarmed mission, which added to the dangers we knew existed each and every day. Dangers we accepted while being able, nevertheless, to exercise moments of normality: whenever the office wasn't busy with cadets in need, we would access a music directory on our computers, and I would try to stump him by playing just a few notes from a variety of hundreds of classic rock tunes for him to identify—he knew them all.

Soon after joining the unit, I also met an Iraqi Colonel who had an office a few doors down from mine. He invited me into his office one morning and asked me what I thought about the academy. He asked if I really understood what was going on with these cadets. I answered that I did not entirely understand, acknowledging that there were layers of complexity beyond my scope of knowledge. He went on to explain that for many of these cadets, money and food for themselves and their families were so scarce that for them becoming a policeman made financial sense. It came down to survival for them and their families. He said that keeping themselves and their families alive lured many of them to join the police—*and* the ranks of terrorism—as it unfortunately turns out. He asked me to imagine an economy so bad that putting your life on the line for an income outweighed your decision between right and wrong. Many of these young men were seductively recruited into terrorism by being offered a promise that if they joined, not only would they and their family be provided for and taken care of comfortably, but if they completed a suicide mission their families would be cared for . . . *forever.* In addition, their picture would be mounted on a wall of heroes and they would be honored as such.

The Colonel went on to say that these desperate men seeking jobs would often take on contradictory roles: not only the job of policeman—but also of terrorist—not because they believed in any jihad, but because their families were starving and would be taken care of by way of recompense. He then informed me that there were terrorists amongst us in the guise of police cadets, and that efforts were being made to identify and extract them. This explained how some of my previous students had suddenly disappeared from my class overnight. He warned me to watch my back, a warning I took seriously. The Colonel liked me and regularly invited me to join him for morning tea. Through his guidance I became a much more informed and astute advocate and counsellor, connecting with most of the cadets who came in to see me for help and consultation, just as I had become in my role as an instructor.

We were very aware the academy could come under attack at any time; that was a given. Most of these cadets welcomed the efforts the West was making to help. Some did not. We also knew there were many extremists who co-mingled, undetected, among us, following direct orders from Iraqi terrorists cells. One of our greatest concerns was getting hit by a missile in the canteen area that fed about a thousand cadets and internationals at a time—three times a day. This seemed like the most logical place for attack. By striking the canteen, the terrorists' community would wipe out, in one shot, as many of us as possible and receive international news attention.

Now, my usual morning routine involved attending the academy as the sun rose before the cadets attended their classes in order to get paperwork filed: I often had a number of transfer requests that needed to be signed by the academy director after determining which of the cadets should be expatriated back to Iraq for any one of a number of issues, including mental illness and extreme depression. Most of the cadets who attended the academy had not been adequately or properly vetted, and one of my duties was to determine which ones stayed and which ones went.

A couple of months after joining the Advocacy and Counseling branch, a young cadet who had been dropping by my office regularly warned me that an attack on the academy was being planned from within. He knew it was going to be soon but didn't know exactly when. I alerted our security division immediately but all would continue to be business as usual. There was no question of sending anyone "home" in spite of this information of a threat of an imminent terrorist attack; no one gets to go home during a war. Simply, we were required to remain strictly alert. But, as it turned out, we didn't have to wait long for the moment of forewarned crisis. For, a few days following the warning, on an early morning, with the temperature about 110°F (43.3 Celsius) on the Jordanian Desert, and a foul and fetid stench emanating from a nearby pig farm and lingering mercilessly in the air, **the moment** arrived . . . a moment which my partner Jarmo and I had discussed and in anticipation of which we had strategized, as much as one *can* strategize over the what and where and when and how of *any* terrorist attack. The "why" had long since ceased being a question for us—trained to accept the *de facto* reality of acts of terrorism rather than ponder their senselessness.

And I was glad to be in Jarmo's company as the moment arrived on this morning among mornings. But on this morning among mornings, nothing would exist outside of **the moment.** On this particular morning, Jarmo was at my side and we had just left the director's office, which was a few hundred feet through the desert from our building, after having our documents signed. We weren't far from our building when we noticed *them* . . .

For days, countless cadets—some terrorists and some their supporters—had been gathering makeshift weapons from within the camp: sticks, rocks and whatever potentially harmful implements they could get their hands on to attack and seize the Academy as per the orders which had issued from their terrorist leaders. Today was the day. Two hundred and fifty or so cadets were prepared to attack and had ventured out of their barracks; while another two thousand seven hundred and fifty cadets remained in their bunks, choosing not to participate. Not all of the two hundred and fifty to take up arms were full-blown terrorists, but they were ready to follow those who were. Suddenly, Jarmo and I were alerted to the swift approach of about forty of these armed and angry Iraqi cadets emerging threateningly from behind our building; and, with lightning speed, surrounded us, obviously intent on giving us a severe beating—or worse. They had simple orders: to forcibly control and destroy the Academy. As to whether they had been given the *kill* command—I can only speculate. But if I were a betting man, I'd drop all I had on that being a "yes." What was clear to me, however, in that moment, on this blazingly hot morning, was that not much of what I had discovered about terrorists mattered. Jarmo and I knew we were in for the fight of our lives; and he glanced down at me, patted my head and said, "This is going to hurt, little buddy." I looked up at him and answered, "Yeah buddy, it sure is . . . "

Although I was frozen with fear for a moment as the thought that I may never see my two daughters again, I was determined to fight with everything I had, and quickly focused in to meet the attack of the angry mob. And as their menacing "whoops" and cries and screams smashed against my ears, my heart raced at breakneck speed as if it would puncture my chest of its own volition. But then, *then,* something startling occurred, as, almost simultaneously, within the chaos and cacophony, a distinct voice emerged . . . I could hear one of the men shouting *my* name, "Mr. Paul! Mr. Paul!" Dominating the screams, he was barking commands in Arabic; and without one of my trusted language assistants by my side, I had no clue what orders were being given. But suddenly, as suddenly as we had been grabbed with unmistakable force, the men released their grip on us and backed off *en masse.* The attack stopped and the circle they had made around us parted. Just like that. With a shock almost equal in force to the promised attack itself, notwithstanding my relief . . . our relief. Yes. Stopped. ***Just stopped.***

One moment, hostages about to suffer a severe beating or death, the next moment freed. Jarmo and I, as you can well imagine, were reeling with both the shock and the relief. But we waited with bated breath, with some skepticism, wondering what exactly had happened, and whether the reversal of taking us hostage was firm, or whether it was some ploy to play with us. For second-guessing the actions of terrorists is a futile and dangerous occupation at best. However, as they cleared a path for us—almost like the parting of the Red Sea— I mused at our good fortune, and that we were provided the opportunity to leave unharmed. We knew some blessing had occurred, a miracle I felt, with us the most grateful recipients.

As I regained my complete focus, I scanned for the cadet who had given the order to stop and, lo and behold, recognized him as one of my former students! He had the biggest grin on his face and there was kindness in his eyes. He gestured that we should make it to our nearby advocacy building, all the while with the radiant smile on his face, reflecting his own pleasure at having done the honorable thing. At that moment I realized we could find humanity in terrorism.

Jarmo and I made it safely out of the academy that morning, and I credit the miracle of our safe passage out of possible death to the fact that I had always treated that young cadet and each of my cadets with dignity and respect. He was rewarding me in his application of some unwritten law—a code with its own principles of justice— informal, yet based upon a unique sense of right and wrong.

The foregoing account, of course, is a situation of classic hostage-taking by an external force. And, believe me, notwithstanding the outcome of our being freed, the experience was, to say the least, traumatic—with all of the concomitant factors which accompany trauma: fear, panic, a sense of helplessness, a rapid rise in heart-rate/blood pressure, among other reactions. *What,* you may ask, is the connective tissue between being taken hostage by external forces and being taken hostage by one's *self?* What are the markers which announce to oneself that one is under attack from one's own thoughts and emotions and headed for a situation in which you sabotage your self—your peace of mind, your freedom of thought and of choice?

Well, first and foremost, regarding thoughts and emotions which hostage your free and easy state of mind, it is essential to note the *speed* and urgency with which they arrive to encircle you (just as we had been encircled physically by our would-be hostage-takers in our desert mission): one moment you're free of them; the next they strike and have you in their grip. Being alert, prepared and ready to fight, is crucial to your survival in a physical hostage-taking. And so it is with *self*-hostage taking. Having the skills and energy to handle hostage-taking thoughts and responses is essential. Knowing and, moreover, embracing the power of our own thoughts, and recognizing and acknowledging the power which the sub-conscious mind (which houses millions of thought fragments and emotional memories) can exert over the conscious mind, seemingly randomly and at will, and at any time, is absolutely essential in order to eradicate and nullify the power of destructive, negative thinking.

Physical hostages, when seized, are deprived of the choice to move about freely and carry on with their lives as a result of the actions and demands being forcibly imposed on them by someone else. The hostage is a captive against his/her will and is at the mercy of the hostage-taker. To resist may realistically result in violence against them and/or death. The hostage most often experiences hopelessness and is at a complete loss of choice and control. And these very factors apply similarly to the situation of taking yourself hostage—or allowing yourself to be taken hostage emotionally and/or psychologically through corrupted thought processes. And they apply when you find yourself hostage to toxic relationships— with yourself or with others—be it negative self-talk of any kind, self-defeating internal monologues, a haunting sense of guilt long overdue for a purge, or remarks from someone toxic to your self-esteem, perhaps crippling expectations imposed upon you by family or friends or employers . . . all are discouraging, all are disheartening, all are harmful to your overall sense of well-being and, moreover, to your actual well-being. And that's how you take yourself hostage. That negative self-chatter going on in your head telling you that you're not good enough, not worthy enough and a million other things that have no place or right to be there.

In conclusion, let us remember, and remember well, these two steps:

Step1: Understanding the process of hostage-taking—and how taking yourself hostage or allowing yourself to be taken hostage in thought or in relationships for instance, is the first and foremost to rendering that process null and void . . . dysfunctional.

Step 2: Recognizing, acknowledging and *accepting* that you are endowed with innate, dynamic, personal power to interrupt the process of taking yourself hostage. You have the absolute power to un-hostage yourself.

Accepting your personal power to change your thought patterns is daunting for most. We become comfortable in our M.O. Change implies that we must inject new effort, new energy into a new awareness, new consciousness—to become vigilant of our thoughts and actions. We become more responsible overall for ourselves. And you may feel that you already have the weight of the world upon your shoulders and cannot bear the burden of more responsibility. But, there's the irony, folks! By freeing yourself from negative thoughts and relationships which have you bending under their yoke, you become inordinately freer to carry on with your life and to handle other responsibilities with greater agility. Investing in yourself in this way has the effect, therefore, of lightening all of the things which you consider a burden overall. You will, thus, find yourself in a win-win situation when your self-speak switches (permanently) from words like (for example): "I'm so stupid for _____."—to "I'm human, after all; I'm learning; that's not something I want to do in future; I'll do such-and-such instead . . . "

"Neither dead nor alive, the hostage is suspended by an incalculable outcome. It is not his destiny that awaits him, nor his own death, but anonymous chance, which can only seem to him something absolutely arbitrary. He is in a state of radical emergency, of virtual extermination."[5]

—JEAN BAUDRILLARD

Next, let's examine two headline hostage-taking studies.

Hostaged by force, case study #1: Patty Hearst[6]

Around 9:00 PM on the evening on February 4th, 1974, there was a knock on the door of apartment #4 at 2603 Benvenue Street in Berkeley, California. As the door was answered, a group of armed men and women rushed into the apartment seizing a shocked 19-year-old college student by force and beating her fiancé. That young woman was Patty Hearst. She was thrown in the trunk of a car and from that moment she became a hostage. Patty Hearst had been kidnapped by a group of armed radicals who called themselves the Symbionese Liberation Army, or "SLA." Led by a hardened criminal by the name of Donald DeFreeze, the SLA wanted to incite a guerrilla war against the U.S. government and destroy what they called the "capitalist state." Domestic terrorists, their ranks included women and men, Blacks and Whites, anarchists and extremists from various walks of life.

It was believed that Ms. Hearst was originally kidnapped to get the country's attention in addition to a large ransom for her return. She came from a wealthy and powerful family; her grandfather was newspaper magnate William Randolph Hearst, a famous 19th century newspaper mogul and founder of the Hearst media empire. The SLA's plan worked and worked well: the kidnapping stunned the

---

5. Jean Baudrillard was a French sociologist, philosopher, cultural theorist, political commentator, and photographer

6. www.fbi.gov/about-us/history/famous-cases/patty-hearst-kidnapping

country and made front-page national news. But things took a strange twist in the Patty Hearst kidnapping and hostage matter.

Soon after her disappearance, the SLA began releasing audiotapes demanding millions of dollars in food donations in exchange for her release. They hoped to make her a "poster child" advancing their cause. Over the next few months, Patty Hearst joined her captors in their acts of terrorism and became a victim of what is known as the "Stockholm Syndrome." She had been taken hostage by force and later empathized with and joined her captors—a not-too uncommon occurrence among captive hostages of sustained duration. We'll examine the Stockholm Syndrome in a later chapter.

Hostaged by force, case study #2: Ingrid Betancourt[7]

On the 23rd of February, 2002, Ingrid Betancourt was campaigning for the presidency of Colombia. A former Senator and anti-corruption activist, she was on route to a remote village which was under the control of a group known as the FARC, the Revolutionary Armed Forces of Colombia. She thought she could pass through to the village and beyond without trouble, but she was wrong. After being kidnapped at gunpoint by the Colombian rebels, FARC, and held hostage, Ingrid Betancourt spent six and a half years in the Columbian jungles, before finally being rescued some six years later, on July 2nd, 2008. Having been held hostage and never knowing what her fate would be, she stands as another well-known example of a hostage taken by force.

In these two cases, Hearst and Betancourt, the victims were taken hostage by force at the hands of an external enemy. Each of these stories is unique yet similar in essence. Each was kidnapped with a different agenda in their captors' minds. One fell victim to the Stockholm Syndrome; while the other found ways to cope and to find hope within despite never knowing if the jungle would be the site of her grave.

7. https://en.wikipedia.org/wiki/Íngrid_Betancourt

The sad reality is that there are thousands of kidnappings and hostage-takings each year, across the globe; and the numbers have increased exponentially in the last decade. Nigeria's Boko Haram alone have taken hostage hundreds of school girls and women, purportedly brainwashed them, and now use them to perform further violent acts at their command. Or whether it is Somalian pirates seizing any nationality of ship(s) off the coast of Africa in the Indian Ocean, or ISIS hostaging random individuals to no good end, the cases of hostage-taking are legion . . . far too many to list. For the range and nature of hostage-takings include spur of the moment hostage-takings in crimes gone wrong, domestic violence abductions, kidnappings for ransom, and human trafficking, to name some of the types. Nevertheless, as tragic and sad as these cases of human hostage-taking and trafficking all are, they are not, in and of themselves, the primary *focus* of this book. Rather, our main purpose in the here and now is to examine the dynamics involved in taking *ourselves* hostage, an act which, while it does not involve the violence and threat of physical hostage-taking associated with external force, nor the overt terror of the SLA, FARC, ISIS or any of the other international groups in active operation in this, the 21st century, *does,* however, cause loss of freedom and freedom of choice and a life lived within the shackles of a self-created prison. Your self-created prison. And so, we shall now examine our third "case study" which, while fictitious in identity, represents a day in the life of anyone who falls victim to the negative, even destructive, self-sabotaging consequences of his or her own thoughts and/or emotional responses. So, onward, with faith and courage, which we need when looking at *self.* For, it is far more challenging to look *within* than to look outside of ourselves for answers, although the solutions are nowhere but within ourselves. But then you know that, or you would never have picked up this book, nor would you be reading it now.

Taking yourself hostage, case study #3:

Fictitious study: Dawn has broken in your town. You awaken from a restless night at the sound of your alarm and rush to get ready without taking time to plan your day. Your obligations are beckoning you and you've slept in. You're in a rush and don't take any time to plan your day or to choose the attitude with which you'll greet the world. You imagine your day will work itself out. As you quickly exit your front door after wolfing down an unhealthy breakfast of processed whatever's, thoughts of your upcoming day flash through your head.

You think about how you hate your job and about your boss who always puts you down, but you still hurry to get to work on time. You imagine *if only* you had tried harder in school and taken a different path to pursue your dreams, that maybe you wouldn't be looking for excuses to call in sick. And today is Friday; but you don't have a date for tonight. You still haven't found the courage to ask out that cute guy/girl at work. Why? Because you have sabotaged yourself by asking, "What if they say no?"

The more you think about your job, your day and your love life, the more you convince yourself there must be something wrong with you. You feel you're not smart enough. You're afraid you're not ambitious enough or good-looking enough. Yeah, in your mind you've convinced yourself that your life pretty much sucks. Your energy is drained already and you have just gotten on the highway. You're so tired. You, my friend, have become a hostage to yourself . . . a victim of a syndrome of self-perpetuating, self-defeating thoughts that have permitted your circumstances to control you instead of you controlling them.

"Hostaging"[8] Mind and Body:
You take yourself hostage first in the mind;
the body naturally follows

In many ways, when you become hostage to yourself, you can expect to experience a similar sensation of captivity and loss of hope as the hostages you've read about in the two earlier case studies. Although

---

8. "Hostaging" is NOT a word you'll find in the dictionary. I created it. Meaning: "to make or take ourselves hostage"—i.e. captive.

it may not be your physical body that is taken hostage at the hands of someone else by force and/or violence, when you hostage yourself, you hostage your mind—the hostage-taker being your thoughts and your internal monologues. Far too often, self-doubting negative chatter in our heads becomes our dominant thought pattern, a pattern difficult to escape.

When we experience adversity, setbacks or a multitude of other human conditions or "states" so common in the average modern stressful lifestyle, some of us feel we don't have the courage, strength or ability to cope. We feel overwhelmed by an activating event, a trigger or by something that is said to us, with the result that we slip into a sabotaged way of thinking that prevents us from moving forward and finding a key to free ourselves from those thoughts and to feel strong again. The triggering event or words that were said to us is/are so often brought on by others, outside of our control; but despite that, it activates responses from us, the results of which keep those sabotaging thoughts in our minds and affect our subsequent behavior.

Thoughts often turn into interior monologues within ourselves. When any sabotaging self-chatter is given "stage time" in your mind, it has a way of growing and infecting your feelings and the state you're in. This affects your subsequent mental images on the issue hogging center stage; and your state of happiness and peace suffer depending on how well the performing dominant thought is doing. Your confidence, for one, is affected; and left unchallenged these thoughts can quickly feel "right" (or natural) to you the longer they keep hogging the center stage of your mind. For instance, in the example I provided earlier about my own experiences in grade school and being told I was dumb and would never amount to anything: those thoughts took root in my mind, and being unequipped to deal effectively with them, I believed them. The longer those thoughts looped back and forth in my mind, the stronger they became, and the more "real" they felt to me. I accepted what I was told without a fight, and those words manifested themselves in a number of different ways affecting my behavior and beliefs. *I became a hostage to those thoughts because they controlled me and I did not control them.* My internal monologues surrendered to the "I can't do this" and "I may not as well even try" loop. That cancerous thinking rooted itself into my belief system so deeply that I lost sight of the power and control I needed to dig myself out and truly believe in myself and in my abilities to change my circumstances.

You may argue that I was just a child at the time, but the process is the same in adults as it is in children. Children can easily become victims to the same sabotaged thoughts and hostage themselves in the very same ways as adults. In fact, childhood influences are largely at the root of this negative thinking. Children play movies that loop in their heads too. As we grow older, we are expected to acquire greater life experiences and should by then have developed the ability to deal more effectively with our thoughts and emotions. By the time we reach adulthood, we expect to be equipped to take responsibility for our own lives and not leave it up to others or to chance. Sadly, many of us are not. Many adults have not developed the defense mechanisms they need to protect themselves from this harsh world. They often give up too easily or simply don't fight the negativity that eventually hostages their thoughts. Does this sound like you?

Opening the door to destructive thinking is bad enough, but letting those thoughts in and showing them the room they'll be staying in is wrong on a whole other level. When they knock, your job is to call your internal 9-1-1 (your personal "get out! squad'). The good news is that we have control over the mental images and thoughts that pop into our heads demanding center stage. By discovering how to more effectively choose the right ones for us we can develop the mental muscle required to push out the bad and allow in the good. The unconscious mind will respond well with training.

Consider that rational and empowering thinking is affected once you give in to thoughts and voices of despair, fear and self-doubt. Like weeds, those voices can grow overpoweringly within you, taking your thoughts hostage. It can be as simple as telling yourself, "I can't possibly do this." Once that thought gets locked in—and settles in—it grows stronger with each repetition of that thought. You acclimatize to it and it grows stronger; and as it takes root, it develops into a belief you eventually accept as truth.

The "hostage-taker" has at this stage successfully moved from simply trying to coax you to believe that toxic idea, into a full-out kidnapping of a belief you at one time did not hold true. Suddenly the thought, "I can't possibly do this" becomes real to you in the moment—it becomes the predominant thought and activates your subsequent responses. The trigger is pulled and the damage follows; you can't possibly do what it is you intended to do.

Simply suppressing the hostaging thought or trying to forget it won't work. It will almost always come back. To really get a handle on controlling it, you should examine it until you discover its "root cause" if possible. This will help you to track its origin; and once you've done that it will be easier for you to see the whole picture clearly. That way you can decide the validity of it and correct what needs to be corrected or simply call it for what it is: a lie told to you or one you've made up yourself.

Our thoughts affect our bodies and our actions. There is a *principle* that says, "The head leads and the body follows." Originally coined by researcher Rudolf Magnus (1873–1927) who observed this to be the case in mammals he studied, martial artists have made use of this principle in their methods of self-defense for centuries. This principle applies to us and how we hostage ourselves as well. If our heads— our thoughts—are taken hostage, then our bodies will follow; our thoughts will direct our bodies to take certain actions or not. That's the behavior that flows from our thoughts. Not only will your thoughts lead you to physically take action or to avoid taking any, depending on how severely those thoughts have affected you; they can also lead your bodies to experience an anxiety and stress that can result in fatigue, headaches, accelerated heart rate, sweating, dizziness, shortness of breath, tremors, twitches and so forth. The head leads, and the body follows.

The activating thought leads to a hostaged thought and that leads to response. The response will be influenced by your dominant thought. But you can control these.

How the enemy strikes

For some of you, you know exactly how hostage thoughts get into your head. Maybe you suffered from low self-esteem at an early age; listened and internalized the harmful opinions of others or of the media as it or they tried to impress their idea of the "ideal" human being on you. It's tough growing up, and the schoolyard can be a cruel place as can the workplace and any other place in which people gather. We tend to judge ourselves far too harshly and far too often. We—ourselves—are far too often our own worst enemies. We're unique creatures in this universe and why are we so hard on ourselves? We may be quirky, silly, a bit of a nut or downright unusual. Others may have told us so but really, why the hell should that matter to you? It's OK to be different. That's a spice in life. Why let the opinions of others lead to thoughts of discouragement or sorrow? There are a million-and-one ways negative thoughts get into our heads. We may be blessed with the awareness of how they got into us and if so, that's a good start. But for some, we may have no clue how the hostage-takers got in.

Have you ever found yourself in a dark mental hole and wondered how you got there in the first place? This mental hole consumes your thoughts, emotions, quality of life and your actions; and you may have felt depressed and hopeless. No one pushed you to that dark place. However, the triggers that indirectly pushed you to run into that dark place could have come from a number of places: loss of employment, loss of a home, loss of a relationship, rejection of any type, and on and on. Each trigger, like the sound of a gun being fired, caused you to move further away from the shots. Fear, sadness and uncertainty were too hard to face and the only door that made sense to you was the one that was the easiest to open. But it led into a dark hall, and with each trigger that was set off, you moved further into that dark tunnel. Imagine that the tunnel is one you've seen in a miner's shaft. The further you moved into it, the darker it became and the more complex it was to find your way back into the light, back to where it had all begun.

The process of getting there was gradual, step by step and perhaps even unconscious but now you find yourself in that shaft and the more you keep walking into the darkness the longer it will take you to get out. You can't move in two directions at once. It's impossible. Simply giving in and choosing to stop and stay isn't going to get you out either. But it's a start.

Thinking negatively and destructively and getting caught up in those thoughts is what led you to open the door and take yourself hostage. The door swung closed behind you and you moved deeper into the abyss each moment you let those thoughts sink in and dominate your mind. Friedrich Nietzsche once said, "If you gaze for long into an abyss, the abyss gazes also into you."[9]

That wasted energy is keeping you from moving away from the monster you created and preventing you from un-hostaging yourself. Replaying the imagined possibilities you've twisted and developed in your mind because of those triggers is like watching a horror flick looping back on itself, over and over again.

Your goal is to stop that imagery from repeating itself in your head. The more you worry about whatever it is you've conjured up in your mind or what has led you to that door in the first place, the longer it will take you to get out. Far too often we attach the wrong meaning to what is happening in our lives; and without certainty, our minds can lead us to imagine the worst when it's really not that bad. I'll be discussing this later in the book.

For now, if you are in that deep dark tunnel, **stop** moving forward. Stop and look back for the light to the doorway. Say this: "I am not a hostage to _____." (You fill in the blanks here for whatever it is that got you there in the first place). Say it. Believe it. Own it.

Despite how those intrusive thoughts got into your head, the important thing is to recognize they're in and that they are toxic to you. Focusing on them will not make them go away. As you see, your mind will work at making them bigger than they are. And if they are big? It's not the end of the world. Once you've become aware of them and their effect on your behavior and outlook, you can plan to do

---

9. Friedrich Nietzsche. Beyond Good and Evil, Aphorism 146. German philosopher (1844–1900)

something to rid yourself of them—no matter how challenging the situation is. You can find a way out and face the lesser monster just outside the door. Once you get there, you'll see it's not as big as the one that kept you hostage in that tunnel.

Left unchallenged with no action on your part to get yourself out of that dark place, your thoughts will influence how you react to the adversity, situation or circumstance you find yourself having to confront. And because of their power to control your feelings, the action you take to squash them must be quick, intentional and effective. You must move toward the light and face whatever it is that got you there. Once you stop, take a deep breath. Tell yourself you're not a hostage to your circumstances and that you're stronger than your circumstances. Because, guess what? You are. If you don't, you'll slip further into the abyss; and what awaits you at the end of the tunnel will be much harder for you to fight. And that creature has a habit of bringing along his friends.

Is the secret to all this simply positive thinking? Yes and no. It's not enough to simply say the words, "I'm not a hostage to this." That's one very important step. The next step is to face whatever it is that hostaged you, understand its origin and attach the right meaning to it. *Know it for what it is and NOT what you imagine it to be.* Be aware by being your own detective.

Awareness is power

Awareness is power, and by tapping into your gift of awareness you can develop the ability to change the current moment you're in. To be aware of the effect your present and dominant thoughts have over you when they're harmful is to be aware of the first step in effectively quashing them. That awareness must prompt you to take whatever action needs to be taken to evict the hostage takers. Like a doctor who examines a patient, knowing what the patient is suffering from is the first step in effective and complete treatment. Knowing what thoughts are keeping you hostage is the first step in treating yourself. You become your own surgeon. By treating the cause, the symptoms will be treated. Awareness is one of the keys you require to help unlock the captor's door and free yourself from being hostaged by them. Understand this: your predominant thought can be changed. The thought does not lead directly to a consequence in your life until you respond to it with action.

Become vigilant to your negative thoughts. Be mindful and aware of them and the power they have over you but also be aware that you have more power over them. Develop the ability to listen carefully for clues of an attack. Pay attention to that mind-babbling you have going on in your head and be willing to take immediate action to change the channel. Tune your inner chatter's channel to one that is positive and task-oriented. By task-oriented I mean one in which you'll assume responsibility to do something about what it is that hostaged you or tried to.

For example, if you don't get that job, don't start the chatter in your head with: "I'm not good enough. I'll never find a job. Nobody wants me." Instead, why not try: "Well, I've gained some good experience from this interview. I'm going over my resume again. I wonder if that interviewer would give me some feedback. I'll ask. I'm going to get a perfect job!" Then do something about it.

You must be willing to take action, my friend. It is this moment in time that is most important to you and the only one that you can immediately influence and change. You have no power to change your past, and the future has yet to be written. What happened in the past has passed—it's done. That interview, for instance, is over. There's no going back. What is going to happen in the future is largely up to you, but it hasn't happened yet. Perhaps in the example I just gave, a follow-up call to the HR office to ask for feedback on the interview would help immensely. You don't want to sabotage the best from unfolding as planned simply because you have hostaged yourself to a thought or a state of mind—such as, that you're not good enough. In this moment, awareness of who you are and what thoughts are handcuffing you from being where you want to be is power. Awareness is a powerful construction tool that is far too often overlooked, and you are obligated by a law of life to be self-aware and to conduct periodic self-evaluations to help you remain determined and focused. This is critical to help you change and identify what needs to be changed in your way of thinking and in your life to get what you want from it.

Imagine yourself being conscious of the impact your thoughts have on you: which ones exist to strengthen and support you and which ones don't. Imagine how thoughts lead to feelings and emotions, which also lead to a state of mind, which in turn leads to an action or a series of actions. Imagine recognizing the thoughts that immobilize you and then examining how those thoughts first appeared and how to rid yourself of them. Then imagine new outcomes and better results for yourself. Imagine this as the process because it's how un-hostaging of yourself works. There is no consequence of action until you enact that thought. Recognize that holding on to sabotaging thoughts can hurt your view and worth of yourself, and that is *never* a good thing.

You are the "keeper of your gates," the "master of your thoughts" after all. That's the way nature intended it to be. Being aware of the reasons for the existence intrusive thoughts invade us is power. It's the first step to freedom from them. If you don't take time to examine your life, the state of your happiness and the level of your current happiness, you miss out on essential remedies that will help place you firmly on the journey of total happiness. How you choose to process a thought and what it means to you begins with awareness.

Awareness is only the first step: Your *will* must also be engaged

Some of you, despite an awareness that you've been taken hostage by your self-defeating thoughts, find yourselves either paralyzed, unwilling or unmotivated to take control of those thoughts and to deal with them. It may be that you're gripped by fear and feel frozen and unable to move past your current beliefs, circumstances, and the *voices* that have taken you hostage, the interior monologues. You may be waiting for someone to rescue you and, consequently, abandon responsibility to act for yourself. Or you may simply be unaware that you have hostaged yourself. Maybe you're just too discouraged to deal with it, choosing to believe those other intrusive thoughts that sprout from the original ones such as, "It's too hard for me to deal with," "I'm too fed up," and "I can't take it anymore."

You may experience feelings of defeat either by recalling times you've tried and failed or by listening to others instead of yourself. It may be that you feel unequipped to deal with your setbacks and adversities for a number of reasons. You may feel unable to develop stronger attitudes and better defenses against life's challenges and the thoughts others have put in your head. You may feel powerless to pursue new relationships, leave toxic ones behind or to heal broken ones. You may feel it's impossible to discover and develop new talents, achieve financial security and reach unlimited success. Whatever it is that has taken control of your thoughts, by remaining hostage to them you are leaving the outcome of your life and destiny to an incalculable outcome. That kind of thinking will get you nothing but an unfulfilled life.

Whichever one of these barriers took root to prevent you from dealing with your captors, you owe it to yourself to eradicate them. You're the one who, although most likely unwittingly, let those thoughts in, after all. Sure, the messenger may have been someone or something else completely beyond your control, but no one other than you has the power to allow those thoughts to stay. You are our own thought-control manager—the responsibility to filter your thoughts lies within you and you alone. Man or woman up: you're stronger than you think.

So that's what being a hostage means. Someone who has been taken by force or threat, held against their will and whose lives and happiness are held to an incalculable outcome; OR you, although not seized physically, become hostage to yourself whenever self-destructive thoughts, feelings and situations are permitted to take control of your mind overall. Begin now by telling yourself: I will no longer be hostage to whatever does not serve my happiness. I can free myself from this—and I *will.* Believe it—own it. Make it so.

In Conclusion: Never leave your destiny in the hands of anyone but yourself

If you remain in a state of unawareness or simply choose to ignore that you've become your own hostage, you leave your destiny up to random chance or to anonymous others. Life then becomes mere existence, even subsistence, as opposed to a gift to be enjoyed and appreciated. Awareness is power; and you can use your power to bring about whatever change you so choose. But you must want to and you must have the willpower to create and enact change. You don't have to remain a hostage to your self-defeating thoughts; because unlike a hostage taken at knife or gun point, when it comes to your thoughts and feelings, you are not without choice. You can free yourself and take action to prevent yourself from being taken hostage again. This will require periodic self-examinations and awareness. We're all susceptible to a great deal of "noise" and monologues entering our heads, and it's up to us to filter the good from the bad.

When you hostage yourself, you do so by: firstly, allowing any and all intrusive, sabotaging thoughts to remain in your head unexamined and unexpurgated; and secondly, by submitting to this self-defeating pattern, which leads you to accept and believe their fiction. As such, you fail to filter the good from the bad, to determine their cause and effect, and to conduct the necessary *surgery* to repair it. Without proper self-examination and the right kind of filtering system, your self-talk can turn dark. You must consciously choose to be your own healer and to deal effectively with your hostage-takers *before* they deal with you. It can be done. We are in control of our thoughts, and knowing this is the source of empowerment itself.

CHAPTER 1 SUMMARY

◆ There are two kinds of hostages: Hostages who are physically seized and deprived of the choice to move about freely and carry on with their lives; and those who hostage themselves mentally, by thoughts that deprive them of the choice to experience the best for themselves to reach their dreams and goals.

◆ Thoughts collect and coalesce into interior monologues within ourselves; when harmful thoughts are permitted to take root, they have a tendency to grow and affect our state of happiness and peace. Being aware they exist is the first step to their eviction.

◆ It is *this* very moment in time that is most important to us and the only one that we can immediately influence and change. We have no power to change our past, and the future has yet to be lived. Making the right choices right now is what matters, and that often requires self-evaluation and brutal honesty. Don't judge yourself too harshly though. You are a unique and beautiful creature of the universe. Trying to conform to society's or someone else's image of you can, in and of itself, hostage you.

◆ A hostaged thought can lead the body to take action—or not. Thoughts generally lead to action and the wrong kind of thoughts and beliefs can result in taking the wrong kind of action.

◆ If we remain in a state of unawareness or simply choose to ignore that we've become our own hostages, we leave our destiny up to random chance or to anonymous others. Awareness is power.

CHAPTER 2

Self-Examination

Jimmy Donovan was well known to every senior cop in Durham Region for his reputation as being one tough, violent and cop-hating son-of-a-gun criminal. Whenever any cop had to deal with Jimmy, it usually meant it would take five or so of us to take him into custody along with one hell of a fight. We had no pepper spray back then (not that it would have worked on Jimmy anyway) and no Tasers. Fists, small "Billy clubs," service revolvers and sheer determination were our use of force options back then. That was pretty much it.

Jimmy loved to fight; and it was rumored that in the early 1970s he had done time in the Kingston Penitentiary for God-knows-what; and during his incarceration, several inmates captured their cell block jail guards, set parts of the jail on fire, and took guards hostage, holding them as bargaining chips for a list of demands they wanted fulfilled. Jimmy was allegedly on a "kill" squad, if it came down to that: he would be the enforcer whose job it was to kill hostages.

I had never met Jimmy, nor had I heard the stories about him until after one early cold morning. I was on my second cup of coffee when I received a radio-dispatched call for service to assist ambulance attendants with a "man going berserk" in a residential neighborhood in Oshawa. I was a single-man-unit (simply, the only one in the cruiser— no partner) and pulled up to see two ambulance attendants sitting by their vehicle with blood on their faces; and a tall, thin man in his "tighty-whities" underwear running around holding his head and screaming in obvious pain. Upon seeing me, the attendants got up, wished me luck and told me who I was dealing with. I told them I'd never heard of him. They advised me to call for lots of back-up and that Jimmy was suffering a migraine. He had assaulted them both, and they were leaving.

It was a cold March morning in the very early 80s and I found myself alone on the street with an underwear-clad Jimmy Donovan, who was not only in pain but in a hell of a bad and fighting mood. His long, stringy hair was soaked and he was missing most of his teeth as he clutched his head screaming. Back-up was five minutes away; and almost everyone who heard my call for assistance was on their way once they heard with whom I was dealing. I figured some of the senior cops simply wanted a chance to take a few pokes at the guy for past encounters.

Jimmy was dangerous and they all knew it. The warnings I received over the police radio gave me that "Oh damn, this is going to hurt" feeling in my gut, and I thought I'd wait for my back-up unless it became absolutely necessary to take action. Yeah, well . . . some of the best thought-out plans don't always go your way. Jimmy turned around and spotted me. Likely the sound of the police radio alerted him to my presence, and he looked like a bull about to charge its prey. I had to think fast; so I raised my hands to show him my open palms in a gesture that I meant him no harm; and the first thing I thought of saying was, "You look cold. Let me grab a blanket for you. I'm not here to hurt you . . . just here to help." I slowly walked to the trunk of my police cruiser and opened it to grab a blanket. Jimmy glared at me intensely but didn't attack. He watched my every move with drool seeping from his mouth.

I showed him the blanket and walked up . . . extending it to him. He took it, wrapped himself in it, and immediately calmed down. That was a "Thank you God!" moment that made me feel somewhat better, but I knew I still had a big problem on my hands. Jimmy was still in pain; and although I had been on the job for only a couple of years, I knew better than to drop my guard with him. He hated the police and I was in full uniform right down to the hat I wore on the top of my head. If he was a bull, I was the matador, and my uniform the *red target* he had come to attack so often. I had to take advantage of what seemed like a crack in the door of trust. So I pushed at that crack and asked Jimmy, "Why don't I drive you to the hospital? You look like you're in pain, and the ambulance is not coming back for you. You can ride up front with me." Call me naïve, brave or simply stupid— the words came out of my mouth before I had time to completely assess the situation in which I had just placed myself. The hospital was only a few blocks away; but with Jimmy as my passenger, that would be a dangerously long ride. Jimmy got into the front passenger's seat, bowed his head, and sobbed.

I called my new destination in to the dispatcher and alerted the control center that I had Jimmy on board. The urgent comments from my fellow officers clogged the air band making it next to impossible to hear anyone, but every one or two seconds a few words actually got through . . . phrases like "you're crazy," "he's dangerous," and "meet you at the hospital." Jimmy and I arrived at the hospital a few minutes later without incident; and I walked my passenger into the emergency branch and demanded a room with a door I could close behind us, out of proximity to other patients. I felt that would be safest. The nurse obliged us after she recognized who my passenger was, and I made sure to close the door behind us. Jimmy sat down in a chair and a doctor walked in just then to ask him for his symptoms, whispered in my ear there was nothing he could do for Jimmy and left to get a sugar-based pill, wanting Jimmy out as soon as possible.

Moments later the door swung open and in rushed four of my colleagues ready to fight the vicious beast who had been my passenger. They looked like the keystone cops, and their aggression immediately provoked a once-calm Jimmy into springing from his chair seething at the mouth, with fists clenched and ready to fight. He threw off his blanket and the room suddenly became tense and unpredictable like two gangs about to beat each other up. The bull was about to attack!

I placed myself between my colleagues and Jimmy and raised my hands waist height and shouted, "Back off!" to my fellow officers. "I've got this under control. Get out now. You'll know if and when I need you." And they did. Things don't normally move quickly in hospitals in such a case as this, but the doctor did want us ALL out of there; and he returned a half hour later, gave Jimmy a shot of something, told him he should feel better soon, and left.

I drove Jimmy back to his place, an apartment in one of the high rises outside of which I had first found him. He told me he had never met a cop like me before in a voice that was calm and friendly. He asked me to meet his fiancé, and I figured, "Why not?" I walked him to his apartment and was surprised to meet such a beautiful and intelligent woman. Jimmy wasn't gifted with good looks, but she certainly was. What an interesting match, I mused.

I had been attending a Baptist church back then and whatever made me invite Jimmy and his girlfriend out to join me one Sunday, I'll never know—but I did. I left them my detachment telephone number and name on the back of a religious tract I carried with me, and Jimmy said he would think about it. I left thinking I'd never hear from them again and also thinking how treating Jimmy that night with dignity and respect saved me from quite possibly being a patient at the very hospital to which I'd taken him. My self-evaluation throughout the moments of that experience taught me a valuable lesson in the importance of diplomacy in lieu of force, a lesson which I would never forget.

Two weeks later I was surprised to hear from Jimmy's girlfriend asking if they could take me up on the offer and attend church with me the following week. I picked them up the next Sunday morning. Jimmy had managed to find an old, frayed three-piece suit that looked like it had been found in a dump. But it was clean, his hair was washed, and his grin exposed his almost toothless smile to the world. And it was gratifying. His girlfriend was dressed immaculately. Off we headed for church.

Our church Pastor at the time was a remarkable man. He could remember everyone's name, and embraced newcomers warmly and graciously, as he did Jimmy and his girlfriend, thanking them for their attendance and welcoming them to the church. Most of the congregation knew me well, but the Pastor's welcome was about the only warm and welcoming greeting Jimmy and his girlfriend got that day. I expected more from the congregation, but it was not forthcoming. Nor did it come the following Sunday nor the Sunday after that, in spite of the Pastor's messages about love, kindness, acceptance and hospitality . . . all of which seemed to me to be falling on deaf ears—obviously, I thought, because people were afraid to welcome a hardened criminal into their church. But Jimmy returned again and again, wearing the same suit week after week, smiling his toothless grin to one and all in the congregation, in a true and brave effort to feel welcomed . . . to belong. The church members did not respond in kind, however; and I couldn't help but think that if he had been made to feel welcomed and accepted, Jimmy might very well have found a new home.

The Pastor and I were the only ones to make Jimmy and his girlfriend feel welcomed; and the smile Jimmy had first brought with him gradually faded each week he attended until one day, he didn't bring it with him. I began to question whether the Pastor's messages of love for our fellow man was sinking in for those who showed up each Sunday to hear it because I hadn't seen any evidence that it was, and it angered me. Jimmy thanked me for taking him to church all those times but said he would not be going back. We had come to know each other quite well, and I couldn't help but feel how so many good and faithful churchgoers had missed an opportunity to truly shine and put into action the messages they had attended church each week to hear. I realized it was not enough to simply hear what should be done—you have to consciously think about the messages, let them take root in you and live their virtues. Regularly. You also have to examine your life to see how the words and thoughts of the messages apply to you; only then can they move you to direct your behavior. Self-examinations are a must.

Jimmy left town a couple of years later and died in an armed confrontation some time later. To this day, I believe his story could have ended very differently. If only. . . .

The Power of Your Thoughts

"You are today where your thoughts have brought you;
you will be tomorrow where your thoughts take you."
—JAMES ALLEN, BRITISH PHILOSOPHICAL WRITER

The power of your thoughts and what you repeat to yourself has a tremendous influence on your overall happiness, behaviors and successes. They also have influence over your state of mind which is your mood or mental state at a particular time; for example, sadness, defeat or grief. Your moods—or states of mind—are left up to *you* to choose. They don't choose you. *You* choose them. My brother Robaire has incorporated and highlighted this very concept into his highly-convincing performance as a mentalist. A successful lawyer by day and a mentalist by night, his "State of Mind"[10] show captures the audience's imagination and mesmerizes them with wonder. A frequently asked question during one of Robaire's performances is—*did I just witness what I just witnessed*?! Your states of mind can be redirected; and in Robaire's show, the audience co-operates in the "state of mind" demonstration—enjoying the fun, and finding the entire experience entertaining and mystical. But in your day-to-day life, it's not fun when your state of mind becomes one of sadness and distress.

In your quest to be free of hostage-taking thoughts, it's imperative to examine where you are in your thoughts by asking yourself first where they took you yesterday and secondly, where they've taken you right now. If this simple exercise results in a grim snapshot both of yesterday and this precise moment, you've got a problem. Yes, it is this moment that truly matters to you—not the past and not so much the future. If the recent snapshot of your state of mind yesterday reveals unhappiness and today's image is the same, you are a hostage, my friend.

Begin by focusing where you are in this moment and whether you're happy with who you are right now or how you're feeling. Ask yourself, "Is there more I could be doing to improve my happiness and that of others?"

"For the wise have always known that no one can make much of his life until self-searching has become a regular habit, until he is able to admit and accept what he finds, and until he patiently and persistently tries to correct what is wrong."
—BILL W

---

10. Robaire: www.stateofmind.ca

The merits of self-examination

Self-examination and self-discovery with the goal of seeking to understand where you are at this moment is an important tool in helping you escape your *thought* captors. Think of the points I bring up as tools accessible to you in an invisible escape pouch you carry for the times you're taken hostage.

Another important escape tool is asking yourselves the right kind of questions to help you understand your motivations and values: for instance, "What do I fear here and what steps should I be taking in my escape plan?" By examining yourself fully and honestly, you can then choose to apply positive thought-change, adjust purposeful actions, redirect thoughts and get to where you want to be— out of a hostaged mind. Simply listening to a message given by a pastor, priest or motivational speaker (like the parishioners in the Jimmy D story I told) is not enough. You have to believe that message and then live it.

The Greek philosopher Socrates once said, *"The life that is unexamined is not worth living."*[11] Socrates uttered these words at his trial for heresy. He found himself on trial for disbelieving in the Gods of the state and for corrupting the morals of the youth. The sentence was normally death but Socrates had the option of suggesting an alternative punishment. He could have chosen life in prison or exile, and would likely have avoided death. But he was a man of thought and principles and believed that these alternatives would have robbed him of the only thing that made life worth living: examining the world around him and choosing to make it a better place by adhering to the laws of the state.[12]

Socrates understood that examining your life honestly and in detail, was a key to living a complete and fulfilled life. Self-examination is necessary to determine where you are now and to discover what changes ought to be made to get you to where you want to be. Whatever it is that is keeping you hostage is begging for examination.

11. Plato, *The Apology.*

12. Plato, *The Phaedo,* Hackett Publishing Company Inc., 1977.

It's as though you have an assault team of highly trained and heavily armed tactical officers in your mind at your disposal, and they hear the screams of a hostaged thought begging to be freed. It's worthy of examination for the purpose of exposure and extraction. Only when you know what it is that's keeping you hostage can you plan your escape and use your team to the fullest. You hold the tools and the team. Like a lawyer picking away at even the slightest details to uncover the facts at trial, so must we pick away at ourselves to uncover what it is that's keeping us from moving forward.

The pitfalls of the unexamined

Unfortunately, most people avoid leading an examined life. It's not that they don't have time to examine themselves, their circumstances or states. For some, they actively avoid it. The fear of exposing flaws, shortcomings and bad attitudes is downright terrifying to many. When we expose our weaknesses but aren't prepared to work on them, the inaction leads to stress. The pitfall to that is that nothing changes and life goes on its miserable way. You don't get what you want and at the end of that unfulfilled life, the individual will look back on his or her pathetic life and say, "What was I thinking?" It will be too late then.

People who do examine their lives to reflect on where they've been, where they are and where they're going are by far much happier people. None of us has all the answers. No one's life is free from trouble and strife. But those who have a sense of where they belong in the universe tend to have a context for understanding how all the elements fit together and know what they can do to create their own destinies. Self-examination in many ways provides us with a blueprint which capitalizes on our strengths and helps us discover our weaknesses. Once we study that blueprint we will have a much better chance of creating and designing a map for ourselves to get us to where we want to be.

Imagine two people: one with a map and one without. Who do you think has the better chance of reaching their destination? Of course, the one with the map has the best chance. When we take time to examine our life, it also stands to reason that we'll make time to work on improving it. We'll create our own maps to get to where we want to be. The two should go hand in hand, in lock-step.

One of the most difficult things about examining our lives is getting started. We start by asking ourselves the right questions.

> *You **are** the questions you ask yourself.*
> —TONY ROBBINS[13]

"Who are you?" I'm not talking about the name you were christened with or what others have called you to your face or even behind your back. I'm not asking for your driver's license, ownership and insurance documents as some proof of who you are "on paper." What I *am* asking you is who you really are, deep down inside. I'm asking you to examine yourself and challenge yourself honestly to see what you're made of—your character. Take time to consider your answers to the following questions.

◆ How would you describe yourself physically, emotionally and in your relationships with others? Are you happy with who you are?

◆ How would someone else describe you, physically, emotionally and in your relationship with them and others? Are you happy with their assessment of you?

◆ What do you tell yourself every day about how you see yourself? Or how others see you?

◆ Can you list five virtues you see in yourself?

◆ If your spouse/best friend/co-worker/girlfriend or boyfriend could use only five virtues to describe you, what would those virtues be?

◆ Are you confident in yourself? What are your strengths? What are your weaknesses?

---

13. Tony Robbins, author and motivational speaker (www.tonyrobbins.com).

- What characteristic are you most proud of in yourself? What characteristic are you least proud of?

- Where do you see yourself in six months from now? In two or five years from now? What are you doing right now to make your goals attainable?

- What have you been procrastinating on? What has been the reason for your procrastination?

- Are you fulfilled? Is anything missing? If so, what? And if so, what can you do right now in order to begin to achieve it?

- Are you happy? Why? Why not?

- Are you the person you want to be? Why? Why not?

- Have you settled for someone else's opinion of you? If so, why?

- What could you do right now to improve your level of happiness? Or the level of others?

If you answered these questions honestly you may have been surprised by how difficult it was to be brutally truthful with yourself. You may also be surprised at how some of the answers you came up with painted a picture that is worth closer scrutiny to bring about the changes you want to see in yourself. It's not easy describing yourself honestly or imagining how others may see you. I recommend that you keep a record of your answers. Buy a journal and start documenting your life; keeping a daily journal will help you record daily challenges, feelings, accomplishments and successes. It will also serve as a timeless reference you can check to see how far you've come since the beginning of your journey. A journal has been proven to enrich the quality of many people's lives. Your self-examination questions will change over time and that will mean progress.

SELF-EXAMINATION   49

The importance of examining your virtues

Virtues are moral excellences. You may or may not yet possess some or many. Self-discovery must include honest evaluation to first determine your moral standards, and next to determine how you can work on improving the ones in which you are weak or that you have not yet acquired to bring about the changes you want to see in yourself. It stands to reason that if we live according to a high moral and ethical set of standards, our lives will be enriched in ways we might not have originally imagined. Goodness and decency is always rewarded, despite what some might think. The universe has a way of returning to you what you give to it—or to others.

Here is a list of virtues I gathered for you to consider.[14] At the back of this book, in Appendix A, I invite you to reexamine these virtues and complete a simple exercise to consider how they apply to you and which may need more work on your part to acquire or improve on.

Acceptance: the act of receiving someone or something with contentment, understanding and forgiveness.

Assertiveness: the act of finding your confidence and courage as opposed to dwelling on your self-doubt or shyness. Behaving with purpose and direction will help you find the happiness and success that you're looking for. Being assertive will also help prevent you from being taken hostage by any thoughts that are sabotaging in nature. People respect those who are assertive without being arrogant.

Authenticity: the act being true to yourself, your personality, your spirit and your character. Being honest and living your life with integrity. Replacing low self-esteem in favor of high self-esteem and being yourself as opposed to simply a copy of someone else. Being different is not a bad thing—imagine a life without spice. When you see someone who is authentic and unique, that's worth taking a second look.

---

14. In part from www.virtuesforlife.com/virtues-list

Beauty: the act of finding attractiveness within yourself and others will bring you joyfulness and peace as opposed to looking for the ugliness in life and others. Recognizing that beauty is truly in the eye of the beholder and asking yourself if your inner beauty matches your outer beauty. Everyone has their own unique beauty. I know you do.

Caring: the act of feeling and demonstrating genuine concern for others and the world around you. Showing compassion and kindness as opposed to cruelty and insensitivity.

Cleanliness: the act of keeping yourself and your environment uncontaminated, orderly and pure. Rejecting dirtiness and impurity in both environment and thought. Having a clean mind, clean body and clean environment you become that much more prepared to resist intrusive thoughts from finding their way into your thoughts and taking you hostage.

Commitment: the act of promising to live a hostage-free life and to reach the goals you've set for yourself by persevering. Pledging yourself to finding direction in your life and being loyal to yourself and to others. Pledging yourself to succeed and to ridding yourself of any hostaged thoughts that have managed to make their way into your head.

Compassion: the act of demonstrating kindness to your fellow man, conscious of their distress along with a desire to be truly helpful, caring and understanding. Eliminating hostility and judgment.

Confidence: the act of examining yourself to uncover feelings and beliefs in yourself that you can do so much more—and do it well. Believing that you can succeed at whatever you put your mind to. You are assertive and courageous. You pledge to get rid of self-doubt and uncertainty.

Consideration: the act of thinking carefully before you leap. You **Stop**[15] to consider carefully your next move and you won't simply "react" to what happens in your life. In consideration of others: You will show compassion and a caring nature. Ridding yourself of selfishness.

Contentment: the act of being happy and satisfied with the blessings you already have in your life. It is a fulfillment and joy with what you have now as opposed to a dissatisfaction and restlessness for what you don't have. You understand that all that you have can be taken from you in a mere moment. You pledge to take inventory of what blessings you currently have and you're grateful for all of them.

Cooperation: the act of working well with others. It's about teamwork and unity, as opposed to defiance and resentment.

Courage: the act of persevering and facing your fears or setbacks. Being bold and confident, as opposed to hanging on to fear and self-doubt. Courage means moving forward despite the fact that you may be fearful.

Creativity: the act of finding your gifts and abilities and discovering new ideas, new talents and new opportunities. For those you don't currently have but want, you'll develop them. You'll find purpose and detach yourself from what is simply normal. You're going to stand out from the pack.

Determination: the act of finding the strength and focus needed to continue your efforts to succeed and achieve something you're after despite how difficult it may seem to you in the moment. You're committed and tenacious. You won't give in to complacency.

Dignity: the act of facing and behaving and conducting yourself with self-respect. It's about exercising self-control, honor and respect and rejecting egoism and selfishness.

Encouragement: the act of finding hopefulness and confidence from within yourself. Replacing your self-defeating thoughts and internal mind chatter with ones that make you want to beat any set-

---

15. STOP—explained in detail later in this book.

backs down. It's about keeping your head up high and imagining that whatever failures or setbacks you've faced in your past only served to prepare you for this moment to forge ahead with confidence.

Enthusiasm: the act of being excited and truly interested in something you want! An active and passionate energy and desire. It's about being motivated as opposed to indifferent, bored and unexcited.

Ethical: the act of following an accepted and right set of rules, which are morally correct and good. It's about exercising fairness and respect as opposed to being immoral and unprincipled.

Excellence: the act of finding distinction and quality in yourself and others. Pledging to strive to reach the very best you can in everything you do. Setting realistic and high standards for yourself and then reaching them with dignity, honor, passion, integrity and respect. Never being willing to ever settle for being mediocre.

Fairness: the act of understanding equality and treating everyone in a way that doesn't favor one person or group over others. It's about practicing equality and justice instead of finding reasons for grievances and injustice.

Faith: the act of putting your trust in something or someone you believe in (whether it be a program, a person or God). Finding confidence, hope and trust as opposed to apprehension and doubt. Believing that something will happen simply "because you wish it to."

Flexibility: the act of being prepared and willing to make the changes you need to make and try new things. Listening and learning through understanding and detaching yourself from your old ways and thoughts. Letting go of stubbornness. Being prepared to go with the flow if the flow is headed in the right direction as opposed to paddling in the opposite direction and learn new things whenever possible.

Forgiveness: the act of letting go of something you hold against yourself or someone else. Here you should take a few moments to examine your life to determine your ability to forgive something or someone that has hurt or wronged you. You pledge to also learn to forgive yourself as well. By doing so, you'll help free yourself from your hostaged state and find peace. You'll release that anger and bitterness that kept you shackled.

Friendliness: the act of examining your ability to extend the hand of true friendship and respect to others. Discovering who your real friends are and how to be a true friend to others. Pledging to be an example of kindness, helpfulness and love. Being selective when choosing your friends: you are the company you keep, after all. Ridding yourself of shyness and surrounding yourself with friends of worth and value. Making the effort to be a sincere and true friend to yourself and those you choose to surround yourself with.

Generosity: the act of being kind, understanding and selfless. Being a helping hand prepared to serve and help others as opposed to being self-centered and stingy.

Gentleness: the act of having a kind and quiet nature as opposed to one that's harsh and violent. You understand that this is not a sign of weakness, but one of great strength.

Graciousness: the act of being polite in a way that shows respect. Acting with dignity and tact as opposed to rudeness and disrespect.

Gratitude: the act of finding a spirit of appreciation and thanks for what you have, what others give you and for life in general. Finding happiness, joy, peace and contentment in the "now" as opposed to being disappointed with what you have or how things are in the present moment. Despite how bad your situation may appear, you recognize it can always get worse and everything can be taken from you in a moment—without notice. Do you thank God, the universe?

Helpfulness: the act of giving assistance to those in need—without being asked. And when asked, giving that help with graciousness and service.

Honesty: the act of being fair and truthful to others as well as to yourself. Choosing integrity and truthfulness by avoiding deceitfulness.

Hope: the act of understanding that hope is believing and expecting that something is going to happen or change for the best, and believing in your future. Today IS the day everything changes for the better.

Humility: the act of seeing yourself as not being above others. Being modest and equal to others. Not displaying arrogance and pride.

Integrity: the act of being true to yourself and being honest; having strong moral principles, and extending these to others.

Imagination: the act of being imaginative is finding new and interesting ideas and having or showing creativity. Not allowing yourself to fall into the "ordinary." Not always settling for rationalism. Thinking outside the box and having fun doing it.

Joyfulness: the act of feeling, causing or showing great happiness and finding it within yourself. Finding hope, peace and love as opposed to a disconnect and suffering.

Kindness: the act of being thoughtful, caring and compassionate as opposed to being cruel and selfish.

Love: the act of feeling a strong and constant affection for someone else. Possessing a caring and selfless attitude toward others; exercising forgiveness and unity.

Loyalty: the act of being faithful, honest and trustworthy as opposed to having a nature that betrays others or an organization, thought or principle.

Moderation: the act of being reasonable and avoiding behavior, speech and anything else that is extreme or that goes beyond what is normal and acceptable. Exercising diligence and responsibility as opposed to being obsessive and overindulgent.

Modesty: that act of not being too proud or cocky about yourself or your abilities. Showing humility when appropriate as opposed to pushing self-confidence in everybody's face.

Optimism: the act of showing hope and trust in the future. Expecting that good things can happen. Seeing the glass as half-full as opposed to seeing it as half-empty. Exercising hopefulness and joyfulness as opposed to pessimism.

Orderliness: the act of finding ways to arrange and organize your life in a logical and regular way. Being organized as opposed to living in chaos.

Passion: the act of having, showing and expressing intense emotions and desire in or for something, someone and myself. Showing enthusiasm and purposefulness as opposed to indifference.

Patience: the act of waiting for a long period of time without becoming annoyed or upset. Being determined and at peace with waiting. Working toward what you're focused on without expecting results immediately. Exercising patience with yourself and with others.

Peace: the act of finding your state of tranquility and quietness. Express love, serenity and unity as opposed to anger and cruelty.

Perseverance: the act of remaining focused and on track with your efforts to complete or achieve something despite whatever difficulties, failures or opposition is in your way. Being truly committed, determined and resilient. Abandoning laziness.

Preparedness: the act of being ready. Organizing yourself and taking pride in excellence and orderliness. Getting rid of complacency.

Purposefulness: the act of setting goals for yourself and visualizing them and following this up by taking whatever action necessary to achieve it. Having intent in life and being creative, committed and joyful with it.

Reliability: the act of being dependable. Answering to others in a way that doesn't undermine you or your values. Selecting integrity and loyalty as opposed to untrustworthiness. Keeping your promises, appointments and commitments without falling behind.

Respect: the act of giving particular attention that is due to someone or something. Exercising dignity and reverence as opposed to inconsideration.

Responsibility: the act of being responsible as in moral, legal and mental accountability. Being courteous, tactful and trustworthy as opposed to exercising selfishness. Taking accountability for your own actions.

Self-discipline: the act of being committed and determined to regulate yourself for the sake of improvement. Remaining focused and on task.

Sincerity: the act of being free from pretence or deceit; proceeding from genuine feelings, honest and authentic.

Tactfulness: the act of having a strong moral sense of what to say and do for the purpose of maintaining good relations with others and avoid offensiveness. Exercising graciousness and responsibility for the things that you say and do.

Temperate: the act of exercising a habitual moderation in your indulgences, appetites and attitude. Adhering to moderation as opposed to excessiveness.

Thankfulness: the act of exercising a spirit of gratitude and being conscious of the benefits that you receive and have.

Tolerance: the act of having capacity to endure pain or hardship. Exercising sympathy and understanding for beliefs and practices that may differ or conflict with your own. Being patient and tenacious as opposed to remaining narrow-minded.

Trust: the act of having assured reliance on the character, ability, strength or truth of someone or something. Being loyal and respectful as opposed to being doubtful or skeptic. Having a firm belief in the reliability, truth, ability, or strength of someone or something.

Truthfulness: the act of telling and being disposed to tell it like it is; being honest and trustworthy as opposed to being corrupt and deceitful.

Understanding: the act of exercising the ability to try to understand the opinion or feelings of others while making adjustments for differences you may have. Understanding that you don't have to agree, but making an effort to see and respect the opinions of others.

Unity: the act of being joined to someone, a group or a purpose. Understanding that we are all part of the same universe and the same world and that you have a duty to live in harmony, love and peace as opposed to being on your own and lonely.

Wisdom: the act of being well read and knowledgeable. Seeking the advice of others who are more knowledgeable than yourself. Drawing from your past experiences and the lessons learned in order to make the right decisions today and say the right things.

This list of virtues can be used as an effective tool for self-examination to determine where your strengths and weaknesses lie and what questions you should be asking yourself to grow into the person you'd like to be. Asking yourself the right questions and examining where you are right now and what in your thinking, emotions, and behaviors is keeping you hostage, will allow you to return to reevaluate your strengths and weaknesses and come up with a plan and blueprint for change which will propel you forward to where you want to be.

CHAPTER 2 SUMMARY

◆ The power of our thoughts and what we repeat to ourselves in our inner monologues has a tremendous influence on our overall happiness and success. It's critically important that we replace the garbage we tell ourselves about ourselves with phrases and beliefs that are uplifting and empowering. Repeat these daily and you'll come to believe them.

◆ Our moods—or states of mind—are left up to us to choose. They don't choose us. No one puts a spell on your mood. You create them. Doesn't it make sense to pick a good one?

◆ Self-examination is important in helping us escape our captors. Once we discover our strengths and weaknesses we can adjust what needs to be adjusted from there. If you find you're happy with who you are and you've passed the self-examination test, then that's great. But if after you've taken a close look at yourself and you're not happy with some areas of your life, then start working on them.

◆ Ask yourself the right kinds of questions. Who you are and whether you're happy. Where you see yourself in six months or six years from now? Quality questions will encourage change.

CHAPTER 3

Our Enemies

The Enemy "Without": Threat of Violent Thieves and Explosives

I had been a patrol Sergeant for about two years with thirty-two officers under my command—a responsibility I shared with one other Sergeant and a Staff Sergeant. Prior to parading our platoon each day, we would familiarize ourselves with the events that affected our officers, BOLOs (be on the lookout for), special duties and general information, which we would then share with the shift. Safety and security for our officers and the community was our objective, and at the beginning of each shift we'd share this important information. I had developed a good rapport with my officers and with the members of the Tactical Unit who would also join our parade before each shift.

On one particular graveyard shift, I ended the parade with a question I asked every shift: "Does anyone have anything they'd like to add?" One of the Tactical officers reluctantly raised his hand. He proceeded to inform me that the Tactical Unit had been made aware of a team of violent thieves who were armed with explosives, which they had used to strike armored Brink's trucks and blow the doors off the trucks to scoop up the loot. He informed me—and the platoon—that they were exceedingly dangerous and active and that they may be headed into town. He added that his unit had been warned by their supervisor NOT to share this information with anyone . . . including the platoons of uniformed officers.

I was shocked. How could a fellow officer—a supervisor at that—instruct his Tactical Unit to not inform us of impending danger?! Any of my officers might have found themselves at the scene of a distress call involving a Brinks truck—unaware that explosives and armed thieves may be involved. I was furious! At least this Tactical officer had the courage to share this information and may have quite possibly saved my officers from serious injury and/or death.

Following the parade, I brought this information to my Staff Sergeant with the view that this violated the sharing of vital information and had no place within the police department. Every officer deserved to be informed and alert. Surprisingly, my Staff Sergeant cowered at the thought of making "waves" and thought I should simply leave it alone. I couldn't. Suddenly I felt the enemy was not only outside our thin blue line, but among us. I couldn't let it go.

I wrote a memorandum to the supervisor who had instructed his officers to suppress this information asking why. My report was non-threatening and stressed the importance of information sharing for the greater good of all. My report was not well received. In fact, his reply was not addressed to me. It was addressed to the Chief of Police in such a scathing way I could not let it go unchallenged. I had made an enemy from within our own ranks.

The next step involved a meeting with the Deputy Chief and finally a resolution—instructions to all supervisors that information of such significant importance must be shared with every officer. That still left me with an enemy I had never expected, and I sought the author of that scathing report. I waited to find him alone one night after shift and approached him to explain my reasons for taking the action I had taken. I also wanted to see whether he would hold a grudge against me. Working day-by-day with an enemy would be a constant struggle involving stress and exhaustion. I needed neither. He heard me out and shrugged it off. I felt I had done everything I had to do. I had no idea at the time that my actions would, rather amazingly, result in the respect he developed for me.

I was eventually transferred to the Sexual Assault and Child Abuse Unit under his command—a transfer he granted, notwithstanding and unrelated to our original encounter. We developed a satisfying and rewarding working relationship and mutual respect for each other. Funny how once the enemy is identified, you can find ways to approach him/her/it and do what you have to do to restore peace, harmony, and balance.

The Enemy "Within": Waking Up to a World of Zombies

Imagine waking up one day to a world suddenly infected by a freak viral outbreak and discovering that your neighborhood has been invaded by zombies. You find yourself in the middle of this terrifying new world, unaffected by the virus but with a whole new set of problems and challenges. Gripped by fear and terror, you realize you had better do something fast or you'll find yourself on a zombie menu and you'll turn into a blood-thirsty zombie yourself. You have just woken up; so at first you imagine you might still be dreaming. You close your eyes . . . but after opening them again and looking out your window, you discover it isn't a dream. And imagining the zombies will all go away won't make it so. You have tried it already and it didn't work. The zombies were still there when you opened your eyes, and your day is just about to get a lot worse if you don't do something immediately. Fear grips you and prevents you from moving . . . as though your feet have been cemented to the floor. You feel frozen with no means of freeing yourself. And, you're awake; this is not a dream.

Some of you have watched movies and TV programs like this one before; and you know that in every one of them, it's not going to be easy for the heroes to get away. They'll have a choice to enact either the "fight or flight" response—face and fight the zombies, or take flight . . . run . . . real fast. "Run, Forrest, run,"[16] you shout to the screen and then watch to see which of the survivors will become one of the walking dead. It all seems so hopeless. Some of the characters make it, whereas others don't. Some freeze and some take action. Your heroes soon discover that in order to survive they'll have to fight the zombies straight on by planning and implementing a specific and strategic course of action in order to survive. They discover that sur-

16. *Forrest Gump,* 1994 movie directed by Robert Zemeckis.

vival and victory can only come through deliberate planning and action. The zombies are everywhere and they see your heroes as nothing more than a source of food . . . their next meal.

It would be the same for each of us if we found ourselves waking up in that world. If you're not equipped to out-think and overpower your enemy . . . I would suggest you run and don't stop. Night is falling and it gets scarier and more terrifying at night, and you can't run forever. Eventually you'll get tired of running and you'll simply give in. You won't have the energy or the will to keep up the pace and the zombies will find you. They'll get you.

Well, you don't have to live in a zombie-filled world to experience much of the same hopelessness the characters in those stories do. Sure, you're not being chased by zombies; but let's equate the "zombies" to negative thoughts and the destructive internal mind-chatter that creep into your head. Imagine those negative, self-defeating voices and thoughts to be the "zombies" in your own life. They can show up unexpectedly and overpower your good and positive thoughts—leaving you to choose between "fight or flight." These intrusive thoughts—these zombies—don't disappear just because you hope they will or by sticking your head in the sand and pretending it's all a dream. Rather, they pose a real threat to you and to your overall mental and spiritual well-being. Simply wishing for them to be gone won't make them evaporate and disappear.

When fear is your gatekeeper

You become a hostage each time you allow intrusive thoughts to take control of your beliefs and of your inner monologues. Once they're in they have a way of creating the one thing that most often keeps you from taking positive action: fear. Fear has a way of suppressing courage and often prevents you from taking specific and deliberate action because you equate that fear with a sense of pain. Once you equate fear with pain, you might simply give in to those voices in your head telling you to "stay put," "you're no good," and "there's no point in even trying," or whatever other fear-laden zombie thoughts are deposited in your mind. Remember that once a thought like that gets in, it can and often does become your predominant thought. Your unconscious mind will then work overtime at trying to store it, and it can become your worst enemy. With fear as your gatekeeper, you'll find yourself losing the battle against the zombies and they'll eventually find your hiding place. When your mind is filled with thoughts that fall short of empowering you, you've lost out to your attackers. Don't worry though—that can easily change, and you can get right on track to un-hostaging yourself.

Your enemies appear in many different forms

Your zombie thoughts (aka zombies) can take on many different forms and attack you in a myriad of ways. For that reason, it's important to become aware of the ways in which they might appear so that you can first see a potential attack coming; and next, have a plan in place to fight off the attack before it has a chance to take you hostage.

For some people, and you know who you are, you're already under attack. Not to stress: awareness is power; and with it, you can get an upper hand if you recognize who your enemies are.

For some of you, the aggressor might be an **_All-or-nothing_** attack[17]: an attack in which you see what happens to you in terms only black and white. What happens to you is either all perfect or a total failure, no matter how big or small the event. In the case, for instance, of an individual, yourself perhaps, "on a diet," a single moment of indulgence in which you have one spoonful of ice cream, might have you looking at that moment and saying, "I've completely blown my diet, I'll never lose weight"—after which you proceed to abandon the diet and devour the entire tub. The unconscious mind will respond to your dominant thought. The all-or-nothing victim never sees the full picture. Their monologues are either extremely happy or extremely sad. They don't look for the positive which exists in every situation.

17. Cognitive distortions: http://psychcentral.com/lib/15-common-cognitive-distortions/0002153

Others might be targeted by an **Overgeneralization** attack: an attack in which you experience a setback as a never-ending pattern of defeat. In the case of a romantic rejection or loss of employment for example, you might fall into using phrases like "this always happens to me," and "I'll never find . . . " etc. You get the picture. On and on it goes. You feel defeat and don't bother to examine the activating event for what it is and how it came to be. You don't look for the root cause and your overgeneralization prevents you from being realistic and from moving on with courage and determination. You remain, instead, in the stale pattern of feeling defeated.

Still others might be targeted by a **Filtering** attack: an attack in which you take the negative details of an event and magnify them while filtering out all positive aspects of the situation. For example, you may pick out a single or unpleasant detail and dwell on it exclusively so that your vision of reality becomes darkly distorted. You fail to understand the entire message or event and pick only the hurtful or negative points of what was said or implied. You don't filter it all through fairly. For example, your girlfriend or wife tells you look amazing but you could have worn a different tie. Suddenly, to you, that's the only thing you focus on—the tie doesn't look right so, "I must look really bad."

While others might be targeted by a **Jumping to Conclusions** attack: an attack in which, for example, without anyone saying so, you already know what *they* are feeling and why *they* are behaving the way they are. You believe you already know how people are feeling toward you without examining the facts or considering the evidence. You don't bother to determine the reality because you've jumped to the conclusion already, so it must be right. Or maybe you've just anticipated that things will turn out badly, and you're convinced that your prediction is already an established fact. Those zombie thoughts often come as, "I knew it! I just knew it!" followed by further negativity.

Then there are those who might be targeted by a **Catastrophizing** attack: an attack in which you expect disaster to strike, no matter what. This is also explained as "magnifying or minimizing." You exaggerate the size of your problems, discomforts or shortcomings and see them as being much bigger monsters than they are. You hear about a problem and use "what if?" questions: ("What if tragedy strikes?" "What if it happens to me?"). For example, you might exaggerate the importance of insignificant events (such as a minor mistake you made, or someone else's achievement over yours). Or, looking at it from a different perspective, you may inappropriately shrink the magnitude of significant events and things until they appear inaccurately tiny (for example, our own desirable qualities or someone else's imperfections). You can end up overlooking them. Think about the potential outcome of a new love interest if we were to "minimize" his/her faults . . .

Moreover, some of you might be targeted by a **Personalization** attack: an attack in which you believe that everything others say or do is some kind of direct, personal attack on you. You may also compare yourself to others trying to determine who is smarter, better-looking, more successful and so forth. A person finding himself/herself under a personalization attack may also see himself/herself as the cause of an unhealthy external event for which they were not responsible. An example of this may be, "We were late to the dinner party and caused the hostess to overcook our meal. If I had only pushed to leave on time, this wouldn't have happened."

Some people might be targeted by a **Control Fallacies** attack: an attack in which, if you feel externally controlled by something or someone, you see yourself as a helpless victim of fate. For example, you might say, "I can't help it if my report was less than perfect—my boss rushed me." The misconception of internal control, on the other hand, has us assuming responsibility for the pain and happiness of everyone around us. For example, you might ask, "Why aren't you happy? Is it because of something I did?"

Still others might be targeted by a **Fallacy of Fairness** attack: an attack in which you feel resentful because you think life ought to be more fair, more just. You're under the false impression that life is designed to be fair to you, becoming resentful and hurt when things don't work out the way you expected they should. If you go through life applying an imaginary measuring ruler, judging every situation by its "fairness," you'll undoubtedly end up feeling cheated. Things will not always work out in your favor, even when you think they should. Your inner monologues will hostage you to a false belief that life should be fair.

And some might be targeted by a **Blaming** attack: an attack in which you hold other people responsible for your pain and misfortunes, or you take the other approach and blame yourself for every bad thing that happens to you. For example, you might say "Stop making me feel bad about myself!" You fail to remember that nobody can *make* you feel any particular way, that only *you* have control over your own emotions and reactions.

As well, many people are targeted by a **Shoulds** attack: an attack in which you have imagined and created a list of rules and expectations on how others and you, yourself should behave, no matter what. If you've been attacked by the "shoulds" virus, people who break your preconceived rules make you angry, and you feel guilty and let down when you violate your own rules. You demand a great deal from yourself and from others and you tend to punish yourself and others unjustly because of the rigid expectations you put in place. For example, you might think, "I really should get to the gym. I shouldn't be so lazy." Musts and ought to's are big zombies. The emotional consequence of being hostaged by them is a feeling of guilt. When you direct "should" statements toward others, you often feel anger, frustration, resentment and generally let down.

For some of you, you might be targeted by an **Emotional Reasoning** attack: an attack in which a cognitive distortion occurs and your unconscious mind convinces you of something that isn't true. These self-defeating thoughts usually show up to reinforce negative thoughts or emotions you may be already harboring. Telling yourself things that sound rational and right only serve to keep you feeling bad about yourself or your situation. For example, in the case where you tell yourself, "I always fail when I try to do something new; I fail at everything I try"—similar to the "black or white" (or polarized) thinking whereby the victim only sees things in absolutes—that if they fail at one thing, they must also fail at all things. If you added "I must be a complete loser and failure" to your thinking, that's also an example of overgeneralization—taking a failure at one specific task and generalizing it to form your identity. You believe that what you feel in the moment must be true. If you feel stupid and boring, then you must actually be stupid and boring. You assume that your unhealthy emotions reflect the way things truly are, as if to say: "I feel it; therefore it must be true."

Again others might be targeted by a **Fallacy of Change** attack: an attack in which you expect that other people will change to suit you if you just pressure or sweet-talk them long enough—if you just wear them down. You feel a need to change people because your hopes for happiness seem to depend entirely on them.

Or some might be targeted by a **Global Labeling** attack: an attack in which you generalize one or two qualities in yourself or others, and turn them into a negative global judgment. Global labeling picks the negative and ignores any evidence to the contrary, creating a view of the world that can be stereotypical and one-dimensional. Labeling yourself can have a negative and insidious impact on your self-esteem; while labeling others can lead to you to make snap judgments, lead you to experience relationship problems, and to develop prejudice. These are extreme forms of generalizing, and are also referred to as "labeling" and "mislabeling." Instead of describing an error within the context of a specific situation, you will attach an unhealthy label to it and accept it as a global truth. For example, you may say, "I'm a loser!" in a situation where you failed at ONE specific task. Or if someone else's behavior doesn't agree with you, you may attach an unhealthy label to that person, such as "He's a real jerk." Mislabeling involves describing an event with language that is highly self-defeating, emotionally motivated, self-sabotaging (when applied to yourself), even abusive—of self or others.

Then there are those among you who might be targeted by an **Always Being Right** attack: an attack in which you are continually on trial to prove that your opinions and actions are always right. Being wrong is not an option to those who suffer from this virus, and they'll go to any lengths to try to prove their rightness. For example, they might say, "I don't care how you feel, but I'm going to win this argument no matter what or how it makes you feel because I'm right and you're wrong." Being right is often more important than the feelings of others—even of their loved ones—for the sufferer who engages in this particular cognitive distortion.

And finally, there's the **Heaven's Reward Fallacy** attack: an attack in which you expect your sacrifice and self-denial to pay off, as if someone is actually keeping score. You feel bitter and unfulfilled when the reward doesn't come.

Some or all of the "zombies" listed above may not apply to you, whereas others may see them as real hostage-takers. Any one of these fallacies can affect your thoughts, feelings and actions. We can only process one thought at a moment, remember? The dominant thought affects the unconscious mind. It can turn your thoughts dark and keep you from enjoying your life the way they were meant to be enjoyed. If you're hostaged by these attackers, it might seem easier to give into them rather than fight. It may seem easier to run and hide from them instead of facing them to determine how and why they took you hostage in the first place. The problem is, you can't run forever; and if you stay put, they might just get the best of you and the story won't end well.

Self-sabotaging your state of mind, your thoughts, will have its way with you if you don't do something to prevent the attack, or if you do not fight those thoughts once they're in. The power to do so, remember, lies in your awareness of the process. Being aware of who/what your attackers are forms the basis of your resistance. Being vigilant of the process of thought-hostaging, and especially of your role in it, and not allowing yourself to remain passive, as if you are a bystander rather than the mind under invasion, is fundamental to remaining in control of the domain of your own mind. And if a role model helps to remind us of the importance of resisting being taken hostage by our own thoughts, we need only remember one of the greatest examples of resistance of all times—the French Resistance Movement during World War II—which was in no small way responsible for France's eventual freedom from the oppressor. Armed with their vision of freedom, undaunted by fear, the French designed an efficient underground network to stave off being possessed by the invading enemy. The conclusion: triumph!

CHAPTER 3 SUMMARY

◆ We don't have to live in a zombie-filled world to experience hope-lessness and discouragement. Our own thoughts and internal monologues can do a fine job at accomplishing that on their own. Instead of being flesh-eating bloodsuckers, thoughts that keep you from joy and success can drain the will and happiness out of you. They take you hostage and come in many varieties . . . but the good news is that you can escape them, unlike the fictional zombies who will physically eat you.

◆ Fear is the biggest excuse in giving in to non-action. Fear will keep some people captive forever. But I urge you not to let fear keep you from trying anything. Ask for what you want. Ask for that date, that job, and whatever else you want. Don't let fear be your gate-keeper. Plan to win; and if you fall flat on your face the first time, get up and try again. It may very well be scary at first. But the more you try, the less fear you'll experience until fear disappears. You may experience rejection at first, but *never* take it personally. Get rid of fear or be hostage to its tentacles. Indeed, it is the very *root* of the hostage phenomenon which can corrupt the best intentions in the world.

CHAPTER 4

Developing a Plan

New Year's Eve, 1984. I was a training officer and was partnered with Jeff Hewett, a newly hired rookie who followed direction quite well and seemed eager to do the best he could. Jeff was a "yes sir" kind of recruit, happy to be there and happy to wear the uniform. We were working the afternoon shift when we received a radio call to attend a rural area in close proximity to Sunderland, Ontario, to assist in a ground search at the scene of a homicide. It wasn't until we arrived on scene that we were informed that the victim of the homicide was believed to be 9-year-old Christine Jessop.[18]

Christine had disappeared from her home in Queensville, Ontario, on October 3, 1984, after being dropped off by a school bus at 3:50 PM. She was described as a young girl who loved life; and being dispatched to the scene in which her lifeless body was still present was not how I would have chosen to spend my New Year's Eve—or any eve, for that matter. She was an innocent little girl, abducted, sexually assaulted, and murdered; and I felt an over-whelming sense of sadness as I was assigned my duties that night. Jeff and I were tasked along with other officers to conduct a ground search for potential evidence. The night was cold, crisp and clear. The ground was frozen, and we were on our hands and knees along-side several other officers moving forward slowly, sifting through the grass and brush for any piece of evidence that might help iden-tify and catch her killer. I could feel my bones freezing up under my

18. www.attorneygeneral.jus.gov.on.ca/english/about/pubs/morin/morin
_esumm.pdf

thin uniform pants. A chill got to me. But it wasn't solely from the ground beneath my knees.

At one point during the night, I was asked to assist in carrying Christine's remains to a van that would take her to a facility for forensic examination. As I approached her lifeless form, I saw an image I will never forget throughout my entire life. Her head was missing, she was on her back, and her legs were spread apart in an unnatural fashion. One sock hung loosely from her foot, and what remained of her decomposed body was mostly skeletal. Animals had chewed much of her remains, and it was suspected that they had carried off her head. I won't go into any further gruesome detail here about what I saw of her, but it suffices to say it was heartbreaking. It made me ill with an image, a memory I can never erase.

What does this have to do with a motivational book you may be asking? The investigation that was conducted into her murder illuminates the challenge, but the necessity, of effectively processing devastating events, the breadth and width of which exceed what are normally labeled as stressful. You'll see how this connects to the importance of dealing with your own stress and adversity. For starters, the sadness I sensed when I first arrived on scene had to be set aside while I focused on doing the best job I could despite the ugliness of the circumstances of which I was a part.

Ours was not an experienced Police Department back in 1984. Detectives were trained, yes, but not to today's standards. Accountability and planning was not as important as it is today either. Who knew it was going to snow the next day, covering the ground in a thick blanket of white crust, crippling the efforts of a new shift of officers assigned to conduct a subsequent ground search? Well, the Officer-in-Charge should have known and should have planned. But his lack of preparation meant no tents were erected to shield the grounds from the snow and facilitate the search to keep it going as it had been. This was one of many mistakes made during this long investigation—and one of many that would later be scrutinized, dissected, and criticized.

Don't get me wrong—I'm not writing this to cast aspersion on the coppers who worked long and hard on this case. Many of them I respected and admired. Some I did not. The purpose of telling you how problematic this investigation was is to focus on the importance of being prepared, aware, knowledgeable, and determined to do the best you can in your own quest to eradicate self-sabotaging thoughts, the subject of this book. That's why a systematic, well-thought-out, assiduous plan and subsequent course of action are both essential to any successful undertaking—especially when dealing with our self-defeating thoughts.

Following the trials of Guy Paul Morin, the man accused of Christine's murder and later exonerated, the Lieutenant Governor in Council directed that a Public Inquiry be held; and, on June 26, 1996, a commission was issued appointing the Honorable Fred Kaufman to examine the administration of Justice in Ontario.[19] Several note-worthy recommendations were made for the improvement of police investigations, and I'm happy to report that the service provided by my former police service unit improved immensely as the errors made in that investigation were identified and eradicated from future investigations.

This foregoing example serves to briefly cast light on an aspect of the human being and his/her behavior and choices: at times, you stumble, you fall, and you become aware of what can potentially hurt you or keep you from moving forward. Many successful people fail several times before getting it right but they keep trying and that's a key to their success. Others stumble and fall only once. They stop trying and fail to benefit from their mistakes or to discover ways to avoid failure a second or third time, instead of holding themselves accountable for improving their lot. These people never succeed, but remain mired in one or more of the "Fallacies" outlined in Chapter 3.

When setbacks occur or when you become hostage to yourself, you need to enable a system that not only alerts you of your state but also deploys methods to get you back on track—methods that empower you as opposed to disempowering you.

19. www.attorneygeneral.jus.gov.on.ca/english/about/pubs/morin/morin _esumm.pdf

You become hostage to self-destructive thoughts and disempowering inner monologues by choice. When the words and actions of others affect the way you feel about your situations and yourself they become accomplices to an act of sabotage—the *hostaging* of your thoughts. Simply put, you can hostage yourself completely on your own or by letting others affect you by what they say and do. Often enough, the two entwine to guarantee the sabotage or hostaging. But *you* make the ultimate choice of how to interpret what happens to you. *No one* else does that. No one else can . . . not without your permission. And because you are the author of your own narrative, when you allow others to affect you negatively, you inadvertently hire them as the mob that becomes the accomplice in your very own demise.

How you feel and how you react to an event that happens in your life is entirely up to you, notwithstanding that you may not at first realize that truism. You are the only one who is in charge of your responses, feelings and actions. No one has the power to make you feel sad or bad, no one makes you feel angry; and in most cases,[20] no one prevents you from moving ahead and living your life the way you want to live it. No one but you that is, because it is endemically your choice. Thus, while people and situations outside of your control can inflict or cause you physical, psychological, or emotional pain and/or harm; and while anyone can say things that are meant to be hurtful to you, when it comes to how you feel about what they say, how you feel, and how you choose to react—is genuinely up to you. One caveat is that the moment of choice can sometimes be mercurially brief, with the result that if you do not seize it immediately, it evaporates without recourse or return. And this is why you must be prepared, as I have said repeatedly and shall continue to throughout this book . . . prepared for the assaulting thought which can and will, given a breath of a chance, take you hostage.

By taking yourself hostage by choice, albeit somewhat unconsciously, and permitting others to become accomplices to your

---

20. As we will see later in a true-crime story of kids kept captive, others can effectively control our movements and the direction of our lives, but they can't control our thoughts and will.

sadness and condition, you are choosing to react negatively when life throws you a setback or when someone says something meant to hurt your feelings or direct your thoughts and monologues. That reaction reflex may be something you've developed over time or something you saw others do and then adopted for yourself. Despite how you may have learned to become reactive, you have made a choice: to react without first STOPPING[21] to assess the situation intelligently and thoughtfully. If you fall prey to knee-jerk reactions to everything that happens, you abandon your right to make the best choice for yourself in the moment when choice *must* be made, a choice required if you truly want to positively influence the outcome of the situation challenging you. By simply reacting, you disregard one of your many gifts and abilities: the ability to choose how to react in the face of whatever happens to you as opposed to reacting without thought or acting impulsively.

If it is, therefore, by **choice** that you must react or learn to react; then, surely, with practice, you can train yourself to become less reactive and develop the ability to act "thoughtfully"—with the penultimate goal of freeing yourself from being kept hostage any time a hostage-taking invades the domain of your mind. The techniques for so doing are few, simple, and effective.

Of course, admittedly, at times, you are simply unaware of your reactive states—you may not have conducted the self-evaluation so necessary for identifying those culprit states which lead to self-hostage situations. Remember that awareness is power and remaining unaware means you're not acting in defensive mode. You're simply living your life one day at a time, exposed to disappointments and discouragements, setbacks and trauma just like everyone else on the planet. When a setback occurs, the self-talk in your head turns dark; and when that happens, you have been taken captive. Totally unprepared, you've been taken hostage by a knee-jerk reaction. To avoid this, it is imperative to spend time preparing your defense mechanisms.

---

21. STOPPING, or to simply Stop is the first in the acronym S.T.E.P.—a process that will be discussed in a later chapter.

Creating your own Systematic "Empowering" (and Enabling) Management Plan[22]

This section might sound intimidating at first for a book on motivation; but I assure you, it's not. The idea is to help you develop a system you can access immediately to empower yourself by examining how, in this case, the Canadian government prepares for emergencies using a systematic approach that works. These next few pages will summarize how their plans are "systematically" put into place so that you might also benefit from this approach and use it whenever you find yourself under attack by yourself. Understanding what works will help you to systematically take control of the way you think, and reprogram your mindset to reap the benefits of un-hostaged living.

Respecting the guideposts will allow you to take control of your thinking so that you'll be able to live by your choices and desires and not by those of others. It will help you embrace a mindset of power and control and help you develop control over your thoughts and actions. Fortunately, you don't have to understand exactly how the mind works. That's too big of a task and expectation. Simply know that this all works—for you.

It is the duty and responsibility of all Governments and Ministries to protect the people under their care from disaster. Whether those disasters are caused by nature—natural hazards such as hurricanes, earthquakes, flood, drought, and so on—or man-made—governments establish objectives, guidelines and courses of action on how to best deal with disasters once they occur, as well as a series of steps to prevent or minimize the damage.

They do this by creating an E.M.P.—an "Emergency Management Plan." This is a systematic approach to identifying and minimizing the impact of multiple risks to life, property and our environment: risks associated with geological, meteorological or biological hazards; risks which arise from "intentional human actions" such as chemical

---

22. References: Canadian Government, Public Safety Canada, www.publicsafety .gc.ca/cnt/mrgnc-mngmnt/index-eng.aspx

or nuclear attacks through acts of terrorism or sabotage; risks which derive from "unintentional human actions, such as chemical, nuclear or others hazards resulting from accidents, hazardous spills, release, explosion, fire, among others. Every possibility is examined along with risks associated with each, after which a plan of action is developed. And it serves us well herein to examine the strategy of assessing risk as it applies to the management of our own lives, especially in the domain of the health of a free and un-hostaged mind, one of the underpinnings of a life lived, not in fear, but rather in the comfort of personal security.

Emergency Management Planning provides a foundation for coordinating and integrating all types of activities needed to build, sustain, and improve the capability to mitigate against, prepare for, respond to, and recover from threatened or actual natural disasters and criminal acts including terrorism or other man-made disasters. It's "systematic," which means that it is done according to a fixed plan or system: it's methodical. And it makes use of every resource available to it in order to implement and "enable" the right action to be taken by the right experts. It's a team effort, drawing on the expertise of others; and it's also considered a "living document," meaning that it can be added to and improved on through experience and lessons learned.

We would each benefit by developing our own "self" EMP—our SEMP; but instead of using the word "Emergency" in our plan we replace it with the words "Empowering" and "Enabling." To "enable" is to give the authority or means to do something. This is precisely what is required to keep ourselves from becoming hostages to ourselves and to free us from captivity when we find ourselves taken hostage.

Accessing your SEMP

Eleanor Roosevelt once said that no one can make you feel inferior without your consent. The corollary is true that no one can make you feel bad unless you let them. It's not always easy to remain unaffected by the words or actions of others, especially if their messages are hurtful and were meant to hurt. The fact is, to have the ability to remain unaffected by the insensitivity of others is a learned skill. Some of you may have been taught this vital skill from good parents, a great mentor, wonderful life lessons, or by emulating other strong people. But many others have not. We'll examine how to develop this essential skill throughout this book.

As you grow into adulthood you should come to the realization that your life is really yours to live. Your parents and guardians, for most of you, are no longer telling you what to do, nor are they with you every minute to help direct you. You're left on your own to make it through life. You've been released from the nest, as it should be. No one else is going to live your life for you—nor should they. And no one else is going to feel or think for you either. Choices and decisions are yours to make. It's up to you, and no one else, to rescue yourself if you're taken hostage. To leave your fate and happiness in the hands of someone else is a recipe for disaster. You can develop the KSAs (the knowledge, skills and ability) to fight off your attackers and create a SEMP that works for you. The good news is that you have the ability to create your own mental images and goals; and by doing so consciously, you are not allowing your fate to be left up to chance.

Your SWOT team

"SWOT" stands for Strengths, Weaknesses, Opportunities and Threats. It is a crucial piece of any Emergency Management Plan and for good reason. When determining how to best prevent or deal with hazards of all types once they occur, a team of individuals is selected and tasked with identifying their SWOT, which in turn helps them create a solid Emergency Management Plan. They identify strengths, weaknesses, opportunities and threats—keeping it specific, realistic and relatively simple.

And so it should be with you. By conducting a periodic and honest SWOT analysis on yourself, you can identify what your strengths, weaknesses, opportunities and threats are to determine how that information can help you effectively plan and deal with the hostage-takers when they arrive. For example, are you the kind of person who can find strength by reading, watching or listening to motivational material often? Whether a book, an upbeat motivational speaker, a spiritual passage, yoga or other uplifting activity, are you the kind of person who can use that when you're being attacked by negativity? Or in the case of a weakness or threat, are you easily led astray by others and associate yourself with people who bring you down and fill your head with intrusive self-defeating thoughts? Is the company you keep preventing you from moving in the direction you need to, and thereby weakening you? And as for opportunities, are you the kind of person who can identify and/or create them?

Being thorough and honest with your SWOT will help you create a strong Systematic Enabling and Empowering Management Program. Keep it simple. We all find relief and happiness in different activities. Whether working out at the gym, doing yoga, reading a good book, watching a good movie, or taking a walk in nature, or engaging in a multitude of other things, discovering what helps you deal with (and prevent) the hostage-takers from settling in, is an extremely important part of your success plan. Discover what works for you when you conduct your self-examination, and use it. Examine why you may be an easy target for whatever gets you down, and do something about it. By asking the right kinds of questions, the right kinds of answers have a way of surfacing.

Here's another example of preparation. How many times have you found yourself without electrical power in the middle of the night, searching for a match to light a candle or a flashlight to illuminate your way? Those who have experienced power shortages frequently plan for them, and they have their matches handy and their flashlights within reach. Their understanding has provided them with awareness that a power shortage could occur, and this awareness motivates them to plan ahead. I lived in a rural community and we often lost power. Sometimes it would last for days in the dead of a Canadian winter. Planning ahead of time what meals we could prepare under those conditions, stocking up on extra blankets, and having candles and a generator handy helped immensely.

In the external world of good guys and bad guys, before a hostage is taken, he/she has no clue what is in store for them. In the blinking of an eye, their reality changes and escape is not an option. Had they known what was going to happen, that awareness would have motivated them to take different steps to prevent their capture. They may have taken a different route, for example. The same is true with you—now that you've become aware of how easily you can be taken hostage by yourself, by your thoughts and by your past, you can plan not to be taken. Whenever a thought of doubt or self-defeat enters your mind, your awareness can now act as one of your guards and help set in motion your "empowering" management plan before you're taken captive by those thoughts. This awareness releases the guard, and you can then activate your other defenders to keep you safe.

In case this sounds easy, it is not necessarily so. It takes willpower to stick to a plan that, in the beginning, may be attacked by a persuasive enemy, so to speak. For example, when deciding to have that one piece of cake while on a diet, your hostage-takers will arrive to tempt you "just this once"; and although you may stop yourself at first, how easy will it be for them to persuade you to give in? Even though you've been successful at stopping and considering the effect that one piece will have on your diet, your hostage-takers will be relentless with suggestions such as, "It's just this one time," and "C'mon, you only live once." This applies to eating, skipping a workout, having a drink, or listening to/accepting someone else's ideas in contradiction to your own, and a multitude of other things. To give in to someone else's way of thinking will be a loss at the evaluation stage and your defense plan will have failed. Keeping your goal in mind by having performed the self-awareness exercise earlier will help you see the destination you have created for yourself, which, in turn, will help you resist the temptation to give in. You'll find a better substitute for whatever weakness tempts you.

You may experience a sense of awkwardness at first when you direct your guard to remove the sabotaging thoughts from your mind. But like anything, once you practice something long enough, you develop fine skills that enable you to complete a task with relative ease. It becomes easier the more you work at it. The muscle gets stronger the more you exercise—as does the brain. Developing self-defense for your negative and self-defeating thoughts in addition to regularly practicing and using the skills you develop will lead to your victory over them. Those self-destructive thoughts won't stand a chance against you and your guard, and after a while the zombies will seldom show up to take you on. They will see how powerful you've become and how far you've come since your training and they'll be reluctant to try entering your space because they'll know that you have developed a new habit—one that wins.

With awareness, comes responsibility to yourself. Develop a habit to immediately deploy your self-defense guards and eliminate all negative and harmful thoughts—they don't serve you. Replace the "I can't" with "I can," and develop this skill until all you hear in the monologue of your mind is, "I can do this!" Now don't even think of using a statement like, "This is going to be tough, but I can do it!" The moment you use "this is going to be tough" in your thought, guess what? Your unconscious mind conditions itself to think "this is going to be tough" and you may find yourself making that your predominant thought. That won't help you defeat the negativity holding you back. Be aware of what you tell yourself and leave all the unnecessary self-defeating fillers out.

The Pain and Pleasure Principle

One of the principles we should examine before we proceed further is the "pain and pleasure" principle. In so many areas of our lives, including taking the time to develop a simple EMP for instance, the effect pain and pleasure has on our actions can be that one thing that keeps us from taking that first step.

When you associate taking a particular action which may involve pain, that association will in many cases keep you from taking that first action. It works this way: as humans, we're designed to avoid pain. However, ironically, the association of pain we link to taking any particular action leaves us open to be taken hostage, effectively shackling ourselves from taking the first step because of the pain we associate to it. We send messages to our beliefs that if we take part in that action, something's going to hurt—physically or mentally. Messages like, "It'll be too hard," "That's going to take a lot of time and effort," and "I can't handle that kind of diet or exercise." Whatever the messages we send ourselves, once they've managed to get in (the consequence of not having successfully fought them off with our EMP perhaps), they may keep you from even trying to take that action because of the association to pain you have given them.

With that in mind, who is then holding you hostage from taking action? The answer is: yourself. You are the one who convinces yourself, "I can't;" "I'm not good enough;" "There's no way I can do this;" "It's too hard;" or, "It will hurt . . . " You associate taking certain actions with pain. Making new associations and believing in yourself and your abilities to undertake your goals despite the pain you have associated to the undertaking is an essential component to success and happiness. It will require you to create new associations to link the actions you avoid taking to the principle of "pleasure."

Since the beginning of time, man has avoided pain. Great thinkers have examined to just what lengths we'll go to avoid it and, how doing so can affect our behavior and actions. Ancient Greek philosopher Epicurus (341–270 BC) and British philosopher Jeremy Bentham (1748–1832) have both examined the role pain and pleasure have in directing human behavior. "Nature has placed mankind under the governance of two sovereign masters: pain and pleasure." (Jeremy Bentham) Sigmund Freud also examined the theory that our minds seek pleasure and avoid pain [*Project for a Scientific Psychology*, 1895]. More recently, Tony Robbins has passionately been sharing and teaching these principles to millions and challenges his audiences to begin making new associations to the actions they have been associating to pain.

We avoid pain. We know to do so by common sense; and as we can see, some brilliant philosophers have examined how avoiding pain affects what we do. If taking a particular action then is something you associate with "pain," then naturally you'll avoid it. I'll give you an example: if thinking about going to the gym is painful to you, you'll avoid going to the gym. You'll come up with excuses to keep you from going and you'll talk yourself out of it. You'll convince yourself that it's going to hurt. You'll tell yourself that it's going to take too much time. You'll tell yourself that you won't like it. And consequently, your mind will convince your body to avoid it (the pain). Your inner voice will tell you, "Why would I put myself through some-

DEVELOPING A PLAN ◆ 83

thing like that?" The impetus of the process: a look in the mirror or a feeling of being not as fit as you'd like to be. That becomes a dominant thought that turns into an inner monologue. When your inner monologue contains self-defeating words and phrases that you don't immediately reject and deploy your Empowering Management Plan to keep out, defeat begins to take root. This grows into feelings of abandonment before you even try, and you become hostage to those feelings and subsequent thoughts. Pain associations take root and you'll avoid the pain at all costs by giving in to the abductors.

If, however, you were to choose to look at pain differently and enable your positive (pleasurable) management team to associate more upbeat thoughts to taking that action and tell yourself that going to the gym is a "good thing;" that "you'll like how it makes you feel and look;" "how much healthier you'll be for having gone;" and "focus on the pleasure associated with the benefits of going;"—then your mind will begin to create new associations to going to the gym. You'll begin to look at the pleasure and reward that going will bring you. A breakdown of this process may be: a look in the mirror and/or a feeling of not being as fit as you'd like to be. That becomes a thought that turns into an inner monologue. The inner monologue contains self-defeating words and phrases but you immediately reject them and use your Empowering Management Plan to keep them out. You stop for a moment to ask yourself why you're avoiding going to the gym and what is the source and origin of those thoughts. You examine the benefits of regular exercise and choose encouraging monologues that grow into feelings of pleasure you now associate to regular gym attendance and workouts, thereby preventing yourself from being taken hostage by the thought of pain with which you once associated exercising. Pleasure associations are now created and you'll look forward to your first workout by not having given in to your abductors.

Developing new pleasure associations

Once you begin to practice this regularly, your brain will develop new associations for you; and going to the gym will no longer appear as a dreaded chore but it will become a wonderful opportunity to help you become fit, healthy, and beautiful. You'll begin to feel all the exceptional things associated with working out; instead, the "pleasure" you'll receive from regular workouts will become your new associations. Fake it until you make it. You'll go from having associated pain with working out to associating pleasure with it; and the dread you once associated with the gym will be replaced with the pleasure you now attach to the experience.

When I was teaching at the police college in 2001, I had let myself go physically. My weight at the time was 193 pounds. I'm 5'8" and I wasn't physically fit. I wasn't pretty. I remember teaching a class, and as was customary in most of the classes I taught, the students would want to have a class photograph taken with me. So we gathered around for the picture, it was taken, and I received a copy of it a few days later. We didn't have the convenience of instant digital and share photography back then. What I saw was very discouraging. I had a belly on me, and I looked awful. I didn't look healthy at all. And I remember thinking to myself that this is not the way that I wanted to live my life. After seeing that photograph, I made a decision. I decided that I didn't want to be overweight anymore and that I wanted to live a healthy lifestyle and slim down. So I started out on a path of regular and consistent exercise. And I also kept a journal. I made it a regular habit to exercise daily and to keep a journal entry each day to document my progress. Over the next few months, I dropped from 193 pounds down to 170 pounds. I lost 23 pounds in just four months, replacing fat with muscle. And by developing a much better physique, I felt happier; and this resulted in me not only being physically and emotionally healthier, but I felt overall better about myself. I studied techniques on weightlifting, resistance training and diet. I had a plan and I followed through on that plan. As I maintained my journal, I would from time to time read my earlier journal entries, and this provided me with wonderful encouragement—I could read about my journey to health. My first journal entry on my road to a healthier lifestyle was something like "Today, I was able to do 10 sit ups. It hurt. I'm going to try to do more tomorrow." It was that simple. And as the months went by, my entries were a lot more positive. The things that seemed hard at first became much easier—and I could do more sit-ups and lift heavier weights and feel better for it. Because I had made that choice and that decision, and followed through with action, my consistent behavior resulted in a much healthier body and mind. I'm now resting at 160 lbs. and more fit than I've ever been. And I'm 59.

Now at first I didn't know everything there was to know about fitness and resistance training, but I made it a point to find out. The more I exercised, the more I discovered what my body could handle; and through the guidance of others who knew much more than I did and the literature I read, I was able to reach my goal. Today I weigh 160 pounds and I have a muscular physique. Being a man in my 50s, I'm quite proud of that accomplishment and I plan to continue with this healthy lifestyle for the rest of my life. I've made it a lifestyle. I can actually say that my physique looks like one of a healthy 25-year-old. And how did this all come about? Again, it was simply by making a choice and decision and following through with consistent action. Don't be concerned that you don't know everything there is to know about the goal you set in your mind.

At the time I associated the idea of heading to the gym with pain, so I conveniently made excuses for not going. "Where am I going to find the time in my busy day?"—or—"Man, working out hurts!"—or—"I'll never look like any of the other fit guys in those gyms anyway, and I'll look stupid!" were but a few of my objections. But then I examined what it would mean to me to get in shape. And I began to create new associations instead: "You can do this!"—"Think how great you're going to look and feel!"—"Hey, the journey of a thousand miles begins with a single step and you're taking the first!" The more I focused on these new associations, the more important they became to me. Now fifteen years later, I'm in the best shape I've been in since my early 20s. I feel great, look great, and hate missing a workout. My quality of life has improved, and many people often mistake me for being fifteen years younger than I am. I've become an example for so many younger (and older) men. All these benefits can become yours—by making new associations, by examining your current associations with a different point of view and then choosing to take action. Imagine how great you'll look and feel, how the quality of your life will improve, and how you'll retain youth well into your 80s and 90s. You owe it to yourself. And that's just a single example.

You can develop new associations with anything: a change in your diet, studying a new language, playing guitar or any other challenge you wish to undertake. Whatever you once associated pain with, you can begin to associate pleasure with by first releasing those hostaged thoughts and voices that are telling you, "It's not going to work;" and replacing them with "This is going to be great!" You'll simply be using that little voice in your head to change how you look at the things that once caused you pain, and then take positive action to change the associations and follow through with a plan. You'll make time for the goals that become important to you because they will become your priority.

One more example before we go on: public speaking. For some it's a fate almost worse than death. How do we go about creating a pleasure association to that if we have a huge pain association attached to it? Well, simply by changing the way you see public speaking. By choosing to see it as an opportunity to come out of your shell, an opportunity to make new friends, build confidence and achieve something you once feared even trying to achieve—take it off your bucket list.

As opposed to hostaged thoughts like, "I'm so nervous I'll stutter and look like a fool;" "People are going to laugh;" "I'm never any good in front of people;" your inner monologues and thoughts will become—thanks to your new EMP and training—something like this: "Okay self. I've been so looking forward to doing this! I'm going to have fun doing it!"—"This is going to be great!" I did this very thing on October 22, 2015, when I spoke before one thousand people at the TEDx Toronto conference. It was truly amazing! Creating new associations of pleasure with the action of public speaking will change the way you look at it and provide you with that confidence you need to just *do* it.

Will it be easy? Perhaps not at first. It will take that willpower I talked about earlier in this book to create new beliefs in yourself, to change the hostaged thoughts you once held about public speaking (or whatever goal it may be), and to change your negative associations to positive ones. Whatever your challenge: going back to the gym, eating healthy, cutting down on indulgences that aren't good for you—with determination you can experience a transformation. Remember that saying, "Fake it until you make it" as mentioned earlier. Well, now you look for the pleasurable outcomes by taking actions you once associated to pain; and then you take the first step of your journey, replacing your once hostaged thoughts with empowering and exciting ones "until you make it." Until they become your new associations. Creating new pleasure associations helps conquer the hostage-takers and helps you reach a rich, fulfilled and happy life.

Using pain to your advantage

As much as pain can be your crutch under certain circumstances, it can also be your motivator. You are the one who decides what to link pain and pleasure to after all and how long you're going to continue attributing "this or that" pain associations to your experiences. By examining where your pain originated from, or why it is that you associate pain to a particular action, you have the ability and right to choose why it has value. It helps you break down root causes to the level of associations and thoughts, and helps you determine whether that pain is fact-based or simply fear-based.

Fear is the #1 reason people don't take action. Knowing where and how the pain associations originated can help motivate you to fight back with determination and consciously choose to create new empowering associations. It will depend on the situation, but I caution you not to spend too much time and energy examining the cause under a microscope. That's counter-productive. Sometimes you just have to jump in head-first.

Let's say you were physically abused as a child or you're currently in a relationship with someone who abuses you mentally. There's not much point in creating a pleasure association to that, now is there? Nor should there be. But examining it for what it is can help you understand who the real aggressor is and also help you come to terms with your current feelings. Awareness is power and when you expose the wrongdoers for who and what they are, you can begin to validate yourself and use that pain and belief in your worthiness to motivate yourself to enable your empowering management team. (Remember your SWOT Team). Exposing that "fact"—the one that you were abused or are being abused and that you're not to blame will grow into a powerful motivator by turning your inner monologues to ones that assure you that it's not your fault, you don't deserve this, you can take back your power and control, and you are worthy to do exactly that. The thoughts that once kept you hostage deserve to be evicted and pushed away by reclaiming power and control over them. You've examined where they originated from and determined they have no place in your life; so now it's time to use that pain to your advantage and quash those abductors for good. No one else can do that for you but you.

Far too often, people spend too much valuable time, money and energy trying to understand every single aspect and reason for their current pain and depression. They are often encouraged by "experts" and psychiatrists to relive past experiences and trauma in an effort to determine why bad things happened to them, when the best thing they could possibly do for themselves is to realize that shit just happens. Admitting that it's not your fault, it's in the past, and it has no right to keep you from happiness now is the first step to empowerment and complete recovery. Calling it for what it is and choosing to no longer give in to the hostage-takers that carry the messages, "Why did that happen to me?" is power. Why did it happen? It just did. It's over. Now it's time to move on.

The past is but a memory and it was simply a stop on your journey—it was not your final destination. There's nothing you can do to change your past, and dwelling on it only keeps it with you, dredging up painful memories and feelings of guilt and fear, to name a few. It's like carrying a heavy weight with you everywhere you go—especially when you visit your therapist to "put it all behind you."

Nevertheless, before putting the past to rest, the process of cleansing it of any residue which might cling to your future, is healthful and necessary. It is important to visit how and why you feel the way you do about certain things. You can't simply avoid discovering where they originated, because all the thoughts of, "I'm stronger than this," and "This can't bother me," won't last, unless you understand the source of those thoughts—acknowledge their origin. Once you do that, you can then reclaim your power and tell them: "Enough already!" And that should be a quick process and not a process that keeps you in the office of a therapist month after month, year after year. Enough already. Today, decide to no longer be a hostage to your past.

From *The Lion King*[23] to us: a simple lesson about pain

My daughters and I enjoyed watching many Walt Disney animated feature films together as they were growing up, and one of our favorites was the 1994 release, *The Lion King.* I'm reminded of a short clip/dialogue from that film between the animated characters: "Simba," a young lion, and "Rafiki," a baboon, about the past:

> SIMBA: Going back means I'll have to face my past. I've been hiding from it for so long . . .
>
> *(Rafiki whacks Simba on the head with his stick.)*
>
> SIMBA: OW! Geez, what was that for?!
>
> RAFIKI: It doesn't matter! It's in the past! *(He chuckles.)*
>
> SIMBA: Yeah, but it still hurts.
>
> RAFIKI: Oh, yes, the past can hurt. But the way I see it, you can either run from it, or . . . learn from it. *(Rafiki swings his stick, but Simba ducks.)*
>
> RAFIKI: Aha! You see? So what are you going to do?
>
> SIMBA: Well first, I'm gonna take your stick. *(Grabs Rafiki's stick.)*

---

23. *The Lion King,*1994 Walt Disney animated feature film.

Leaving your past pain behind you is always your best bet, especially when you learn from it. Use it to propel you into taking action to never let past pain hurt you again. Say it out loud: *I am no longer a hostage to my past.* Now, believe it.

The power your thoughts and beliefs have over you

Let's explore the power that your thoughts and beliefs have over you. Examining this will help put into perspective what you've been reading so far and provide you with a better insight into how you can so easily be taken hostage. It will also help you better understand how your SEMP (System Empowerment Management Plan) can work to prevent or deal with—and enable you to recover from any hostage-taking incident that comes your way. Understand too that your thoughts and beliefs have the power to hold you hostage for as long as you let them. You require a strong, strategic plan in place. Hostaged thoughts can prevent you from bringing out your personal best and keep you from reaching success and happiness. They do so just as easily as empowering thoughts and positive inner-monologues, that inspire you to take whatever steps you need to in order to reach the goals you've dreamed of reaching and achieve the things you want. Which of these two you choose to deploy—hostage or hero is a choice only you can make.

Your thoughts are powerful catalysts. You have the ability and means to develop and train them to be your advocates, and to be strong and reliable. As much as they can lead you to feelings of despair, chaos, fear, guilt and doubt, they can also work just as effectively at creating powerful beliefs in you to help you take the necessary action to achieve your personal best. Unchallenged and untrained, your thoughts and beliefs can keep you hostage to fear, self-loathing, guilt and death[24] wishing. You go where your thoughts take you, and what actions they cause you to take are really up to you. Zig Ziglar once said, "Getting knocked down in life is a given. Getting up and moving forward is a choice."

---

24. Brian Keenan. *Hostages.* Brian is a former Beirut hostage and author.

Imagine a world where you are in charge of creating your own destiny. You pull out a note pad, a blank sheet of paper, and start writing the best outcomes and life you could imagine for yourself. There are no limitations on what you can visualize, write, and create for yourself. You just picture it and write it down; and naturally, by not limiting yourself you can imagine only the best for yourself. Do it now. Imagine it and write it down. You deserve only the best because you're worthy of it.

Now, look over what you've written for yourself with a sense of hope and excitement in what you've created and imagined for yourself. It might feel like that moment you bought a super-lotto ticket and imagined what you'd do if you actually won the jackpot. You're not gullible—you know that buying that super-lotto ticket doesn't guarantee you a win. It simply buys you a dream you have fun with until the next draw comes along. In the back of your mind, you're telling yourself, "Hey, it COULD happen!"

What you just wrote for yourself on that sheet of paper or in that diary isn't as hard to win, unlike a lottery. The lottery is left up to chance, but your dreams are left to choice and hard work. Unlike the lottery ticket, those dreams in your personal life, without the expense of buying the ticket (leaving it entirely to chance and ridiculously high improbability), are possible to win. It's not enough to write them down and simply imagine them though. To bring them to realization, those personal dreams require your attention and focus. You can make those dreams come true—with determination, a plan, and action.

Your odds at creating a happier life are far greater than your odds at winning the lottery

Choosing to no longer hold yourself hostage to fear and the negative, self-destructive thoughts that have prevented you from moving forward thus far is key. It's not simply writing those dreams down that matters—that's the first step. You must also believe that you are entitled to your list of wishes and will no longer settle for anything but the quality of life that you not only so richly deserve, but to which you are entitled. Those negative thoughts and fears that held you back? You can use an imaginary eraser to rub them out or strike them from that list you've created on "Why I can't be where I want to be?" Why? Because your thoughts and beliefs are yours to create. Thoughts and beliefs are powerful and take control over the direction in which you move; but the amazing thing is that you get to create them, remember? Creating powerful, focused thoughts and beliefs consistently will lead you to a life-altering habit—one that gives you new hope and provides you with a new challenge.

It takes effort and determination to build effective methods and habits for overpowering your negative self. You can't expect to overcome hostaged thoughts if you only work at it once in a while. Nor should you expect to develop fear-free, strong thoughts and beliefs if you only exercise those muscles once in a while either. Just like developing a strong body or learning a new language takes consistent work and effort, so does developing a fit mind—but everything worthwhile normally takes considerable effort. But the good news is that it's free.

Imagine it this way: you open a bank account and you make a deposit. You decide to deposit $500 into the account and your goal is to have your bank account increase so that it will provide you with safety and security. But then you don't deposit any more money into it. In fact, you begin to make regular withdrawals. Eventually, you're in overdraft. Is it a surprise your bank account didn't grow? I think not. You failed to make regular deposits and the consequence was that the bank account couldn't grow. In fact, the withdrawals you made ended up putting you in overdraft. The same is true if we don't continue to make constant and positive deposits into our thoughts and feelings.

Now imagine your car. A car is a mode of transportation and we depend on it to get us from one place to another. Imagine buying a brand-new car [like a new thought] but then never maintaining it. If we don't maintain our cars, eventually they'll break down. The oil needs to be changed, the engine needs to be tuned up, and regular maintenance is required if we expect that car to get us to our desired destination without breaking down. The same applies to our thoughts and feelings: they need to be regularly maintained and cared for if we expect them to get us to where we want to be.

And guess what? It's okay to fail. It's okay not to get it right the first time. It's okay if it seems hard to achieve something at the beginning. It's okay to try again more than once, and you must try again until you get the results you want. Keep making those deposits and maintaining them and building on them once you do. That may mean reexamining your SEMP (System Empowerment Management Plan) and modifying it from lessons learned, but that's okay. More than okay.

CHAPTER 4 SUMMARY

- Many successful people fail several times before getting it right but they keep trying and that's why they succeed. Others stumble and fall only once. They stop trying and fail to grow from their mistakes. They fail to develop awareness on how to avoid failure a second or third time and don't hold themselves accountable for improvement. Be prepared to fail but never give up.

- Identify your strengths, weaknesses, opportunities and threats. By doing so, you can turn to the things that give you strength and avoid the things that make you weak. You may find opportunities you never knew existed because you're now looking for them. You may also expose threats that are harmful to you and avoid putting yourself in their path, whatever or whoever they are.

- When we associate taking a particular action that's good for us with pain, that association will most often keep us from taking that very action. Pain associations can be modified into pleasure associations, but it takes work. Once we develop new pleasure associations to replace the ones we may have once hated, nothing can stop us.

- Make regular deposits into your life account. Don't settle for the minimum. Maintain yourself, make frequent investments in yourself, and watch your personal life account grow.

CHAPTER 5

Choices

"It is our choices, Harry, that show what we truly are,
far more than our abilities."
—J.K. ROWLING,
HARRY POTTER AND THE CHAMBER OF SECRETS

Four years after joining the Durham Regional Police, I reached a distressing point in my short career and thought of leaving it. I had originally joined full of piss and vinegar, as they say, ready to fight crime and lock up people like my dad. My training officer was a lazy bugger; and I didn't learn much from him except where some of the best sleeping spots were, how to avoid calls for service, and how to get away with drinking on the job. Once in a while he would get in the mood to do what we had been hired to do, but that was rare; and I returned to the police college not having learned much from that man. I was very disillusioned.

Once the second half of my formal police college training was completed, I returned to my police service with new hopes. This would be it, I thought, the chance to do what I had signed up to do. But that's not quite the way it went. Night after night, my Staff Sergeant assigned me to different partners—all experienced officers with several years on the job: Police Constables—career constables, as they were referenced. These were officers at the time who had resigned themselves to the fact that they would never advance within the service, and they had settled with that.

The problem with that for me was that night after night, I would have to listen to their constant griping and negativity—the dissatisfaction they felt with the police department and how the department had failed them. At first I thought it was only one or two of the guys on my shift that felt this way; but I soon discovered that the cancer these guys spread with their thoughts and words had infected most, if not all, of the platoon—and I was beginning to feel the effects take over my thoughts as well. The platoon was made up of mostly senior constables. We newbies were few and far between because we had been hired after a long hiring freeze. It's amazing how, when repeatedly subjected to such negativity, you begin to believe it as well. It seeps into your very being and poisons your mind. But that's not what I had come to embrace in myself since discovering in my teen years that I could do just about anything to which I set my mind. At least, those had been my ideals; and now I found myself questioning why I had joined the police force and whether it was the job for me. I should have gone with a career in acting, a passion of mine throughout my school years, I thought.

Four years of police service had passed and it felt like forever. Maybe I would quit and follow up with my acting passion. That wouldn't be so bad after all, I thought. And it would not have been, except for one thing: I joined the service to protect people and I hadn't quite done enough of it. I found myself as if surrounded by a bushel of nuts infected by pesticides and I was becoming one of them. A choice had to be made and a decision reached. I gathered the courage to approach my Staff Sergeant with a request: don't assign me to a two-man car; leave me on my own. I'll produce for you, or I'll go, plain and simple. He did. From that night on, I was pretty much on my own. Now it was up to me to prove to myself that I could do what I put my mind to: arrest harmful people and serve the public. Throw on my Batman costume and fight crime. Okay, no Batman outfit—just my police uniform.

I soon received complaints from the guys on my platoon. During the night shift, I'd pull over a suspicious vehicle to check out the occupants and run their names into CPIC (the Canadian Police Information Center), our database. The problem was that this was often done at 2 or 3 AM—when the guys who were up to no good came out. And it was interfering with the beauty rest some of the senior guys looked so forward to getting on the night shift. They didn't like it, but I started to make arrests. A lot of them. I pulled over cars in which the occupants were wanted on warrants for robbery, breaking and entering, and drugs. Every night I'd make arrests and find insecure properties. I'd arrest impaired drivers and catch bad guys breaking into places. Sure, I'd get back-up after calling in for assistance, but the ones who showed up most often would have preferred to sleep. Whereas for me, I found what I had missed: passion for the job and satisfaction in knowing that I was accomplishing what I had first set out to do. I almost, however, missed out on attaining job satisfaction by allowing the nay-sayers to infect me. I almost settled and gave up. But I didn't. I pushed forward despite the infection my mind had suffered.

I was soon being recognized as a bit of a super-cop by my bosses; and my Staff Sergeant was so impressed by my work that he gave me just about everything I asked for. As well, he provided me with an excellent letter of recommendation when I first applied to transfer into the detective office. The choice to act effectively had paid off, and I never looked back on my career with uncertainty. Doors opened for me, and I moved through them time after time.

> *"May your choices reflect your hopes, not your fears."*
> —NELSON MANDELA

Up to this point, we've examined what it is to be a hostage, how you can hostage yourself and why you keep doing it. You've seen how messages, both good and bad, make their way into your head; and you've seen the importance of examining the origin of the bad ones to determine why they were allowed in. You now understand the importance of asking yourself whether there's any credence to the thoughts that affect your actions for the purpose of self-discovery and improvement, and to determine whether or not they belong. You know they don't. No one gave them an invitation. You also know not to spend too much time examining every minute detail of their origins because that only leads to years of therapy; you've decided that you're the rightful owner of your power and control, and you're making use of it.

You've discovered how easy it is for you to blame yourself for the bad things that happen in your life; and consequently, you can experience guilt—even when you have nothing to feel guilty about. You've also looked at what to do if you had something to feel guilty about. The past is the past, and it is from this moment on that matters. That message is worth repeating.

You can choose to make all the necessary changes to improve your current state of happiness; and you deserve to forgive yourself and others when they earn it. You've understood that you may have been conditioned to feel guilt, shame, and responsibility for something that you were powerless to prevent. But no more. Say it out loud: "I am no longer a hostage to guilt or shame."

I've written how certain feelings and monologues in your head affect your right to move forward, past certain events or triggers, with the knowledge that what happened to you in the past does not have to control you or define who you are or who you will be. I've written about being realistic and reminding yourself that you're limitless and that you can choose to create new images and dominant thoughts for yourself; to talk to yourself differently and to choose the thoughts and feelings you want in your life. You've read about your strengths and abilities and understand how, by taking specific and directed action and by creating new associations you can go beyond crippling beliefs, to experience and create empowering new beliefs. Now let's examine choices more in depth.

Freeing yourself from guilt

There is evil in this world. That you know. All you need to do is turn on the news, read a paper, or watch a horror flick to be reminded that life is often cruel and can challenge the fabric of which you are made. I've met people who have seen evil in the face. I've met people who had their power and control shaken from them in acts of violence, leaving them shattered, insecure and lost. They experienced feelings of guilt for something that happened to them and over which they had absolutely no control. Imagine walking happily down the street, minding your own business, when you are suddenly hit by a motorist who has veered off the road. Then feeling guilty about it—I didn't say hurt—I said guilty.

Freeing yourself from feelings of guilt is a choice. Determining where that guilt originated and why is an important step in your journey to free yourself from your hostage-takers; that—you now know. The following is a representative *conversation* that I had with the victim of a sexual assault who felt guilty for being victimized. You can imagine these words being said to you if you are experiencing feelings of unnecessary guilt. This example is not exclusive to victims of sexual assault. It applies to any circumstance which may lead you to feel guilt.

It's a sad but true fact that many victims of sexual abuse blame themselves for what happened and feel they can't (or shouldn't) report it to the police. Fears of not being believed, of being made to feel dirty or responsible, of humiliation and so forth, creep in. Society is, in part, to blame for planting those thoughts in the minds of victims. That needs to change.

For the purpose of this exercise, I'll call the victim of the assault Mary:

> *"Mary, I first want to tell you that what happened to you was not your fault. You told me that you're feeling a great amount of guilt and that you're blaming yourself for what happened. But that's just not true. You're not to blame here. He's to blame. You did nothing wrong. What you're feeling is normal, but it's not right. I want you to realize that something was taken from you. Something happened to you. Someone exercised their power and control to hurt you—that was not your fault. You were the victim here— you're not to blame, and what you're telling yourself right now is that you're still a victim. I'd like you to think of yourself differently. If you continue to feel that you're the victim and that you're to blame, then you're allowing that man to continue to exercise his power and control over you; but believe me, you're stronger than that. You really are.*

You have the ability to take back your power and control and not only to tell yourself that you're a survivor, but that you are a super and powerful survivor. You don't have to let what happened to you control how you feel about people and what you do or how you feel about yourself. You're stronger than this. If you leave here feeling that you're a victim, then that is going to transfer into every other aspect of your life. It will affect how you feel about yourself, what kind of relationships you have with other people, and what you say and do. That would be giving him the message that he is still in control. And he's not in control anymore. You are. You're not to blame and what happened to you was wrong. But it happened "to you," not because of you. Mary, sometimes bad things happen to good people. And when those things happen we are left with a choice. We can choose to remain affected by what happens to us, or we can choose to be strong and move past what happened to us. It's really up to us. We can continue to live our lives with courage, hope and happiness because we choose better for ourselves.

You are not the things that happen to you. Your past does not have to equal your future. When you leave here today with some of those bad thoughts swimming in your head, and you tell yourself that you were to blame, I want you to imagine taking those thoughts and beating them up the moment they come into your head! Drown them! I want you to replace those thoughts with thoughts that will let you take back your power. When those voices start telling you bad things, tell yourself something like . . . Hey, this happened to me and it's not who I am. I'm stronger than what happened to me, and I am a power survivor. What happened to me doesn't define who I am—I do. And I'm strong. And I am a survivor. My past does not have to equal my future. I am in control of my own destiny and I choose to be a winner. I choose to be happy. I choose to be powerful. I choose to be the best me I can be! Mary, if you leave here today and you choose to be a survivor, then that will also show in everything you do. It will show up in the relationships you have, how you feel about yourself, and in what you tell yourself—and I assure you that your life will be happier for you making the choice to be strong."

Sometimes you need to be reminded that something bad that happened is not your fault and that you can give yourself permission to be strong again. The *above dialogue* is just one example of the many conversations I've had with victims. Keep in mind that I would also actively listen to what they had to say and how they were feeling. You really have to be aware of what you tell yourself before you can effectively change. And in some cases, the pain is so deep that you need a helping hand to help guide you through the darkness.

How you welcome your day is your choice

We're faced with decisions and choices every day. We decide what to wear, what to eat, how to get to where we need to be, and how to make a living. Our days are filled with choices. Some are simple, whereas others are not.

Before you start your day, you owe it to yourself to take a few minutes to consider an unlimited and empowering set of personal choice enhancers. You should decide not only on what outfit to clothe your exterior body, but more importantly, what "inner outfits" and "choice attitudes of the day" you'll be wearing for the world—and for you to enjoy.

Imagine that you own a closet in your mind. In this closet is a huge wardrobe. It is filled with the finest and most beautiful garments on one side and the ugliest on the other. They are all labeled. On the one side you have happiness, love, hope, kindness and compassion, to name but a few; whereas on the other side you have sadness, discouragement, fear, anger, regret and more. We all enter this closet at the beginning of each day, whether consciously or not. It's our choice what to wear—inside and out—in the mind and on the body. We can choose to wear a happy face or a sad one, a positive attitude or a negative one, an "I'm closed off and don't give a heck" body and/or mind pose or one that welcomes the universe. We choose how to dress our internal selves as well as our external selves all before we walk out the door. These choices are ours to make, and our closets are filled with the most beautiful garments imaginable—ours from which to choose. We didn't even have to buy any of these; they are provided to us for free.

Far too many of us don't consider choosing a particular internal "outfit" or attitude before we step out the door. We sort of "go with the flow'—and one picks us. Maybe one stuck from yesterday like an old piece of gum on the bottom of your shoe. Not a pretty picture. How personally rewarding it is to take a few thoughtful moments at the beginning of each day to choose the behavior and attitude you will wear and share with your world! Will you choose to wear one that reflects happiness or one that mirrors sadness? Will you choose to wear a garment that embodies success and happiness or one that announces failure and sadness? Will you decide to clothe your inner self with a positive attitude or a negative one? Will you choose to be a survivor or a victim? It really is up to you. Whichever one you choose will attract the same to it. A smile will attract a smile and a frown will attract a frown. It's a simple law of attraction—like a magnet; you'll attract whatever you're displaying or giving.

Here's an exercise I encourage you to try before you set out to meet your day. Consider how you greet your husband, wife, children, boyfriend, girlfriend, parent, friend, boss, co-workers and strangers. Consider how you choose to treat yourself; what will you tell yourself before you start your day? What mantras will you choose, if any? Will you tell yourself you're beautiful? Handsome? Successful and limitless? Or will you tell yourself you're ugly, unworthy, a loser and hopeless? By making simple positive daily affirmations and choosing a positive outfit with which to clothe your inner self, you can instantly improve the quality of your day and the happiness you'll experience from so doing. Positive affirmations will make a huge difference in the overall blessings that will come your way, and you will be rewarded for the attitude you choose.

The importance of mantras

A mantra is a basic belief repeated to oneself. The right mantras repeated regularly have the ability to improve the quality of your life. Begin by simply telling yourself: "I'm beautiful!"—" I'm worthy of happiness!"—"I'm limitless!" or whatever you happen to want to say. Repeat whatever phrase it is you don't feel you're experiencing fully at the moment but would like to. A common one so many people don't believe but must is, "I'm good enough."

Why tell ourselves that one in particular? Because so many of us don't believe it, that's why. The truth is, you are "good enough." Everyone is. This affirmation helps to build confidence, as do all others. It's not enough to simply repeat the words; repeat your affirmations and mean them. Believe each affirmation or "fake it until you make it." Internalize the words and do it for each and every affirmation you make. Let the faith you have in yourself be greater than the fears you have. Affirmations are positive statements and messages. Affirmations that we consistently repeat to ourselves become imprinted in our brains and have a pronounced effect on our happiness. Positive, self-serving phrases can change our lives for the better because they act as a counter-weight to negative messages we hear daily through radio, television, other media, and people. They also counter-weigh messages we may have received as children or that others have left us with, well into adulthood. Affirmations affect the subconscious mind, and who better to bless us with these beautiful affirmations than ourselves? Why not tell yourself, "I am beautiful!"—"I am worthy!"—"I can do it!"—"I am unique!"—"Today is going to be a great day!"—"I have so much to be grateful for!"—and "I belong!" Challenge yourself to believe in yourself. Begin telling yourself the things you'd like to hear spoken to you by someone you love and respect. And believe it. The law of attraction reminds us that whatever we focus on with great passion has a way of manifesting itself and becoming a reality. Why shouldn't that be you and what you tell yourself repeatedly? Why not tell yourself you're the best and that you're unstoppable? Today could be that day that changes everything.

One of the easiest ways to change and improve the quality of your life is to change and improve the quality of your thoughts. A new and better perception of yourself can be accomplished by using powerful affirmations repeated on a daily basis to condition your mind to create positive attitudes about yourself, which will result in significant improvements in how you see yourself. Once you make it a habit to repeat empowering mantras daily, you can then reach into the closets of your mind and grab the best outfits to wear with conviction and purpose. It's up to you—and no one else—to get rid of the beliefs that do not empower or strengthen you. It's time you clean that closet out and keep only the best outfits for yourself. If you do this, your life will instantly improve. Guaranteed.

Your past does not have to dictate your future

Those who have chosen to reclaim Power and Control over their thoughts and beliefs do not hold onto the past. The past does not define them, nor does it define you. It may build you, strengthen you, and educate you; but it has no right to control you. I've witnessed the birth of fresh, new and strengthened attitudes in my day by some people who experienced the worst possible experiences in their lives. Their choices not to live in that mindset resulted in transformations that freed them from being hostages to themselves to becoming "Power Survivors." They didn't hold onto the past and didn't let their pasts hold onto them. You are not your past mistakes or experiences nor are you bound to be controlled by them. You decide what to keep from the past and what to burn; it's all up to you. Your choices and decisions are as powerful or as weak as you choose them to be. By becoming self-aware of what has made you or keeps you hostage, and choosing to love and believe in yourself despite what some of your former thoughts and experiences have told you, you can now make the choices and decisions that empower you to be the best you can be. Your past does not have to equal your future. The future has not yet been written. The past has, and some things are better left behind. Keep the good memories and burn the others. Say this out loud, now: I am no longer a hostage to my past mistakes or bad experiences. The past does not have to equal my future. Now, believe it and it shall be yours.

Becoming a Power Survivor

For most Power Survivors I've met, their transformations were almost immediate. It's like a light bulb turned on in their minds and it took only a few moments for them to adjust to the new light but they had found the switch—and the new light they experienced was good. A Power Survivor is someone who, when faced with extreme pain, suffering, injury or unexpected setbacks not only goes on with their life choosing to accept whatever setback or pain that they've been dealt and to become stronger for having experienced it. Some experienced severe trauma and some experienced a hopelessness out of which they never thought they could dig themselves. Having found themselves in a dark place, faced with fear and uncertainty, they chose to overcome their circumstances and many actually drew strength from them. Whether hurt by the actions or words of others or circumstances that are not within your control, you too can gather the courage to meet difficult challenges and be strengthened by them. Power Survivors tell themselves not to listen to the harm-filled voices holding them hostage, and they choose to create positive monologues for themselves despite their circumstances.

When you choose to become a Power Survivor you commit yourself to creating better thoughts for yourself and to speaking to yourself more positively. You commit to making better decisions and consequently better choices, all leading to strengthened beliefs and actions. You use the pain you experienced to become stronger. This sets you free from your former hostaged self—free from the images, thoughts, words, beliefs and feelings that kept you feeling scared, uncertain, inferior, weak, helpless or unworthy of happiness and success.

Overcoming adversity

Imagine living in a relationship or home in which you're told day in and day out that you're "ugly," "stupid," and "worthless." Whether it comes from a parent, school bully, boy or girlfriend, husband or wife . . . Imagine being told that nobody else will ever love you and you had better just accept your fate and deal with it. When you hear messages such as these over and over again, you might just come to believe them. Now imagine being caged like an animal for over ten years of your life—locked in one form of cage or another and never truly experiencing authentic love, freedom or the right to choose your own destiny. Fact is often truer than fiction, as you'll read about later in this book in Chapter 12—which includes the description of a horrendous crime against two young boys who were kept in cages for years on end. The cages were real. But Power Survivors emerged from that nightmare. What happened following the rescue of those kids in cages would surprise you and make you believe that anything is possible!

When it comes to your head and what messages swirl around in it, many of the destructive ones in there didn't show up all on their own. They had your help and the help of others who fed you harmful words, put-downs, and bad attitudes. And the ones shoved in there by others? They stuck because you let them, and you grew to believe some, if not all of them. Depending on how you interpreted what was said to you and just how much self-belief, self-love and self-worth you had in yourself at the time, determined how deeply-rooted those thoughts and beliefs became. They say "sticks and stones can break your bones but words can never hurt you." Try convincing someone who doesn't know how to un-hostage themselves and has been deeply hurt by the words of others of this. That's a wound some feel powerless to heal.

When I discovered the power that choices and beliefs could make in us, that and the affirmations that it's not our fault for so much bad that happens, I began sharing that message with broken people that I came across and worked with, as in the case of "Mary." So many people take such a heavy load on their shoulders by thinking that they've done something wrong when bad things happen to them and that it's just too much to handle. And also in the case of some individuals who may have deliberately caused harm to others, by their words or actions, they often don't realize that they too can forgive themselves. They can forgive themselves first and then seek the forgiveness of others. We are all simple humans, experiencing a sometimes complicated existence, and when we fall or are pushed down, we need to get back up. Sometimes we are victims. Sometimes we are perpetrators. But we are all human, worthy of forgiveness and happiness. We fall down. We get up. It has to be that way to be right with the world. Unattended, life can turn sour on a dime. But life, in its natural essence, is joy . . . a gift . . . and gifts are made to be enjoyed.

Glue when cracked

We can all break—and some people have been so deeply bruised and cracked by others that it's no surprise it led them to despair. It doesn't mean they're beyond help. It simply means that they have reached a point in their lives where they desperately need strength, support and a new set of empowering beliefs—along with some grounded hope to guide them through the storm.

We all need to remind ourselves that nothing is permanent in this life and that we have it within ourselves to move forward, despite how tough it may seem in the moment. And sometimes we need the support of others. Whether directly or indirectly, we all need the support, help and the comfort of others. And that's okay. If it were not so, why then were we put in a world with so many other people? Why were we born completely helpless and dependent? We needed help and protection as children and we grew to become independent, sure; but understanding that our strength can be supplemented by the words and the helping hands of others is a powerful and necessary tool. Everyone needs love and everyone needs a helping hand from time to time. It's a condition to being human.

In cases where I've provided a helping hand or encouraging words—for those who were willing to hear the messages of hope, strength and even forgiveness—something changed in them. Instead of staying on a path of sorrow and self-pity, feeding themselves a diet of bad thoughts, words, and beliefs . . . they chose to begin a better *diet* of strength and deliverance. This healthier diet was made up of empowering thoughts, images, hopes and goals. This new improved diet they discovered was focused on talking to themselves more forgivingly, more powerfully and more encouragingly. The more they stuck to this healthier diet and spoke to themselves more understandably and powerfully, the easier it became for them to believe it.

Understanding that you aren't responsible for all the bad things that happen to you and that when you are, you have the right to forgive yourself through reflection, change and love and move forward, is life changing. That journey is worth taking. Unlike the journey into guilt. That journey can never end well. Choose, rather, the journey into self-forgiveness. The moment you decide to kill the monsters of self-doubt, guilt and discouragement when they first appear, the easier it becomes to for you to travel in new directions. Killing a monster before it gets a chance to grow is far easier than killing it after you wait for it to gain strength and grow. If you're cracked or do crack—you can glue yourself back together and move on. Use super glue and be stronger than ever. Say this out loud, now: "I am not a hostage to my guilt. I am stronger than the guilt that kept me hostage." Now, believe it and make it yours.

Perfect practice makes perfect

The result of any new diet (or in this case, new habit) is **change**. Choosing the right diet is crucial to the results you want. If you choose to indulge in a bad diet, you'll get bad results. Such is the case in choosing the right diet or exercise program if you want to see solid and lasting results. You now know I'm a bit of a gym nut; and I've noticed that some inexperienced weight lifters often have the right goals and attitudes in mind at first, but they lack the knowledge of how to get what they have envisioned for themselves. They lift improperly, often putting their bodies and muscles at risk of injury; and because they lack the know-how, they'll be slow to benefit from their workouts—that is, if they experience any progress at all before either injuring themselves or simply giving up.

In order to truly benefit and improve yourself, especially with something new, you have to practice doing that something correctly. Practice doesn't make perfect. Perfect practice makes perfect. Get whatever new habit you are committed to forming right by making it a priority to learn how to do it correctly in the first place, and keep at it for the best and most rewarding results. Sometimes all you need is a personal trainer to teach and encourage you. Find him or her in *every* aspect of your life. It doesn't take long to achieve great results in whatever undertaking you choose, providing you are doing it *right.* By using the right methods and continuously repeating it that way, you develop "memory muscle." By developing and practicing new and improved attitudes within yourself, for example, you develop new mental-muscle memory, so to speak. That muscle gets stronger in time. Be the one to take control of where you want to be and don't leave it up to others. Make solid choices and live by them. Do it right— or not at all! Not doing it right puts you even further behind than you were before attempting the new habit-forming improvement by causing a sense of failure which exacerbates your sense of failure or hopelessness or both.

Your choices are for you to make—no one else. You are defined by those choices and your happiness depends upon making the right ones, from the attitude you choose each day to the thoughts you keep in your head.

Life is "empty and meaningless"

I first heard these words spoken by my amazing acting coach, Robyn Kay Pilarski. I didn't buy into the idea at first but once it was explained to me it began to actually make some sense. At least at some level I could use to keep my brain from drawing the wrong conclusions.

Does this "empty and meaningless" concept mean that YOUR life is empty and meaningless? No, it doesn't. Your life is full of meaning and purpose. It should always be. As I understand this existential concept, it simply means that as humans, not everything in life has meaning except for the meaning that we attach to it. Our emotions and thoughts are affected by the meaning we attach to events and circumstances in our lives. "Life"—or what happens to us in life is at first meaningless. We're born into a life without personal meaning at first; and until our brains begin making sense of what is happening in our space, it is without meaning.

We are the ones in control of our emotions and the ones who determine whether what happens to us is good or bad, right or wrong, dangerous or safe and so forth. We are "meaning-making" machines and our brains work overtime to make some kind of sense of everything that happens to us. We base our conclusions partly on past experiences, how we feel about ourselves in the moment, what society teaches us, and what we have discovered about life to this point. A huge problem develops, however, when we choose to attach the wrong meaning to what happens to us. Attaching the wrong meaning often leads to anxiety, frustration and hurt.

An example that my acting coach, Robyn, provided was about relationships. Suppose you've just met someone you like. You seem to both hit it off. You decide to text that person but you don't get a text back for quite some time. Suddenly, your brain tries to attach meaning to the unanswered texts, and your self-defeating monologues begin to pipe in as your brain is scurrying to figure it out. Maybe, you tell yourself, they mustn't like you or they must be seeing someone else. You ask yourself what you did wrong or whether you're even their type. By that time you've attached meaning to the un-received texts and you decide to get even. You go out, see someone else, maybe two or three people, and work yourself into a state of sadness and rejection only to get a text later on saying, "Hey babe, sorry for the late response, my cell phone died and I just got your message. I was thinking of you too [smiley face]." Now you understand, but in the meantime the emotions you attached to not receiving that text in return got the best of you. So the idea is this: not receiving the text when you expected to was empty and meaningless. There could be a million and one reasons why you didn't receive one right away. You were the one to attach meaning to it. Next time something like that happens, why not simply say, "Life is empty and meaningless. It's empty and meaningless because it's empty and meaningless . . . " and go on with your day?

I had the same thing happen as I was writing this book. A very successful and respected worldwide organization reached out to me to ask if I would be interested in providing a talk on a subject matter on which I was an expert. Of course I jumped at this amazing opportunity and said yes. After preparing a proposal for the topic I'd be presenting, I was informed that from a list of a thousand applicants, I had made the short list of twenty. Twelve speakers would be selected and would be informed of their success the following Monday. Monday came and I received no call or email. Tuesday came and still nothing. Fortunately, I applied the concept that hearing nothing at this stage was life being "empty and meaningless," and on the Wednesday I heard back. A decision had not yet been reached but I stood an excellent chance of being one of the twelve. My brain could have easily attached the wrong meaning to not hearing from them at a specific time.

So now I'm going to step out on a limb here and apply this concept to more serious matters, for which I mean no offense. I was an exceptional Sexual Assault investigator, and I truly felt compassion and understanding for my victims. What I'm about to suggest is one way of approaching the idea that circumstances can be meaningless at first UNTIL such time as we attach the right meaning to them. After an assault, most sexual assault victims attach meaning to what has happened to them. It's usually the wrong meaning. They attach self-blame and shame. The moment our brain takes over trying to make sense of an event that is senseless or meaning-less is the moment the wrong conclusions are almost always drawn, leaving us feeling devastated, traumatized and defeated.

By removing knee-jerk meaning to a senseless attack, victims are then in a place to comfort themselves in knowing that the assault meant nothing in first light. By not immediately attaching meaning to the attack, you prevent feelings of guilt and shame from overwhelming and controlling you. It's far more empowering to step back, take your time to evaluate and then say, "This was not my fault. I did nothing wrong. I'm a good and remarkable person. I think I might just enroll myself in a self-defense class, and I pity the fool who ever tries that again."

The same is true with victims of physical abuse. We often allow our little brains to work themselves into a frenzy and stick whatever explanation they come up with at the moment, to try to make sense of an experience before all the facts have been gathered. Imagine if cops were given the right to arrest without facts, detain without just cause, and reach conclusions simply because they needed to get it done "right now."

The negative reactions we often attach to a situation, person or event are often due to the MEANING or ASSOCIATION we have created from that experience or person. Didn't get that job? Why attach meaning to it that will discourage you and prevent you from trying again; it is self-defeating to listen to the voices in your head which might be saying, "Because this happened, I must be worthless;" or "I can't do anything right." Another example is self-talk related to your health; for instance: experiencing pain in your stomach, leg or elsewhere and find yourself thinking it may be the early stages of cancer? Go see a doctor if it's serious enough, but don't attach meaning to it unless you're certain that meaning is legitimate.

Reminding ourselves that we are the masters of meaning empowers us to choose the right emotion based on the facts, circumstances and events. It is that easy. You are limitless.

So the next time you fail to receive that text, that job, that callback or the many other things that pop up on a daily basis, begin by telling yourself, "Life is empty and meaningless;" and then choose the right meaning for whatever the situation is, and take whatever action needs to be taken to move yourself forward.

A little story to summarize this:

I knew a Zen master. I asked him about life. He said, "Life is empty and meaningless."

I said, "That can't be so!"

He said, "And it doesn't mean anything that it doesn't mean anything."

And I still said, "No!"

Then he said, "And that gives you the freedom to make it up to mean whatever you want it to."

And I said, "Ahh!"

(Author unknown)

The right choices matter

I recently met with my cousin Jacques Dallaire[25], author of *Helping Kids Perform*. In his insightful book he writes that if you want to climb out of a hole, you first have to stop digging. This is a common problem for many because we focus so much on the problems we're facing and keep digging ourselves deeper into them. As he points out, the mind can only actively process one thought at a time, and you can't *not* think about whatever is on your mind. As he observes, your dominant thought determines your emotions, the behaviors that flow from it, and ultimately your ability to perform.

The fact is that we are in control of our thoughts. Dr. Dallaire writes that your perception or perspective regarding the challenges that you face will determine your dominant thought; and if you do what you've always done, you'll get what you've always gotten. It is imperative that you stop digging. Stop listening to those voices of self-doubt and put down the shovel. Focus your attention on thoughts that will help you climb out of the hole you're digging, and make the choice to climb out.

CHAPTER 5 SUMMARY

◆ Freeing ourselves from feelings of guilt is a choice.

◆ Before we start our day, we owe it to ourselves to take a few minutes to consider an unlimited and empowering set of personal choice enhancers. Pick the best attitudes to greet the world with and you will be rewarded with each and every choice you make.

◆ Today could be the day that changes everything.

◆ One of the easiest ways to change and improve the quality of our lives is to change and improve the quality of our thoughts.

---

25. *Helping Kids Perform: Mental Skills Every Parent, Teacher, and Coach Should Master!* Copyright 2015, Jacques Dallaire, PhD.

◆ Our choices and decisions are as empowering or as weakening as we choose them to be. Choose to be empowered.

◆ Our past does not have to equal our future. The future has not yet been written. The past has passed, and some things are better left behind.

◆ Life is not empty and meaningless; but we'd better attach the right meanings to what happens to us, or life *will* become empty . . . and meaningless.

CHAPTER 6

Taking Action

"There are risks and costs to action. But they are far less than the long range risks of comfortable inaction."
—JOHN F. KENNEDY

Eddie Forgette was legendary. Well, at least he was among his peers in the 70s when tough cops and cowboys like him were a dying breed. Eddie stood 5'8" tall and he was a golden glove boxer. A troubled man for sure; but he never showed fear.

I had pissed off one of my Staff Sergeants one night shift when I pointed out during a parade that I had been assigned to walk the beat several nights in a row. It was winter and I hated that detail. Generally, this Staff Sergeant would rotate guys through this assignment never sticking one of us with it too long because it was winter and no one wanted to stand on the street corner at 3 AM during a cold Canadian winter with the gusts of wind blowing in their faces. I must have caught him on a bad night because he made it a point to announce to the platoon that no one should ever question his authority. I was stuck with the beat detail for the next several months and became a regular beat cop well into the summer. I learned to enjoy it because I chose to have fun with it and found ways to be productive.

Eddie would often drive around in his police van to check whether I was standing on the downtown street corner like a good little soldier as I had been instructed to, and he would rarely pick me up and allow me a few moments to warm up in his heated van. He was tough to please, but he soon developed a respect for me when he saw I was making arrests and working hard, despite my assignment. I was eventually relieved of my steady beat duties and regained my spot in the rotation, but from time to time I'd be assigned to the beat as everyone was.

One summer night while walking my beat, Eddie picked me up. It was 1979, as I recall, and Eddie told me he needed a witness. He drove to the Satan's Choice clubhouse. The Choice was a biker gang notoriously known in our city. Their clubhouse at that time was simply a residential house on Browning Avenue in Oshawa. They were your typical biker gang and they were into everything you might expect a biker gang to be into: drugs, women, violence, and much more. Nestled in a residential neighborhood, the gang had no intention of leaving it any time soon. This obviously alarmed and concerned the neighbors because of the late night parties, motorcycles, drinking, and drugs that went on night after night in what had been once a quiet residential spot. The Choice had taken it over and the complaints were numerous. Back in the 70s, we didn't have a dedicated unit of officers to fight gangs—we had Eddie. No one else dared to take them on.

On this night as we drove into the neighborhood, I had no idea what Eddie had planned. All he told me was that he needed a witness. It was about midnight and we drove past the many parked motorcycles on the street by the clubhouse, filled with gang members and their women. They weren't alarmed in the least when we drove up, despite being in a marked police van. But I was shaking in my boots. They carried on drinking and partying; and once we had parked, Eddie led the way to the front door of the clubhouse, moving past the many intimidating bikers who were now curious why two cops were showing up on their turf. Eddie calmly knocked on the front door and asked for the Satan's Choice President.

I was scared as hell . . . but Eddie . . . he had a smile on his face. The biker president appeared and calmly, Eddie announced the following to him: "You, me. On the street. If you win, this town is yours. If you lose, you pick up and get the hell out of town." I couldn't believe what I had just heard. The Choice had made no excuses for their criminal activity and they had no plans of leaving any time soon. Eddie had just challenged the president to a fist fight and the prize was the city. It sounded like a cowboy movie—back in the 70s police work was much like the Wild West.

At first I sensed hesitation on the part of the Satan's Choice president, but his fellow bikers all encouraged him to accept the challenge. He was a good fighter himself. Tough too. "You can take him!" they exclaimed; and the challenge was accepted. A few minutes later, both Eddie and the president were on the street, surrounded by the rest of the gang, their women, and me.

I wish I could say that it was a great fight to watch, but I can't. I couldn't have grabbed a bag of popcorn and settled in to watch this one. It was over in a few seconds. After someone shouted "Go!" Eddie unleashed a flurry of fist strikes next to impossible to see (they were at a speed which blazed the eyes of any onlooker) to the head of his opponent, and the president dropped like a sack of potatoes. He was out. Eddie won by knock-out, and the whole thing lasted but a few seconds.

Now I was even more alarmed than I had been earlier. We were surrounded by bikers who had just watched their president get taken down by a single cop, and the price was to get out of town. The president didn't get to be president because he was a wimp. He was known as a tough guy and I wondered what the hell was about to happen to Eddie and me. The once cheering crowd was now eerily silent; and after a moment, about three of the bikers helped their beaten president up, put him onto a motorcycle and they left. They were true to their word. The clubhouse was abandoned by them; and for the next couple of years we didn't have any problems with their gang. They never returned to that clubhouse, and I had witnessed Eddie stare danger right in the face and move forward despite it. He took action knowing full well that there could be severe consequences. To this day I believe had the Satan's Choice president won, Eddie would have honored his part of the agreement as well. Eddie was a man of his word, and once stood in front of an on-coming get-away car (after a bank robbery on the main street) with a machine gun and didn't flinch as the car barrelled down on him. He simply sprayed the car in a hail of bullets. Call it what you will. Was he crazy or just plain brave? I have my thoughts on what the answer is and I learned some valuable lessons from him. Courage, for one. Facing uncertainty head-on, and moving forward despite your fears, for another. Taking the action that needs to be taken to get to where you want to be for another. Do I condone his actions that night he challenged the president to a duel at the cost of the city? Well, I'll reserve my answer on that one. For now.

Success and happiness do not belong exclusively to others

> *"We are what we repeatedly do.*
> *Excellence, then, is not an act, but a habit."*
> —ARISTOTLE

We are all similar by design and different by nature. Some of us choose to simply exist, while others go for what they want and believe they deserve. We sit in awe as we watch others reach goal after goal. We imagine, "Wouldn't it be nice if I was as successful as he is? As she is?" "Why can't I do that?" "Why couldn't that be me?" And suddenly our thoughts are drawn to other less significant matters—the small stuff, and we become distracted from focusing on success . . . we fret about the small stuff until we see that person again moving from success to success, or until we read about a celebrity in a success magazine whom we yearn to be like. Then we start asking ourselves the same questions over again. Why can they do it and I can't? Why couldn't that be me? It becomes an endless loop of "I wish I hads." Until, that is, you *short-circuit* the loop with action.

You may feel that the success they enjoy is exclusively theirs and never meant for you. You may believe it's only within the reach of a "chosen" few, those born with a silver spoon in their mouths. You might have self-defeating inner monologues going on all the time in your head and make up reasons and excuses about what you believe your limitations to be, and why you couldn't possibly achieve the success and happiness that you have seen others having. You may ask yourself why you haven't found the love that others have found, or developed the kind of relationships you see others enjoy with their families, friends, lovers and children. Or you may imagine how nice it would be to make the kind of money that you see others making. And so it goes, on and on like rats on a spinning wheel. If it's change you want, you are responsible to act on that wish and to make it happen. No one else has the ability to do it but you. You need to take action to make it happen. *Cut the loop*!

Comparing yourself to others

One trap so many of us fall into is comparing ourselves to others. Comparing ourselves to people more successful than us is a sure fire way to destroy self-esteem and may cause us to feel shame in ourselves as we imagine the ideal life—who we'd like to be, what we'd like to have, and what we'd like to be doing. But while we're asking ourselves why we can't do something, have we asked ourselves why *they can*? And *are*?

Don't be too hard on yourself if you're focusing on what you don't have right now or why you don't seem to be achieving the things others are. But beware of harmful comparisons. Comparing yourself to others is something you've learned to do over the years. It's what many refer to as a "learned behavior." You were conditioned to compare yourself to others. Your parents, teachers and the media taught you how to do it. But it's harmful.

In my case it came from a bunch of Catholic nuns and teachers in my grade school who kept pointing out how much smarter the others kids were in comparison to me and asked, "Why can't you be more like so-and-so?" For others it may have been a parent who said to them, "Susan is so slim and pretty. Wouldn't you like to lose 20 pounds?" or "Why can't you be more like your brother?" Our society is saturated with the "ideal" beauty, the ideal body, the best clothes and how plastic surgery can fix just about any supposed imperfection society tells us that we have. That fifty-foot billboard or subway poster staring you in the face every day, teasing and shaming you, is only one example of the "flavor of the month."

Comparing yourself to others can result in self-doubt, feelings of inadequacy and shame, leaving you feeling inferior, unworthy and hopeless as though you weren't entitled to enjoy the happiness others do. Or it can leave you feeling you're not perfect-looking enough, slim enough, or loveable enough. So, if you're comparing yourself to someone else right now, STOP that insanity! And if you absolutely must: compare yourself to that less fortunate person you see and be thankful and grateful for what you *do* have that they don't. Only if you must. But remain humble if you do.

Comparing yourself to the seemingly more fortunate will just hurt. It won't help. Stop it. Do take notes in a journal though for the purpose of self-improvement. Don't compare. Asking why another has come to be so much more successful than you have, what their work ethics are, by what means they got to where they are and how you can imitate their success, is a great practice. It doesn't involve comparing; it involves *examining* for the purpose of self-improvement.

I remember reading a Christian bumper sticker that asked, "WWJD?" Translated to, "What Would Jesus Do?" If you happen to admire someone for their excellent business sense, their way with people, their charm, their style, their qualities and so forth—learn from them. I can see no harm in asking yourself, "What Would _____ Do?" And if you know that person or get a chance to talk with them—ask them how they do it. Be a sponge and soak it up.

Judgment

Consider the consequence of comparing yourself to others. It can quite easily lead to judging the individual to whom you're comparing yourself. Judging yourself and others always leads to thoughts that have no place in an un-hostaged mind. You might begin to think you're better than he or she is. Smarter, better looking, more popular, better dressed or a multitude of other judgments can take over your thoughts and along with them, a major shift in your overall attitude which could easily include arrogance. You must find balance between lack of self-esteem and gloating haughtiness.

Remember that life can knock you down when you least expect

it. You can suddenly find yourself jobless or homeless, disfigured or crippled. Working toward total freedom over everything that takes you hostage includes being appreciative of what you *do* have, and not judging others for what they don't. You're not better than they are. I dedicate my last chapter to gratitude, but it's important to mention it here as well when examining judgment and comparisons.

Don't curse your job, your income, your looks or yourself. Everything, including your health, can be taken from you in an instant; so be truly grateful for what you have. If you want more of it, make it happen—but don't take what you have for granted; and treat others the way you'd like to be treated yourself because we never know what the future holds. You can only make plans for the way you would like things to unfold and create this moment as hopeful and beautiful. My personal experience immediately after retiring from the police force is proof that your circumstances can change in an instant and your income can be taken in a flash. I was left with 20% of what I had counted on; and the road to rebuilding was long and hard.

Master of your choices

Some people live in a hopeless state of mind for most of their lives, choosing never to even bother to try moving beyond their current circumstances, or their in-the-moment comfort zones. They abandon the goals they once dreamed of and give up on becoming the people they imagined they could become. Why? Because it's easier to do nothing in the moment.

Being master of your choices and your destiny takes work and some people are simply lazy or uninspired. Some choose not to take ACTION to create change. They'll settle and keep making poor choices and decisions or none at all. They'll give in to roadblocks and closed doors or continue comparing themselves to others and feel unworthy and inadequate. Or they'll settle for what's become familiar to them. They'll remain hostages to their current thoughts and beliefs by choice, and consequently, they'll give up because they will not have become masters of their choices.

They'll build no **SEMP** for themselves, won't check their **SWOTs** and will simply give in. At the end of their lives, on their death beds, they'll look back and say, "I wish I would have;" or "If only I had . . . " How sad that the final moments of a life would be spent never having taken risks and never having done what their hearts had wanted them to do. Never stealing that kiss, never saying what you mean, never stepping out in faith, never taking any kind of risks and never being everything they could have been. To be successful requires going for what you want. I read a posting on a social media site recently that said, "Remember that actor who just gave up? . . . I don't either." Losers often lose because they gave up too damn fast or simply wimped out.

But that doesn't have to be you

Understanding the power your thoughts have over you has been the main focus of the various chapters of this book up to this point. You understand that in order to get what you want in this life you have to un-hostage yourself from the thoughts that are preventing you from getting it. You have to then take action. You are worthy and entitled to what this life has to offer—if you choose to go for it. You are damn near limitless. Stop comparing yourself to others. It will either make you feel inferior or superior. Either way, it won't help get you to where you want to be. Change begins with a single thought, followed by a single decision, and then by a single action. From there it blossoms into a whole new set of beliefs and values. And those decisions are yours to make. Changing one single belief in yourself can change your entire destiny. Start competing with yourself and not others. Push yourself to think better, feel better, and *be* better each and every day. The journey of a thousand miles begins with a single step. Start walking. Hell, start running.

Tenancy at will

Think of your thought storage space as a loft you own in an incredible neighborhood. You lease it out. You are the landlord and thoughts are the tenants. You're the one who allows these tenants to take residency in your mind. Imagine that if you let them in, you can make them leave. It may require some work—the landlord and tenant act has a way of protecting tenants; but in our world, we ultimately reclaim the Power and Control over our loft and can evict the bad tenants we allowed in. Choosing tenants who make regular deposits into your account, take great care of the place, and even make improvements are the ones you want to keep. Tenants who make us happy and not miserable will be keepers.

Aristotle said, "The ultimate value of life depends upon awareness and the power of contemplation rather than mere survival." Being aware of who the tenants are that we're considering allowing into our lofts is a vital step in assertive power of them. It would be wise to do a background check on them before they move in—it only makes good business sense. Get so focused on that step that the next time you have one of these bad seed tenants creep up to your loft, you'll know how to deal with "it." You'll say "no" before it has a chance to move in. Should a "thought would-be tenant" move in before you discover just how bad it is, take a bat with you.

Power and Control: Another look

We've touched on this topic earlier but it's worth another look. In the world of crime (and yes, business), so many offenses are committed by a desire for Power and Control. When it comes to intrusive thoughts and feelings that keep us shackled, imagine that they simply want Power and Control over you. Negative self-sabotaging self-hostaging thoughts want to control your feelings, choices, decisions and overall behavior. Looking at them as common criminals might make it more fun for you to work with. The more they are fed the belief that they can seize Power and Control over you, the more they'll act to do just that. They'll recruit other gangsters as well, and the more determined they'll be to capture you. If you look at it in this way, you can imagine a cat and mouse game and thus prepare yourself to win. It's *your* Power and Control after all, and no common criminal or criminal business type has the right to try taking it from you.

From this point on and forever, be the one in charge of your thoughts and never leave anything to chance or someone else's choice. Prepare, plan, play, and win.

We become what we repeatedly believe about ourselves and what we repeatedly do. Being aware of what we think, believe, and do gives us a greater advantage to reestablish control. Any thoughts that don't empower us do not belong. Give them their eviction notice and kick them the hell out. They're not welcome in your world. You can choose to live in a better neighborhood than you do from this moment on—and you deserve to create that neighborhood yourself if it has not yet been created. Take back your loft. You're worthy of it. You're even entitled to move into it if you choose. Remember: you are damn near limitless; and in your world, you choose where you live, what music you listen to and what food you eat. Choose music beautiful for your soul and words rich with hope, strength and courage because you deserve the only the best thoughts taking residency in your head. Only then can you find the happiness to which you are entitled. Only then can you truly find Power and Control and free yourself from ever being taken hostage again.

Everyone has a story

In our journey to free ourselves from hostaged thoughts and attitudes, awareness has been a significant key in the process. Being aware of your weaknesses, strengths and challenges is essential for your liberty and success. Improving your life involves careful scrutiny of the self; and in developing your best self, considering others and what they are going through will serve you in reaching your goals. People should help people; and when you serve humanity, you serve yourself. Everyone has their own challenges. Everyone has their own story. And being unaware of anyone else's narrative isolates you from humanity, which in turn isolates you from your *self.*

We are all interconnected, far more than we realize

Everyone you see walking down the street is thinking about their lives right now and they're chatting up a storm in their minds. They're chatting about their goals, their successes, disappointments, worries, hopes and dreams. Just like you are. Behind each smile is a whole world of thoughts and internal monologues, some much better than others. You ask someone, "How are you?" and you expect, "Fine, thanks";—but you have no way of knowing how that person is feeling or what they are living in that moment. Their reality and circumstances may not be reflected whatsoever in their smile and their response—"Fine, thanks. . . . " But then you know that, having most likely experienced the same disconnect between your own smile (which seems to say—all is well) and your truth which may not be quite so happy as your smile projects and would have everyone believe.

We keep our personal lives secret to most. It's social conditioning and not a bad idea. Consider that the person you just asked, "How are you?" may be: suffering from cancer; or from the recent loss of a loved one; or loss of their job; or loss of a marriage or important relationship; or loss of their home (may even possibly be living out of their car). The person may have been a victim of rape. Or he/she may *actually* be "fine." You just have no way of really knowing. You don't walk in that person's shoes. Nor do I walk in yours. I have no way of knowing what your circumstances are, unless you tell me. Perhaps you are experiencing one—or some—of the things I just mentioned when you answer someone with a, "Fine, thanks." Everyone has a story, including you. In being the best you can be, consider that everyone you meet is going through one kind of challenge or another. You may not be able to do anything about another person's difficulties; but simply being aware of and genuinely interested in your fellow man will help you on your journey. They too may be hostages to their own self-sabotaging thoughts and inner monologues; and maybe something you say or share with them will help free them from their *captors;* and that, in turn, will help you be the person you were meant to be—a winner.

Life is not always "Rainbows and Sunshine"[26]

Let's face it. Life is hard at times. It's not all "rainbows and sunshine." Many of us are dealt a harsh hand of cards to play in this game of life—some more than others, it seems. We can all experience discouragement and a sense of helplessness; and we generally have no choice but to play the cards we've been dealt. But how we *choose* to play the cards we're dealt is our *ticket* to freedom and happiness.

Simply because we've been dealt a bad hand, doesn't mean that we'll lose the game. Sometimes we need to take a deep breath and remind ourselves that it's just a bad day, not a bad life. When we're dealt one of these bad hands, or a bad day, it simply means we need to plan how to play our next card. And as we consider what to play next and how that will affect the overall game for our success and happiness, we need to plan to win. We need to know how to play the game so as to produce the outcome we desire. Not knowing how to play will result in stress and likely lead to failure. That failure will lead to apprehension. This apprehension can lead us to take the wrong action or not take any at all. And so it goes in a never-ending syndrome—that is, until you decide to change the pattern. Then, at the point of awareness, the conversation you have with yourself will determine what you will do.

We can talk ourselves into either playing the cards we've been dealt with a strategy to win, or fold. Win or lose. Life is not always filled with rainbows and sunshine, but the sunshine and rainbows do not typically disappear forever. A new dawn is about to come. "The sun also rises" (the Biblical quotation that Hemingway chose as the title to his novel about his struggle with his *own* demons). A new day is about to begin; and somewhere in this world, tomorrow has already arrived. The next moment of your life could be the moment that changes everything for the best.

The theme of the very first Rocky movie taught me something I'll never forget. No matter what life throws at you, you have got to find

---

26. *Rocky Balboa,* 2006 movie from MGM/Columbia Pictures/Revolution Studios.

the courage to get up, move forward and "kick butt"—your own if you're not moving fast enough.

In Rocky's fights with Apollo Creed, he demonstrated the pure **will** not to lose. No matter how many times Rocky was knocked to the mat, he got back up and kept fighting. Life is going to knock you down and it is going to discourage you, but the secret to winning is to get back up and keep fighting the good fight. In the film *Rocky Balboa,* Rocky makes a compelling speech to his son. Discouraged by his son's lack of motivation and personal self-worth Rocky tells him:

"You ain't gonna believe this, but you used to fit right here. (He gestures to the palm of his hand). I'd hold you up to say to your mother, 'This kid's gonna be the best kid in the world. This kid's gonna be somebody better than anybody I ever knew.' And you grew up good and wonderful. It was great just watchin' you, every day was like a privilege. Then the time comes for you to be your own man and take on the world, and you did. But somewhere along the line, you changed. You stopped being you. You let people stick a finger in your face and tell you you're no good. And when things got hard, you started lookin' for something to blame, like a big shadow. Let me tell you something you already know. The world ain't all sunshine and rainbows. It's a very mean and nasty place, and I don't care how tough you are, it will beat you to your knees and keep you there permanently if you let it. You, me, or nobody is gonna hit as hard as life. But it ain't about how hard you hit, it's about how hard you can get hit and keep moving forward. How much you can take and keep moving forward. That's how winning is done!

Now if you know what you're worth, then go out and get what you're worth! But you gotta be willing to take the hits. And not pointing fingers saying you ain't where you wanna be because of him, or her, or anybody! Cowards do that and that ain't you! You're better than that! I'm always gonna love you no matter what. No matter what happens. You're my son and you're my blood. You're the best thing in my life. But until you start believing in yourself, you ain't gonna have a life."

The world isn't all "rainbows and sunshine," and the world knocks us down occasionally, despite what we do to avoid it. That's "just the way it is." But as Rocky so accurately says, it isn't about how hard we're hit, it's about how hard we can get hit and keep moving forward. Sometimes our worst enemy turns out to be *ourselves.* We deliver devastating blows to our egos by repeating harmful monologues of self-defeat, convincing ourselves we're unworthy of love, success, happiness or achievement. We can easily begin to believe this self-brainwashing and avoid "stepping into the ring" of life to fight for ourselves. To avoid the pain of failure, we choose to stay down on the mat being knocked back and we think we "just can't get up."

To live life by avoiding the challenges that come with it is to live a life unfulfilled. Fighting for yourself takes guts, determination and stamina. Do you have what it takes? I sure as hell hope you do because fighters are the ones who win. Despite whatever fears are keeping you still once you've been knocked down, you have to pick yourself up by the bootstraps—stand back up, brush yourself off, and move forward. Keep your eyes open and your hands up. Face the beast. That last blow taught you something and you're that much stronger for having taken it. Without experiencing the occasional setback, we have no real idea of how strong we can be.

Facing our fears and moving forward despite their temporary power over us strengthens us to stand up and deal with the challenges of life. Many setbacks are temporary—provided you act against them immediately or as quickly as possible. The more you face them immediately and take direct action, the easier it becomes to dispel and eradicate fear. It is our fears which keep us hostage to ourselves, because fear sets negative hostage-taking thoughts into motion—and, like the bull, once out of the gate, it/they are very difficult to rein in. Fear didn't keep Rocky, an unlikely opponent for the championship of the world, from believing in himself and facing his fear—and that made him a winner. A fictional Hollywood character, yes, but the same principles apply to real life. That's why so many people loved the film. It touched something inside each of us that reminded us that we, too, are capable of getting back up when knocked down. Fear must not be permitted to keep us from doing just that.

Set realistic goals and timelines for yourself. A 130-lb. man may never develop the muscles Arnold Schwarzenegger developed for a number of reasons: body type, genetics, and so forth; BUT that man can substantially develop and increase muscle mass, endurance, and strength. Be realistic, set your bar high, and give it all you have.

The world is a stage, and we are all actors

While I'm on the topic of movies and actors, I'm an actor myself, and I've been handed some good and bad scripts. These scripts, to a writer or a group of writers, often take a very long time to complete. Some are wonderful. Some are not. Some are just plain bad. Those are the ones you know from first read that no thought went into the writing, and you know that the script isn't going to succeed as a film. Even very skilled and talented acting cannot mask a poor script, and people will walk out of the theater or shake their heads after the film and ask, "What was that?" If you're a struggling actor who can't pick your projects like an "A-List" actor, you bear it and grin, as they say; you tell yourself it's the script you've been handed, and that there may be some piece of it you can use for your reel. Unless the Director is open to changing the script, you're stuck with it.

But it's your life we're talking about and you're the Director of it. You're also the writer. And if someone else hands you a lousy script to live, you have the Director's approval to rewrite it. The world is your stage, and you have exclusive rights to choose how your life unfolds upon that stage. If the script you now have in your head is a bad one, rewrite it. Trash the old one and create a new one.

It is critically important when you find yourself living a bad script, or any part of one, that you change it. In writing a better one, create a winning character for yourself . . . and a happy ending. Don't put your life script in the hands of someone else or rely on someone else to write it for you. Write your own and follow it "to a T." Act the way you think the hero of your story would, and keep acting with confidence and determination. The world really *is* a stage and we truly *are* actors. Let's be the leads in our own stories.

Choosing the right script for yourself

You have the Director's approval to write your own script; and, as such, you have an unlimited number of Director's rights. Choosing the right script is up to you. You can choose to write a winning script with a feel-good ending. You can create a character capable of handling whatever comes your way. Create a kick-ass dynamite power survivor who doesn't buckle when life throws a setback your way; then watch that character grow. Your internal script will take whatever direction you give it, so why not write a good part for yourself?

The quality of your scripts will dictate the quality of your life. Successful and happy people have discovered how to write the best scripts for themselves. They believe in their storyline. They see their storyboards differently than most, and they talk to themselves differently. They don't allow negative self-talk to stay on the pages of their life or to affect their box office profits. They've found ways to write and live their stories to maximize their happiness. They kill the monsters before the monsters get to them. They're accomplished and successful writers AND directors.

Quality, not quantity

"The greatest danger for most of us is not that our aim
is too high and we miss it, but that our aim
is too low and we achieve it."
—MICHELANGELO

Most of us look for quality products and services, be it food, clothing, furniture, automobiles, education, and so forth. We look for quality because we know that quality lasts. It stands the test of time. We know quality matters, even in the smallest of things. So it should be with our thoughts. Our thoughts should be of such sterling quality that we naturally expect more from ourselves and our current conditions, particularly if what we have isn't bringing us what we want.

If your current standards for quality thoughts are low, you need to make adjustments. Changing the quality of your expectations means changing the quality of your thoughts and your inner mono-logues. It's mind over matter: whatever is in your mind is what mat-ters; so, whatever is in there should be of the highest and most enduring quality. You can't succeed in writing a quality chapter for your life if you keep using yesterday's inferior quality beliefs. You're in competition with no one but yourself. Beat your old thoughts and beliefs down, and build your new ones higher and better.

Write a happy ending and build your character strong enough to attain that happy ending.

> *"To get up when you are down, to fight more intensely when you are struggling; to put in extra effort when you are in sheer pain, to come back when nobody expects you to and to stand when everyone is pulling you down are what makes a champion."*
> —APOORVE DUBEY

Garbage in, garbage out

If you allow garbage to enter into your thoughts and life, the likes of those brought to you by negative people, negative images, and bad habits, then chances are that the same kind of "garbage" you let in will make its way into your scripts and your behaviors. They'll show up in the details of the script you're writing and directing for your-self. Furthermore, because you're also the actor of your life's story, they'll also show up in your performances and your behaviors. They'll block your success. Your happiness.

Keeping garbage in your mind will end up negatively affecting—even distorting—your character, and will spoil a good script as well. If you're not good at improvisation and redirection, this garbage will become your theme; and you will find yourself out of a job, a rela-tionship, happiness, and success. Your thoughts and actions will be consistent with what and whom you've allowed into your stories—into your scripts and into your life and thoughts. This saturation orig-inates from many places.

Consider this poem written by Dorothy Law Nolte from her book *Children Learn What They Live.*[27]

We are influenced by our environment, what we've been taught, and what we've come to believe: If a child lives with criticism, he learns to condemn . . . If a child lives with hostility, he/she learns to fight . . . If a child lives with fear, he learns to be apprehensive . . . If a child lives with pity, he learns to feel sorry for himself . . . If a child lives with ridicule, he learns to be shy . . . If a child lives with jealousy, he learns to feel envy . . . If a child lives with shame, he learns to feel guilty.

BUT—If a child lives with tolerance, he/she learns to be patient . . . If a child lives with encouragement, he learns to be confident . . . If a child lives with praise, he learns to be appreciative . . . If a child lives with acceptance, he learns to love . . . If a child lives with approval, he learns to like themselves . . . If a child lives with honesty, he learns what truth is . . . If a child lives with fairness, he learns justice . . . If a child lives with recognition, he learns to have a goal. If a child lives with sharing, he learns to be generous. If a child lives with security, he learns to have faith in himself and those about him . . . If a child lives with friendliness, he learns the world is a nice place in which to live.

Are you being fed by someone else's garbage right now? In a relationship or with the company you're keeping? Is it time to change your diet—be it the places you hang out or the stuff you're watching, listening to or reading? You may carry some pretty heavy baggage with you into adulthood and into your current life scripts. But by now, you have hopefully grown to the point where you have the remarkable ability to choose how you think, what thoughts you should keep, how you respond to what happens to you, with whom you choose to associate, and how to write your new and improved scripts. You have freedom of choice and freedom of thought. You can release the garbage and leave it where it belongs: in the past. Remember, you are

---

27. *Children Learn What They Live.* Copyright 1972/1975, Dorothy Law Nolte.

the Directors of your life; and it is precisely what you tell yourself and what you believe that will determine the actions you take, who you will ultimately be, and what successes you will achieve. Avoiding garbage is a sure way of ensuring that your scripts will be richer—and healthier.

Caring for your garden

Far too often in today's busy and unpredictable world, we choose to accept, without question or rewrite, the thoughts and beliefs others impose upon us. And if these thoughts and beliefs prevent you from moving forward, gaining self-confidence, and achieving the success and happiness you seek, then your inaction to rewrite and reevaluate your scripts will allow the thoughts of others to take root within the fabric of your attitudes—like noxious weeds; and they will take up residency and show up in your scripts. Eventually, these weeds of doubt and uncertainty will choke your successful thoughts from being set free and from being rewritten to open the gateway to your achievement and happiness. If you entertain and write a bad script for yourself, then you won't be ridding yourself of the garbage; and you'll allow the weeds to grow. You won't be walking to the podium to receive an Oscar with a script and performance that has been carefully planned, executed and free of garbage and weeds. You won't even be invited to the Oscars.

Because of specific childhood experiences and the beliefs you may have attached to them, you may also be prone to accept disempowering beliefs without question or challenge, allowing them to affect your current feelings and beliefs. This conditioning leads you to a place of insecurity and simple acceptance. Someone else may have deeply affected your current script, and you may feel too tired or afraid to change it. A personal immaturity may develop that prevents you from reaching maturity of thought and action. It may and probably will prevent you from developing the right thoughts and beliefs—and taking the right action to reach your full potential and receive your personal Oscars and triumphs. It keeps you from the success and happiness you deserve. The environment in which you were brought up, and some of the disempowering messages you received as a child, can have a tremendous impact on how you see yourself today. And not only are your childhood experiences capable of affecting how you see yourself today, but so are certain experiences that you've had over the years as an adolescent and adult. Some of us take longer than others to mature, and we may have experienced setbacks that are still affecting us because we failed to have a management plan in place. Or maybe you were just dealt a bad hand of life cards. Whatever it is, your past experiences can have a significant say in what you do now and what you do in the future—again— *if* you allow them to.

Your past experiences can affect how you write the present and your future scripts, and they can cause you to *not* envision a better future—or happier ending for yourself. Do I sound like I'm repeating myself? Good. Repetition is the vehicle of learning and thus knowledge, and I want these messages to sink in. The more you think about the good stuff, the better your outcome will be. It's the law of attraction.

We know that our pasts do not have to equal our futures. We simply must not allow any negative past experiences to affect the quality of our lives now and tomorrow. Whatever has happened to us in our pasts is *in* the past. We are now directing our lives according to how we wish to have our lives unfold. And if we want our lives to be directed in positive and successful ways, then we cannot allow any self-destructive past experiences, thoughts or memories control our current thoughts and decisions today. Bad things happen to good people. It's just the way it is. Once you recognize that whatever it *is,* it has no control over you in this moment or in your future, then you can eliminate any influence **it** would otherwise have over your current scripts. You can write the stories you want to write for yourself without having to worry—or even think about the past. The nasty or undesirable past is a dead issue and has no place in our current or future scripts. Create a happy ending for yourself.

Being too nice

Sometimes we buy into a way of behaving and allow ourselves to be too nice to disagree with someone, or too nice to object to a particular situation when it isn't right or fair for us or goes against our beliefs and our will. We may even allow fear to seize us to the point where our own morality and character will be dictated by the will of others. Being too nice to say "no" when it's just not right for us—or even dangerous for us—can be critically harmful.

Successful people know how to say "no." Being too nice can have harmful consequences. As you've discovered, you can allow yourself to become hostages to your beliefs, thoughts, past, and conditioning; and additionally, you can also become hostage to the behavior and will of others—especially if you're not strong enough to say "no" when "no" needs to be said. Without objecting (or very little) to that which is against your desires and will overall, you might find yourself in the most uncomfortable and wrong situations as your character is put to the test. You might just find yourself in a "Good God, this can't be happening!" moment—one which tests those monologues in your head and tests what you're prepared to say and do about it. You might just be in a spot where fear allows another to dictate what is about to happen; and you will allow yourself to be "acted upon" rather than choosing to act for yourself and in your own best interests. Rather like a physical hostage situation without the gun or threat being held over you.

When this happens, you have a duty and responsibility to yourself, and *only then* to others. Your character is often tested; and if you should fail to live up to who you are and to act upon your new thoughts, beliefs and scripts, you will be letting the most important person in your life down: yourself. It's not enough to *know* what to do; you must be willing to *do* it. You must be willing to not only talk the talk, but walk the walk. You will remain a hostage to yourself if you are not ready to live by the code you create and embrace for yourself. It is not enough to know what to say to yourself or to memorize the script. You need to step onto that stage or in front of that camera with what you know and apply the necessary action in order for it all to work out for you. Stage fright won't win you an Oscar. Beating fear just might.

Facing fear and still making the right choices

In the early 1980s, I was working in the Youth Division investigating crimes committed by kids under the age of 18. It was a Saturday night and I was approached by a senior Detective working in the Adult Division who informed me that several teenagers had just been arrested for a vicious assault in a rural jurisdiction several miles from where I was stationed. Most of them were over the age of 18, but two of them were under 18. That meant I got to deal with them. When they arrived at the station I interviewed the two younger ones, 16 and 17 years of age. Both of them were female.

I was provided with the facts of the case, as we knew them: a group of approximately seven to nine teenagers had gathered at a farmhouse for an overnight party of drinking, drugs and socializing. It was a cold October weekend and it had been raining. They had partied hard and eventually crashed. When they awoke late the next day, one of the girls suspected that a chain of hers had been stolen during the night. She immediately accused one of the younger girls of having stolen it, and the gang decided that they would administer their own form of justice against the so-called suspect, a 16-year-old. They tried her on the spot in a mock court and found her guilty. Led by a couple of the older boys, the poor girl was stripped naked and beaten severely. She was then dragged out of the farmhouse into the cold wet night. There, the beatings continued in a pool of mud and blood. The beatings were so severe, her face was unrecognizable. One of the young punks then decided to urinate on the helpless victim as she lay in the mud, and he was followed by a couple of the other young idiots. The abuse they put this young girl through lasted at least an hour, we were later told, and she was left in the cold wet mud to find her way out or die. They all went back inside the farmhouse leaving the helpless beaten victim behind. But this young girl remarkably managed to defeat the odds and crawled her way over to a farmhouse in the distance where the police were called. A squad of armed cops responded and found the cowering teen suspects all huddled and hiding in the attic of the old farmhouse. It was a night they wouldn't soon forget.

As I interviewed one of the two young suspects, I could sense that not only was she terrified for having been caught by the police and for what would happen to her, but she was genuinely in shock from what had happened. She readily cooperated and admitted her involvement in the assault; but, as is most often the case, she blamed the others for instigating it and maintained she "had no choice" but to follow the others. She told me that she was afraid of speaking out against her friends when the vicious assault took place. She said she didn't take her stand out of fear. She remained "silent" against her better judgment and chose not to say "no." She eventually admitted that she went along with the assault "just to fit in." And what did she get as a reward for being a participant? She was tried in a real court along with the others, labeled as a criminal, and convicted of aggravated assault. There's a night—and a nightmare— she'll never forget.

Life is not all "rainbows and sunshine." It can be a tough *place* at times, filled with the necessity of making an endless number of tough decisions and choices. The thoughts that pop into our heads in the multitude of situations we encounter can create fear and hesitation within us; but it is still, and always, up to us to deal with them in and for our best interests. Our **EMP** (Empowerment Management Plan) guards will help as will our next step: to simply **STEP** . . . (Chapter 7: Stop—Think—Evaluate—and then Proceed).

CHAPTER 6 SUMMARY

◆ If it's change we want, we are responsible for taking the necessary action to make it happen. No one else has the means to do it but ourselves. Success and happiness is not exclusive to just a few. It's ours to take.

◆ Don't be hard on yourself for focusing on what you don't have right now or on why you don't have it. While it is common to do so, your focus needs to shift rather onto how to take the right steps to achieve what you want. Wasting energy on misguided focus robs you from reaching your dreams.

◆ Comparing yourself to others who have more than you may result in self-doubt, feelings of inadequacy and even guilt and shame, leaving you feeling inferior, unworthy and hopeless. It's counterproductive to arriving at your destination—your goals. Instead, challenge yourself and compare your own progress as you work at reaching those goals.

◆ Being the master of your choices and your destiny takes work; and some people are simply too lazy, afraid or uninspired to move forward to get what they want. The power of your thoughts, choices and decisions is what will garner you the rewards you seek. Move beyond negativity and be the master of your own choices.

◆ Think of your thought storage space as a loft you own in an incredible neighborhood. In order to keep it desirable and lucrative, you'll need to maintain it and attract the right kind of tenants. Do your background checks before any tenant takes residency in your thoughts.

◆ Everyone has a story. You're not alone. Choosing to treat others as you would like to be treated yourself will help strengthen your character, which, in turn, will contribute to the development of your focus. What goes around comes around.

◆ *Life is not all rainbows and sunshine.* It can be a mean place and knock you down from time to time. To be a success and get what you're after in life, you have to move past the blows. Picking yourself up and keeping your eye on the prize is what will motivate you to keep going. If you don't, you'll throw in the towel and your worst fears will have won.

◆ The world is a stage and we are all actors. The wonderful reality of that is that we get to write our own scripts and direct our own lives. Leaving the script-writing and directing in the hands of someone else or of circumstances over which we have no control will leave us unsatisfied and unfulfilled in the stories and outcomes of our lives. When you're handed a bad script, **rewrite** it. It is, after all, your life.

◆ Our thoughts should become of such sterling quality that we naturally expect more from ourselves if what we have isn't bringing us what we want. This means taking out the trash and cleaning out the rubbish that is staining the walls of our minds. Get rid of toxic thoughts, people, images, literature, or *whatever* it is that has been preventing you from moving in the direction you wish to go.

◆ Learn—and know when to say "no." Say no—simply **NO**—to the things or people who rob you of your will, and of pursuing the path of your choice. And—say "no" to yourself when you feel weak and about to give up. In conclusion, be nice, but not to the point that being so sabotages you and your goals and/or to the point of inflicting pain upon yourself. For there is no pain like that which you, even if unwittingly, impose upon yourself. What a waste!

CHAPTER 7

STEP: "Stop—Think— Evaluate and then Proceed"[28]

As one of only a handful of Advocates and Counsellors at the Jordanian International Police Training Center in 2005, I had my hands full dealing with the politics of the American-run academy and the needs of the Iraqi police cadets who attended it.

Day after day I would be visited by police cadets who were longing to go back home to Iraq because they missed their families and were concerned for the well-being of their loved ones. Iraq was in a state of war and the cadets had no telephone privileges except for a ten-minute call once a week in a monitored environment. The use of individual cell phones was strictly prohibited for safety reasons. The academy did not want information being conveyed back to Iraq and potentially to terrorists who were intent on using whatever intelligence they could gather to effect an attack.

The day following these monitored telephone calls, our office would be visited by a half dozen or so cadets who had not managed to reach their loved ones. They would express their concern and request a follow-up investigation in an effort to receive assurances that their families were safe. That was no easy task. With the many different towns, villages and centers around Iraq under attack, trying to reach a police service who could spare to send officers to check on the individual families was next to impossible. But surprisingly, we succeeded at times. I had developed a rapport with

---

28. The credit for the STEP system belongs to the late Dr. Stephen Covey.

a couple of Iraqi officers via telephone; and I'm sorry to say that on at least five occasions, the news they reported was devastating.

Many of the police cadets attended the academy out of a sense of justice. They wanted to make a difference in their country and fight crime and terrorism. Once a terrorist cell discovered the intent of an applicant yet to attend the academy, leaflets were dropped at or near the potential candidate's home warning that if they chose to attend the academy, there would be a severe price to pay. On the five occasions I mentioned, the cadets chose to ignore the warnings; and I had been informed by the Iraqi police that their families had been executed by terrorists. No one was spared, not even the babies.

Imagine if you will, being told that your family, including your infant children, were executed because you decided to ignore a warning from killers to attend a training academy and take a stance against violence. The news I had to deliver to each of these cadets was heartbreaking.

In many Middle Eastern countries, the dead are buried the same day they pass or are discovered to have passed or been killed. Unlike traditional western Christian custom, there is no period of time that allows for a wake/visitation and funeral.

Once I had delivered the heartbreaking news and the cadets reacted with understandably deep emotion, I would make an offer the academy encouraged us not to—I would advocate for their return home. Here is where the S.T.E.P. system worked for them. After their initial grieving, each of these cadets collected themselves and informed me that they had thought about it. Two of them took a day to consider their circumstances; but in each of these cases, the cadets told me they had thought about it and were determined to stay to complete their training. They informed me that returning would not accomplish much under the circumstances—their families were gone and buried.

I can't say I would have been as determined as these young men were, but it certainly was a testament to their purpose and determination. They had "STEPped" in the direction of their goals, as hard as it was.

S.T.E.P. before leaping

Making the right and often difficult choices in life like the one you examined in the previous chapter involving the 16-year old teen, and then that of the five cadets I just mentioned, is not an easy thing for many people. But you are defined and judged by your choices, your beliefs and your actions. Had this young girl taken time to exercise *STEP:* **Stop** for a moment, **Think** about her situation and **Evaluate** the consequences of her actions before **Proceeding** and going along with the others, making her a party to the offense (resulting in her culpability in the matter), her life would be very different today.

So it is with your own thoughts, beliefs and actions. From time to time you need to stop and consider what is in your greater interest and resist your self-doubt, fears, and the expectations and wishes of others. You must demand the best from yourself to make the best choices you can and act in your best interests, with conviction, by setting high standards for yourself. You must free yourself from being taken hostage by another person's will and find it within yourself to just say "no" when the circumstances call for it. You are in complete control of the standards you establish for yourself.

The *STEP* principle is simple. In almost every situation you encounter, you have a few moments to consider what your action to the event will be. Despite what you hear, are told or see, you generally have a few seconds to think about how you'll respond. In applying the *STEP* strategy, you process what just happened the following way: first, take a moment to STOP. Simple enough, isn't it? Just Stop. You don't always need to rush in without first giving it thought.

Thought, or "thinking," is step number two. Once you stop, THINK about what you've just heard, seen and experienced. Consider it from every angle possible, weighing how it affects you, how you feel about it and what actions are best for you to take in response. Your mind can often do this in a nanosecond. The circumstances will dictate how long you should take to consider all of your options. Take your time whenever you can—it's your life after all. If a contract is handed to you, does it not make sense to first read through it to understand what your best options are? Most people take it home or have a lawyer examine it—they don't rush to sign what they don't fully understand.

Now comes step number three: EVALUATE what just happened. Ask yourself important questions. For instance, "What does what I just heard mean to me?" "How should I respond to what I've just heard?" Or, "What is my best course of action for dealing with what I've just experienced?" By asking a few simple questions before you act or respond, you may save yourself a lot of grief and leave people with the impression that you're a wise person. Evaluation means assessing, judging, analyzing and examining. Far too often many of us jump to conclusions or take precipitous action without considering the potential consequences. In the case of the young woman I spoke of earlier, had she taken a few moments to use this "STEP" principle, and acted in what was in her best interest as well as the victim's, her life would have turned out very differently. Perhaps had she chosen to say "no," her actions would have positively influenced the actions of some of those around her.

Once you have stopped, thought about an event which has just happened, evaluated your best course of action—then you're ready for the last "step" in STEP: that is, PROCEED. You will be proceeding by word and action having carefully considered what is in your best interest and well as in the best interest of others in whatever situation you find yourself. It's that simple to **STEP** forward. Remember, actions speak louder than words. If you simply speak the words without following through with action fitting to the words you speak, people will quickly lose respect for you and judge you according to your actions and not your words. Expect more from yourself by thinking things through and taking the right STEPs. Be consistent. Failing to be consistent in your actions will return you to old behaviors and doubts, preventing you from being the best "you" you can—and should—be. You'll start letting toxic thoughts direct you again and the dialogues of doubt will return. You'll be feeding the monster and letting it grow with each feed you give it. Face your fears and move forward in spite of them.

Demand more from yourself. Set the highest standards for yourself and aim to maintain them. Choose "the road less travelled" (Robert Frost) and don't let anyone or anything discourage you from following your dreams and taking the most propitious action(s) or making the most focused choices to attain your goals. Don't let anyone keep you hostage. STEP forward—don't be afraid to stumble. Stumble you may in the beginning, but we all stumble before we learn to walk. We all walk before we learn to run. It's your life, and your choices have consequences. Actions, or failure to take action, will manifest itself in some definitive way and leave an imprint in the chapters of your life and your script. If you're not willing to take risks, you won't stumble but you won't learn to walk either. Make your choices and your actions worth applause, even if you're the only one applauding at the moment. Be strong and choose what's best.

CHAPTER 7 SUMMARY

◆ Stop, think evaluate and proceed. Etch this into your brain so that the next time a situation calls for action, you'll consider your best option. And while enacting this STEP process, do not be vulnerable to the various opinions, comments, attitudes of others which can, if not in synch with your goals, throw you off your course of thinking and action.

◆ Say to yourself, right now: "I am not a hostage to someone else's will." Now, believe it. It's yours!

◆ Learn to say "no" more often and with confidence. And you don't have to defend your "no" to anyone—nor should you.

CHAPTER 8

Victim Selection

I had heard of the "Boogie Man." Since joining the police, I now knew he was real. A cold and wet autumn brought with it three reported cases of aggravated rape in the small community of Bowmanville, Ontario, in the late 1990s. I was assigned to the sexual assault unit and given the task of leading the investigation into this UNSUB (unknown subject/suspect). We knew he was brutal. If ever your mother warned you of the "Boogie Man," this unsub was one such being. His attacks were frightful, fast and violent. He selected his victims based on age, hair color and body type. His victims were female, in their late teens, with slim bodies and long hair. He was what we refer to as a "power aggressive" rapist. He hid behind bushes late at night—often in peoples' yards—waiting to pounce on his victims. No witnesses—only the traumatized victims who all reported that he wore a balaclava and gloves, and bound their wrists with duct tape.

Despite the many cups of black, hot and cold coffee I drank to keep me pushing forward, canvassing the neighborhoods provided no leads. His latest victim was a college student who attended a pub in the downtown core on a rainy and cold night. She left the pub just after midnight, informing her friends that she had promised her father she would be back by midnight. She refused to be walked home by a friend, convincing him that she would be fine—she only lived a few blocks away after all and it was a small town. What could go wrong?

This young woman had been so traumatized that by the time I interviewed her she had cropped off most of her hair and had withdrawn from life as she once knew it. I spent every moment I had hunting this rapist down; and three weeks later, I got him. It turned out someone did see a dark pickup leaving that night. It was rather distinctive and had not been parked in the neighborhood in which he had attacked his last victim. It had been parked a few blocks away. That was the lead I needed. I identified the rapist, a hulk of a man. He was a married man with three young children and was known to many as a "pillar" of the community. The community was shocked at his arrest. DNA sealed his fate. He had a history of minor sexual deviances including masturbating in public and peeping into windows. As is often the case, these perpetrators graduate to rape. He showed his true colors following his arrest—both at the police station and later when a skilled prosecutor and my friend, Greg O'Driscoll, took a run at him when he applied to be released at his bail hearing. Greg had the suspect seething with rage and close to jumping into a fit of violence right in front of the Justice of the Peace. Needless to say, the Justice denied the suspect's release.

The point of this story is that victims are often selected because opportunity arises when their defenses are low. The Boogie Man's last victim had been walking home alone on a cold, dark, rainy night. The rain pelted down into her face; and in sheltering her eyes from the rain as she walked instinctively toward home, her defenses were down, her alertness minimized. She became vulnerable, and consequently, an easy target.

Victim prevention

The above story is one example of victim selection. Have you ever wondered if there is anything that can be done to minimize the chance of becoming a target? What steps can be taken to lessen the possibility of being selected as a victim of crime, and for the purpose of this book, a victim and hostage to yourself? In answering these questions, let's examine what victims often do to unwittingly broadcast messages to an attacker that they are vulnerable and easy to take. In the hundreds of interviews of rapists, thieves and break-and-enter "artists" which I have conducted, many have confided in me how and why they selected their victims. And several of those same elements of victim selection translate to our own self-victimization when we choose to sabotage ourselves via negative thoughts. How so? . . . you might well ask. Please read on.

Well, to begin with, I'll introduce you to a term used in police and scientific circles to assist in determining why certain people are more susceptible to being targeted than others. The term is "Victimology," which, simply put, is the thorough study and analysis of victim characteristics;[29] and it is used by criminal investigators to help them understand how and why a particular victim, or a number of victims, are targeted by an assailant or assailants. The reason victimology is important is that the victim makes up roughly half of the profile of the criminal offense, and as such, is as much a part of the crime as the crime scene, weapons, and eyewitnesses are. This is especially true when the police have a live victim, because that victim was the last person to possibly witness the crime, and may be able to provide the best behavioral and physical description of the offender.

Apart from this, the victim's background may provide the police with important information about their past activities or lifestyle which may possibly help lead the investigators to a suspect. This "victim profiling" has traditionally been overlooked in police investigations, but it is an important consideration in successful investigations.[30] For example, depending on the type of crime that was committed, investigators consider things such as: what color is the victim's hair and his/her eyes? What physical build and characteristics does he/she have? What is his/her daily routine and what routes does he/she take to get to his/her destinations? Furthermore, did the victim broadcast a message of vulnerability to the assailant by projecting an image of weakness, inattentiveness and lack of confidence?

29. Brent Turvey

30. *Criminal Profiling, Fourth Edition: An Introduction to Behavioral Evidence Analysis.* Copyright 2011, Brent Turvey, Academic PR.

We are creatures of habit, and certain habits can be killers

*"In the rush to examine a criminal's behavior, it is
not difficult to become distracted by the dangling carrot
of that criminal's potential characteristics and forget
about the value of understanding his victims."*
—BRENT TURVEY

Many of the characteristics that make some people victims/targets, but not others, are the same traits that can potentially make us targets to the thoughts and beliefs we may hold which leave us susceptible to becoming hostages to ourselves. Numerous victims I've dealt with in severe sexual assaults had taken unnecessary and reckless risks. For example, some had chosen to walk down a dark unpopulated street at night or hadn't paid attention to their surroundings or to the people around them. They listened to their music through their blaring headphones and didn't "listen" to the sounds that could have alerted them to danger. They kept their eyes glued to their cell phones or texting away and not on what was in front of, above, or behind them. They walked into an elevator with a stranger after their inner voices and instincts were screaming for them to wait for the next elevator. In short, they dropped their guard or simply had no guard at all.

There are so many different reasons why individuals are "selected" as victims. Our research has provided us with hundreds of reasons; and my interviews of hundreds of criminals have provided me with insight into what motivated them to select the victim they had. One need only watch the popular TV show *Criminal Minds* to get an idea of how the criminal mind works and of how many different reasons there are that make someone a target.

Sometimes it's as simple as being at the wrong place at the wrong time. Despite that, it can also be as simple as dropping your boxing gloves in the ring of life when you should have had them up, with both eyes open and your mind alert. A lack of awareness makes many victims an easier target than those who remain aware and confident in their surroundings. Many crimes can be prevented by simple awareness, observation, and by projecting an attitude of confidence.

With awareness, confidence, optimism, and a mental state of alertness, you are well on the road to success. Without awareness or the right attitude, you can become easily paralyzed by the same self-defeating thoughts time and time again, walking the same unfulfilling paths you did yesterday and the day or months or years before. Or you can choose to go nowhere and bury your head in the sand, praying everything will work itself out without having to make choices, take risks and move forward with a specific destination or goal in mind. I don't deny that there's a certain amount of comfort in familiarity, even if that familiarity serves no other purpose but to keep us in one place. But remaining in one place will get you nothing and nowhere if your desire is to create a better and happier life for yourself.

If you allow your negative thoughts or your past to control your behavior and don't have a positive destination in mind, you won't reach the desires of your heart and the goals your "good thoughts" fought to bring into your world. It is essential to have a destination in mind before you set off on any journey, and that you remain aware not to drop your guard or allow negative and self-defeating thoughts to consume you. With a positive attitude and confidence, the moment any negative thought makes its way into your head, your inner strength and character will quickly dispel it. Being aware of their invasiveness helps prepare your management team to eliminate them before they take root. Being prepared and aware that you've been attacked by them before, you'll prepare a defense. You'll watch for the first sign of them and you will project an attitude of "I'm stronger than what happens to me."

Don't be a victim to self-defeating thoughts. Be aware that they will target your mind if you show any signs of weakness, unawareness and self-doubt. **Release** them. Remain confident and look ahead: see where you want yourself to be. Have a destination in mind and move confidently ahead toward that destination and goal. Do this by eliminating doubt and by knowing where you want to be.

Dealing with empathy
when empathy is "extorted" from you

Behavioral scientists have labeled empathy created as a result of extortion as "The Stockholm Syndrome." The Stockholm syndrome was named after the Norrmalmstorg robbery of Kreditbanken at Norrmalmstorg, Sweden, in which several bank employees were held hostage in a bank vault from August 23 to August 28, 1973, while their captors negotiated with police. Behavioral scientists began to observe that some of the hostages were actually sympathizing with their captors—even after having received severe beatings and being threatened with death. It was suggested that in the minds of these hostages, their feelings of helplessness had resulted in seeing their captors as gods. The hostage-takers had established complete control over the lives of their captors; and "giving in," "submitting to," and actually "accepting" their fate in the moment became to them a far better and safer choice than resisting at the expense of severe pain and/or death.

Remember the pain/pleasure principle? We'll do almost anything to avoid pain. In cases of the Stockholm Syndrome, if the victim obeys his/her hostage-taker, they feel that they might be spared and given a chance to live—or that perhaps their captors would select someone other than them to beat, humiliate, or kill. This fear develops/developed into a form of learned hopelessness. This learned hopelessness and submission in those who experienced the Stockholm Syndrome often lasted long after their captors had been caught or killed. It became ingrained in their minds, in their realities and in the "conditioning" their minds had undergone through the fear and terror they had been exposed to and experienced. And it can develop over a very short period of time. Their circumstances conditioned their minds into accepting a new reality, a new belief, a new set of choices and decisions, and subsequently new actions and behaviors.

We all experience a mild form of this syndrome from time to time. Because of our fears of failure or even a fear of success, we often give in to the hostage-taker of our own thoughts and beliefs;

and we unconsciously choose to abandon hope, adopting a sense of learned hopelessness and settling for what we are comfortable with or accustomed to—an acceptance of remaining "where we are" at the moment—wooed by its comforting familiarity. We choose to abandon our freedom of choice and move forward with our goals and dreams; we convince ourselves that to do otherwise would result in too much personal and emotional pain. We associate change with pain. We condition ourselves to believe that we really have little or no choice over our circumstances, and that we may as well accept our fate and stay in our "comfort zone." We begin to identify and empathize with our current "normality" which is anything but healthy.

As previously discussed, we are naturally conditioned to avoid pain, physically and emotionally. It's simply part of our nature.[31] Emotional pain and the value we attach to it are created in our own thoughts and choices—in our own minds. We often talk ourselves out of taking action by telling ourselves that "It will be too hard," "I'll be too embarrassed," "I can't do this," and "I may as well just accept it." Repeating negative assertions continuously is like setting up a self-fulfilling prophecy; that is, thinking an outcome into existence. Those voices take control and you fall into a false sense of empathy—much like the victims of the Stockholm Syndrome. If you believe victimizing thoughts strongly enough, they become your reality. You condition yourself to narrow-minded thinking. You condition yourself not to believe in your abilities, and to avoid tapping into your full potential to create something greater than what you have, greater than you can imagine. Greater than you are in the moment.

The foregoing process translates into feelings of hopelessness and fear. The moment you relinquish your Power and Control over your circumstances, and you push the "stop" button on your choice menu, is the moment you give in to the hostage-takers—be they negative suggestions from without or thoughts from within, as I have mentioned repeatedly in this work. You choose not to exercise your

---

31. Epicurus, Freud, Anthony Robbins.

power of choice, and you settle for the present moment, thoughts and conditions you have come to know. You pray for a rescue that won't come because you fail to grasp the understanding that rescue for you will not come from the hands of someone else. It will only come from within yourself. The words, encouragement and wisdom of others is absolutely of no rescue value to you unless you decide to make your own choices for your own life and choose to appreciate the blessings you're given and change that negative talk in your head to positive messages instead. This means believing in yourself, talking in an upbeat "voice" and tempo to yourself, fighting the monsters who try to invade your thoughts the moment they arrive and before they have time to take root, taking risks, moving forward and listening to others who offer wisdom and knowledge—but always, *always,* making your own choices.

The Stockholm Syndrome occurs in your subconscious simply because you are permitting thoughts and language into your mind that do nothing to build your personal growth or your will to achieve, and you begin to accept it as your fate, finally empathizing with it. I saw this in victims of crime many times. They convinced themselves—or had been convinced by others—that there was no escape for them and they "may as well accept their fate." With these self-defeating assertions, they abandoned better choices for themselves by remaining "hostages" to their own self-defeating thoughts and beliefs. They fell into a Stockholm Syndrome of their own making. And, if you accept these beliefs out of the fear of pain that you associate with taking action and freeing your own self to pursue your own happiness and success, you create your own Stockholm Syndrome. You end up convincing yourself that you are hopeless and that you may as well accept where you are.

Be willing to succeed

Imagine yourself in a race at school. All the other students and runners line up on the track ready for the race. Well, almost everybody. Some show up but don't even bother lining up at the starting line because they have no interest in running the race—or they imagine themselves losing even before they begin. So they didn't bother going up to the line. The race is just about to begin. After hearing the "Ready, set, go!" you may be one of the runners to give it everything you have. There may be other runners ahead of you and some behind you. But you keep running.

For some runners, they start off strong and they give it every-thing they've got . . . for a while. But because they weren't prepared, they didn't have the stamina to maintain the pace. They became exhausted quickly and saw other runners well ahead of them, so they told themselves that there is no way they can win and they slowed down to a halt. They gave up. And they may have watched the race from the sidelines, noticing how the other runners were making out and who was ahead of the race. As they watched the race go by they may have even begun to cheer for a runner or two. And everybody was anxious to see who would cross the finish line first.

Quite possibly the person to cross the finish line first will still have energy left in him or herself to run even further. How did he or she do that? Who is this person? He or she must have been born a runner. At least, that's what some people will say. So who is this per-son, really? This is the person who heard about the race and told him/herself that they were going to prepare for it. They then condi-tioned themselves by preparing and training for it, running regularly with a goal in mind. That goal was to win. Their internal monologue went something like this: "I'm going to win this race!" "This is going to be fun!" "I've got to train to win!" and "I'm gonna feel so good when I cross the finish line!" Whereas most of the other runners never chose to prepare for that race. They may have wanted to win, but they didn't prepare for it in advance; and because of this, it was sim-ply a wish and not a goal. They obviously didn't want to win that much. It's very possible that their internal monologues were some-thing like, "I'll do the best I can;" "I never win anything anyway;" or, "I'm not going to enjoy this one bit."

Other runners gave up hope of winning even before setting foot on the track once. They felt that there was no possibility of them win-ning at all. So when they heard about the race, they ignored the pos-sibilities and convinced themselves they were defeated even before trying. And they were right. Their negative self-talk became their self-fulfilling prophesy. When we tell ourselves there is no hope—we effectively abandon all hope. When we tell ourselves there *is* hope, we effectively create and stimulate hope. Because there is always hope, and there is always a chance to win.

Runners never thought they could break the 4-minute mile until Roger Bannister, a 25-year-old British Medical student broke the record on May 6th, 1954. After he broke the record, many others followed. We are confined to the extent of the limiting thoughts and beliefs we create for ourselves. We are confined by the walls we build within ourselves and the actions we fail to take. Our thoughts and beliefs can galvanize us into action that will change the course of our lives forever, just as readily as they can prevent us from dreaming and believing. Our thoughts and beliefs can lead us to take chances and reach new goals which free ourselves from our hostage state. Winners are people who take chances. Risks. There are endless possibilities waiting for us and it is up to us as individuals to choose the goals and destinations we want for ourselves. It's up to us to create the beliefs that will empower us to take action and act on these beliefs with consistent action that will develop into positive habits within ourselves, enabling us to reach the goals that we first set out to achieve.

As an aside, it baffles me to no end how so many people I've met who have reached the age of fifty think they're old. Once they tell themselves this, they condition themselves for failure. They believe their years are numbered and their health will naturally get worse. Nonsense! Having that kind of attitude will "make" you grow old. You'll stop living, taking chances and working hard at staying fit and healthy. It's all how you choose—yes, choose—to see yourself. If you subscribe to such a self-sabotaging way of thinking, there's so much you'll miss out on, and you'll reduce the quality of your life enormously.

Be willing to succeed. Prepare for it, believe in it and welcome it. Without preparation and planning, the likeliness of reaching your destination is left up to mere chance.

Leaving hopelessness behind

In my years as a Hostage Negotiator, I came to realize that hostage-takers and their hostages often experience many of the same emotions. For example, among many other emotions, a hostage-taker often feels anxiety, hopelessness and desperation. Similarly, these same feelings are typically experienced by the hostage. That sense of hopelessness is common to both, but for very different reasons, of course. In many instances, the hostage-taker didn't wake up that morning thinking that he would end up taking a hostage that day. And equally, the hostage didn't wake up that morning thinking that he or she would become a hostage. But whatever the reasons that brought them together, they found themselves in a situation in which each of them felt a great deal of hopelessness and anxiety. Their thoughts and actions were affected by anxiety and an inability to make informed decisions or choices due to the overwhelming stress in which they found themselves.

Did all hostage-takers whom I encountered feel hopelessness? No. Some were goal-oriented with a specific outcome in mind. However, for those who were not career criminals or goal-oriented, most experienced a sense of hopelessness, at least for a brief period. My job as a Hostage Negotiator was to establish communication and to de-stress the hostage-taker, with the goal of persuading him (or her) to think rationally and realistically and to release the hostage unharmed—and then surrender.

My intent was to get them from the state of hopelessness to a state of hopefulness. But as you might imagine, when a person is under extreme duress and stress, they are not able to think rationally, and often they don't even hear the words you say to them at first. They experience the "fight or flight" response. The heart beats so rapidly and the mind is filled with so many different thoughts that the stress causes them to be unable to: focus, understand, or appreciate the environment surrounding them. As you know, under extreme duress the body automatically prepares itself for fight or flight. Stress can cause us not to think clearly. Under extreme stress, our brain receives messages and evaluates the amount of danger with which we are faced. We respond with "fight or flight" and we are conditioned to react accordingly. That's why, in many hostage situations, it takes a long time for the negotiator to actually establish communication and be heard by the hostage-taker. He/she, or they, as the case may be, often simply can't hear what is being said due to the overwhelming stress they are experiencing.

Imagine for a moment, a time when you experienced an unexpected and sudden shock, be it big or small. Maybe you were walking down a street late at night and the lid of a garbage can suddenly crashed onto the pavement right beside you, resulting in a thunder of unexpected noise and shocking you senseless! Immediately, your blood pressure rose, your heart began to beat faster, perhaps you began to perspire. Your hands may have automatically risen, preparing to fight. Or you froze for a moment. The thoughts you had were either "I've got to fight" or "I'd better get out of here, fast!" Most of us want to avoid pain and conflict, so the choice to flee sounds like a better option. But when you're trapped, the choice to flee is not an option. And when I was dealing with a hostage-taker, their option to flee wasn't an option either. They were surrounded by heavily armed Tactical Response Officers. And because of the severe stress and uncertainty of the situation, the hostage-taker often could not think rationally or clearly, and often didn't even hear the sound of my voice at first. It's almost like the sound of someone's voice when your head is under water in a pool and you just can't make out the words.

Once I was successful in establishing communication with the hostage-taker, I was able to provide realistic options and a safe means out of their predicament (and into the hands of the tactical team). One other thing I considered could realistically happen. The hostage-taker might opt to make the worst decision they've ever made in their lives: the choice to commit suicide. This happens more than you might think in hostage situations, especially when the hostage-taker feels absolutely no sense of hope. The choice to commit suicide as opposed to being taken into custody crosses their minds; and if it's allowed to take root, those thoughts may overpower their rational thinking. If that happened, they might choose to turn the weapon on themselves or rush toward the Police, committing "suicide by cop." Whichever way it ended, the decision was a final one. There would be no tomorrow.

In addition to dealing with hostage-takers, Negotiators most often deal with suicidal persons and barricaded people in crisis who have the intent to commit suicide. In those instances, I would ask them directly, "Do you intend to kill yourself?" By being that specific, it directed their mind to their intent. Part of the training I received as a Negotiator made me realize the importance of directing their thought back to reality so that I could talk to them about what they were actually considering—and talk them out of it. You do absolutely no one any good by avoiding the use of direct language.

And so it is, as well, with self-talk. Be specific with yourself. If you avoid telling yourself directly what it is you want and how you'll go about achieving it, you'll be essentially committing "success suicide." Notwithstanding that this "success suicide" may be accidental and unintended, the result will be equally profound. If you're not specific with yourself about what you want, how can you possibly achieve it? In cases of actual hostage situations, it was often necessary to repeat the message over and over again, reminding the hostage(s) that there were better choices for them to make. Repeating the same positive messages to ourselves will have a transformative effect on our thought processes. We begin to believe what we're repeating to ourselves. By using this technique with a person in crisis, a hostage-taker or even a victim of crime who had lost hope, I was successful in getting the message across. Repeating a positive message has a great chance of rooting itself in our minds as well as in the minds of others.

This too shall pass

When it comes to making decisions about where you want to be and who you want to be, you can't settle for feelings of hopelessness or defeat. If at the first sign of difficulty, you've conditioned yourself to feel hopeless and defeated, then there is very little chance for personal success and victory over your situation, if any. One of the secrets of moving forward and rising above a situation is to remind yourself that whatever the situation is, in most cases, "This too shall pass." And most often, whatever you are faced with will pass, provided you take certain actions and change your thoughts and beliefs about the situation. And if it's a permanent setback, you need to remind yourself that you are a Power Survivor, capable of choosing how you feel about your situation and how you choose to react to it. You do not have to close the door on your dreams and goals by making decisions that would lead you to "success suicide" or failure. If you feel so desperate that you choose to accept your poor lot—the bad hand that's been dealt to you—without making any effort to improve your situation and move ahead, essentially, you are killing your chances of true happiness and joy. And this can happen even if it's just a case of you simply forgetting to remind yourself that eventually everything will be okay—like a heavy rain followed by blue skies. Remind yourself in those times of trouble, "This too shall pass." And remind yourself that you are strong enough to make sure that it passes quickly by changing your thoughts, beliefs and attitude about the situation, and by taking necessary action. And in the words of Lawrence Welk: "There are good days and there are bad days, and this is one of them."

CHAPTER 8 SUMMARY

◆ Many of the characteristics that make some victims targets but not others are the same traits that make us targets to the thoughts and beliefs that leave us susceptible to becoming hostages to ourselves.

◆ Dropping your boxing gloves in the ring of life when you should always have had them up makes you an easy target to be hostaged.

◆ With awareness and an attitude of confidence, optimism and alertness, we are well on the road to hostage prevention and success.

◆ Because of fear of failure or even a fear of success, we often give in to the hostage-taker of our own thoughts and beliefs and we unconsciously choose to abandon hope, adopting a sense of learned hopelessness and settling for what we are comfortable with or accustomed to—a "where we are" at the moment pitfall.

◆ Be willing to succeed. Prepare for it. Without preparation and planning, the likeliness of reaching your destination is left up to mere chance.

◆ Consider being specific with yourself as well. If you avoid telling yourself specifically what it is you want and how you'll go about achieving it, you'll be essentially committing "success suicide."

◆ One of the secrets of moving forward and rising above a situation is to remind ourselves that whatever the situation, in most cases, "This too shall pass."

CHAPTER 9

Learned Helplessness

Diary Entry, Paul Nadeau—
Wednesday June 15th, 2005, Amman, Jordan

"This week has been intense. The cadets—particularly some in class 18 seem to be running the camp. We believe many of them are militants, terrorists—insurgents. The 'riot' last Friday was really another one of many planned attacks on the academy—and us. This one resulted in an estimated $250,000 (US) damage to vehicles, buildings and equipment. Seven PSD officers were injured as was Brutus, the head of camp security. He and his partner Gerard believe their days as camp security and their continued deployment here are numbered because of their stance against the violence. Go figure this one.

The rumor is another riot has been planned for tomorrow during the day. Last Friday, Colonel Rea prevented a riot squad entering the camp. They arrived from Jordan to help some 20 minutes or so after the riot had begun. This non-action seems to have been motivated by political considerations, including appearance. No action was taken against the inciters of and participants in that attack, and the Jordanians don't seem to want to take any action against the Iraqis. Not even when we are/were under attack.

It is said that Jordan is the poorest of all Arab countries. They have no oil, no water and no industry. They get their water from countries other than their own; and part of the Red Sea was given to them by Saudi Arabia. A major source of income comes from international participation in Peace-Keeping efforts. Poor, yes, but their people are their riches. Such wonderful people. And their King and Queen are such amazing leaders.

Many Jordanians feel trapped in their country. Income is terrible and they hardly earn enough to get by. Leaving the country for school or travel is next to impossible for most young Jordanian men, unless they have power and/or money. Many of these men feel they're living on a volcano about ready to explode at any time; and if you think of it, they're right. The men will be needed if they go to war. I've heard it described as a Western town movie set—nice front to look at, but in reality there is nothing behind the front set. Many feel so helpless and discouraged; they've come to accept their fate and have learned to expect nothing. They've learned to be hopeless; and behind their eyes there is NO hope. No expectation. No will.

I'm working tomorrow. This should be interesting. Hopefully nothing resembling a riot or an attack will take place; but as it has so often been mentioned, it's only a matter of time. . . . "

There are things over which you have no control. Then there are things over which you *do* have control. In everything. As stated earlier in this book—it's not what happens to you that matters; it's how you respond to what happens that does.

You may occasionally react to circumstances with the belief that no matter what you do, there is no hope for you—no way you can make it through your dilemma, get through to someone, or achieve a particular goal. Although the situations you encounter may not be life-and-death situations, the thought process may actually appear to be similar. You are very much a creation of your thoughts; moreover, you are a product of your past and present experiences. In your formative years, you experienced things that shaped the way you interpreted life. Your external environment—your upbringing, the influence of your parents, teachers, friends and schoolmates, played a huge role in how you saw life and how you saw yourself. Good or bad, many of these outside influences determined and shaped your belief system; and subsequently, those influences are/were reflected in the unfolding of your life. As you grew older and wiser, you went from dependence to interdependence and finally to independence. However, for some of you, those bad experiences that you went through as children were dragged into your adult lives, and you're still hostages to them.

Viktor Emil Frankl, (1905–1997) was an Austrian neurologist and psychologist who was a Holocaust survivor. In 1959, his book *Man's Search for Meaning* was published, which chronicles his experiences as a concentration camp inmate. The imprisonment led him to discover the importance of finding meaning in all forms of existence and experiences. What he discovered in those concentration camps can be applied to our own way of thinking when we find ourselves hostage to own thoughts, beliefs and circumstances. We can't control what happens to us externally in life. Just like the weather, many experiences we're faced with are not within our control to change, whether it is an unexpected job loss or a serious health issue. But what is within our control is our ability to choose how to respond to what happens to us. It's not so much what happens to us that is the most important thing, but it is what we do and how we respond to what happens to us that is. Frankl wrote, "When we are no longer able to change a situation, we are challenged to change ourselves." He also wrote, "We who lived in concentration camps can remember the men who walked through the huts comforting others, giving away their last piece of bread. They may have been few in number, but they offer sufficient proof that everything can be taken from a man but one thing: the last of the human freedoms—to choose one's attitude in any given set of circumstances, to choose one's own way."

As you've read earlier, in my experiences as a domestic violence coordinator, I came to realize that many domestic violence victims often felt trapped and often ended up empathizing with and defending their abusive spouses. Again—that "empathy" word. In most of those abusive relationships, the abused spouse was regularly fed a bombardment of damaging messages such as: "You're no good;" "Nobody would love you if you left me;" "You're useless," and so forth. These repeated messages so often resulted in the receiver eventually adopting them as true. Under the threat of physical harm or worse, the domestic violence victim will often suffer from what we discussed earlier: the Stockholm Syndrome. They become conditioned to accept the trap they're in and suffer constant and never-ending pain to the point that they believe what they're fed—accepting their lot in life as the way it is and simply giving in. This is also referred to as "Learned Helplessness."

Learned Helplessness occurs when an outside condition, be it a person or an environment, continuously sends a message of hopelessness to the receiver that is eventually adopted by the receiver to be true. The receiver accepts it as "the way it is" and gives in to it.

In 1967, the concept of Learned Helplessness was accidentally discovered by psychologists Martin Seligman and Stephen F. Maier who initially observed helpless behavior in dogs that were conditioned to expect an electrical shock after hearing a tone. Later, the dogs were placed in a shuttle box that contained two chambers separated by a low barrier. The floor was electrified in one shuttle box, and not on the other. Dogs previously subjected to electrical shock conditioning made no attempt to escape, even though avoiding shock simply involved jumping over a low barrier. That resulted in the observation that eventually the animal will simply stop trying to avoid the stimulus and behave as if it is operably helpless to change the situation. They'll "give in."

Even when opportunities to escape were presented in those experiments, this Learned Helplessness prevented the animal from taking any action. While this concept is strongly associated to animal psychology, it also applies to many situations involving human beings, as in domestic violence as earlier alluded to. In general, when people feel that they have no control over their circumstances, they may also begin to behave in a helpless manner. This conditioning can lead people to overlook opportunities for relief and change. Children are especially vulnerable to Learned Helplessness. Consider a child who performs poorly in school. He or she may come to believe that nothing they do will ever result in success at school: they may easily come to experience a sense of helplessness. I certainly did in my earlier years. Learned Helplessness has also been associated with several different psychological disorders such as depression, anxiety, shyness, and loneliness. Such disorders may also be the result, as I have indicated, in situations of domestic violence; and this I have witnessed firsthand.

So how does Learned Helplessness factor into being a hostage to yourself? By now it should be clear that being a hostage to yourself simply means that occasionally you may allow yourself to feel a sense of hopelessness and desperation. Your inner monologues convince you that no matter what you do to improve your situation, you won't. Additionally, you convince yourself that you may as well not even try. You then become hostage to a false set of beliefs; and because you choose to give in, you prevent yourself from moving beyond your comfort zone and taking risks, from making changes and taking action that would ultimately and invariably result in your success. You feel operably helpless to change the situation and condition yourself to feel helpless. You choose hopelessness instead of hopefulness. But the good news and truth is, the only person preventing you from being where you want to be, is you. Remember that!

"The mind is like a parachute.
It only works if it's open."
—FRANK ZAPPA

Scientific discoveries are being made that crush the age-old saying, "you can't teach an old dog new tricks." No matter how old one is, you can learn new things and create new habits—always. You are limitless. You control your thoughts, and you determine the action that you subsequently take. What you say and do is all largely under your control, and you have absolute control over your thoughts, if you choose to exercise that control. That being said, without exercising control, it makes sense that some of the thoughts you allow yourself to dwell on are preventing you from living a full and happy life. You know this. It's time for you to change the thoughts that prevent you from moving forward to thoughts that catapult you into moving ahead. Make them your dominant thoughts.

You don't have to settle for anything in life that doesn't fit how you see yourself living. Far too often we simply sit back and give in. We don't even try to change whatever it is that we don't like or want in our lives. Whether you're feeling overweight, unattractive, socially awkward or financially insecure, you don't have to feel that way. So many of those insecurities can be changed when you change your way of thinking. But thinking alone won't make it happen. You must also take action to affect change. Act with purpose; and remember the simple truth that we reap what we sow. Your journey to success, happiness and beyond must be reflected in your intentions, attitudes, beliefs, imaginings, language, thoughts, self-talk and the fabric of which you are made. It has to be you. Begin by believing in yourself, your dreams and your abilities. Then talk the talk to yourself first, and step ahead by walking the walk. Fake it until you make it if you must, but it will happen. Each time you exercise the muscles of beliefs and actions, you commit them to memory. If you're stuck in one spot, remember what Albert Einstein said: "Insanity is doing the same thing over and over again and expecting different results."

Imagine for a moment that some of the greatest success stories come from people who experienced adversity, took chances, and chose to take risks and make changes in their own lives. Were they any different than you or me? I don't deny that some of these people may have had better upbringings than we did, or were born in better environments. Some were. Many were not. But despite what the situation is, scientists tell us that our genetic inheritance and biochemistry account for 25–35% of our character; whereas the environment in which we were raised and the people who raised us account for a large component. However, success, confidence and character are also learned behaviors and strengthened by how much we decide to invest in these learned behaviors.

Behind most success stories are people who failed on their first, second, and even third or more tries. But what made them different is that they never gave up. Setbacks and events in their lives led to radical changes in their direction. As you recall from my passage on Power Survivors, researchers have observed that in the cases where humans have suffered enormous trauma—from surviving cancer to surviving human injustices—many of them emerged with an even stronger spirit. Power Survivors began to see things they hadn't seen before, appreciating things they hadn't appreciated before, and living in ways they hadn't lived before. Some of these lives took on new purpose. Almost like so many of those super hero comics I grew up with, where due to some laboratory accident and subsequent trauma, a superhero emerged to save the world. Or a billionaire's parents were killed in cold blood, and that event led our hero to don a cape and fight injustices. You get the idea . . . We are often inclined to believe that for successful people, success came effortlessly. This is far from true when we examine the stories of some of the most successful and influential people of our time and of those who came before them. Why did they succeed where others did not? Passion, drive, hopefulness, tenacity, belief in oneself and consistent, repeated action. And those new attitudes may have arisen out of loss, trauma, and a sense of hopelessness, fear and so forth. We often hear of people who were born into rich families who made all the wrong choices. We also hear of people who were born into poor families and in bad environments who became immense successes.

Take, for example, Oprah Winfrey. Born to a 13-year-old mother, Oprah was physically and sexually abused as a child, and she herself gave birth to a stillborn child at the age of 13. She acted out in ways that got her noticed by the authorities for her disruptive behavior at the tender age of 15. Oprah is just one example of how someone can take her/his life and mold it into something significant, meaningful and successful. Look at this powerful, wonderful woman now! The choices she made for herself worked. She didn't let her past dictate her future.

You are the one who decides where you want to be and how to get there. Milton Berle once said, "If opportunity doesn't knock, build a door." The chapters of our lives are almost entirely written and directed by the author of our lives: ourselves. We are the ones who place limitations on ourselves; and the truth is, we are limitless. What we convince ourselves of becomes largely true. If we convince ourselves in the dialogue of our own minds that we are incapable of success, we're usually right. That bad self-talk will affect how our lives unfold. As I noted earlier, we can't control our external environments.

They unfold in a certain way and are very often not within our control. But what we can control is the manner in which we interpret what happens to us and what we do as a result of what happens to us. We get to choose how we react.

The key is believing in yourself and making the right choices, choosing the right monologues and telling yourself the right things. And when you make mistakes, get back on track. We are imperfect people living in an imperfect world and mistakes are bound to be made. Getting off course is bound to happen. But if we are focused, we can get right back on track. Is it always going to be easy? No. It will take work at first and you may stumble and fall. But that's when getting back up comes in. Imagine for a moment that you decide to take a flight from, say, New York to Toronto. To you, the flight looks straightforward. How could it not be? Draw a line on a map and it appears straight. But the pilot has to deal with winds, turbulence and a number of other issues that take the plane off course for maybe 90% of the flight. The point is, the pilot gets back on track. He/she adjusts and knows where he needs to be. We should make it a habit to program ourselves to follow this line of thinking should we get off track. It will keep us on the right track. And the more we choose to make decisions that are in our best interests—the more we change our internal dialogue to reflect successful thinking and the easier it becomes. The secret is to take that "I can't" attitude and change it to one that says "I can!" And once we do that, we must then follow through with meaningful decisions. And these decisions must then be followed by action—consistent action that will result in consistent success.

"The journey of 1000 miles begins with a single step . . . "
—LAO TZU

" . . . and the idea is to keep moving forward,
one step at a time, until the journey is complete."
—PAUL NADEAU

CHAPTER 9 SUMMARY

◆ We are a by-product of our thoughts and we are influenced by our past and present experiences. The key is to be aware that our past is the past and this moment is the only one that matters.

◆ Some of the greatest success stories come from people who have experienced adversity, taken chances and chosen to take risks and make changes in their own lives. You can too.

◆ Learned Helplessness occurs when an outside condition, be it a person or an environment, continuously broadcasts messages of hopelessness to the receiver that are eventually adopted by the receiver to be true. The receiver accepts it as "the way it is" and gives in to it. If you sense that you are being manipulated, disrespected, objectified, mistreated, and so forth, and feel hopeless to fight it—you're not. Remember that hopelessness is often a learned behavior. You don't have to give in to it. Remove yourself from whatever is drawing you into that state, change your inner monologue and fight for yourself. You can do it.

◆ You are in control of your thoughts. Your thoughts will affect and mold your beliefs. Your beliefs will craft your attitudes and your attitudes will dictate your actions. Your actions are what determine your success. Remember: you're in control.

CHAPTER 10

Decisions

April 10, 2009, was the day I reached 30 years of service with the Durham Regional Police and the day I started to seriously consider retiring with a full pension from the job I loved. The word "retirement" is a scary one for many people; but to me it simply meant closing one chapter in my book of life to allow me to write new adventures in another chapter.

I had often been asked what I would do when I retired. I was qualified in many areas, thanks to my police career: teaching, investigations, consulting and polygraph were simply a few possibilities. International Peacekeeping appealed to me and I had asked my police service to send me on a second mission to Haiti; but my request had been denied as the service felt I couldn't be spared from the important job I was doing. I was their only polygraph examiner and I had provided them with a solution which simply meant replacing me temporarily with the certified examiner I had replaced. He was keen to do it, but my supervisor wasn't.

Now that I was eligible for retirement, I had rediscovered acting with a passion and was being cast often in small TV shows and roles—and I loved it. The RCMP (Royal Canadian Mounted Police) International Peacekeeping Branch was also looking for retired policemen to go on mission and Haiti was in need of peacekeepers. I had wanted that mission a couple of years earlier and I told you how that worked out for me.

I was married at the time, still young, and had a new career in film. The police department was going to pay me not to come to work; they were going to provide me with a full pension, and it all made sense to me. That fall I spoke to my then wife about my thoughts of retiring the following year and she fully supported the idea. With that support, I had now reached a decision. I based it on several factors, including a steady income from my pension, her income from her full-time job, and the income I would be making in film and quite possibly new peacekeeping opportunities. It all made perfect sense. Don't get me wrong: I still loved my job as a cop, and I was very accomplished at it; but I now felt it was time to explore new opportunities with no risk attached.

The following January, 2010, I retired from the service. Acting jobs were coming in and I applied for the Haiti Peacekeeping mission with the RCMP. Three months went by and I was well into the process of working my way toward deployment. One final detail remained and I was off to Haiti.

All was going extremely well, until one afternoon three days before my wife was going in to have surgery. She wasn't too much for socializing with the exception of a couple of good friends she visited regularly. Then, one bright sunny afternoon she disclosed that one of her friends was not in fact a girlfriend from work she had been spending several weekends with over the last few months as I had been led to believe, but it was her lover . . . and . . . she wanted a divorce. To say I was shocked is an understatement. The affair had been going on for a year—long before I approached her with the idea of retiring from the police. I was a professional lie-detector, but I didn't even see that one coming. I had trusted her, and her confession caught me completely off guard. It hit me like a left jab delivered by Rocky Balboa himself.

The next few days were filled with uncertainty and anxiety. She demanded the news of her affair remain between us. She didn't want our daughters or our families knowing the details; I could see why. I didn't want to hurt my daughters and family with that kind of disclosure either, and I wasn't in the best frame of mind to make the wisest of decisions. But decisions had to be made and I made them.

For the first month, the secret of her affair remained hidden. News like that doesn't stay hidden forever however, and the truth eventually came out. I withdrew from the Haiti mission to be there for my daughters. I could never have deployed under those circumstances. It took a while but I got through it.

Now the point of telling you this personal and ugly story has everything to do with the chapter you're about to read. Decisions are made every day. Some are small and some are huge. Some are made carefully whereas others are made in haste and under emotional duress. Some are permanent and others are not. Some can be revisited and revised or modified whereas others are lost forever. Some decisions hurt you or others, and some bring about great rewards and benefits. The fact is we all have to make decisions. It is crucial to do your best to make the right ones; and even if things don't quite go the way you planned, that's okay. You pick yourself up, dust yourself off, and move forward. You simply do . . . what you must.

> *"If you obsess over whether you are making the right decision, you are basically assuming that the universe will reward you for one thing and punish you for another. The universe has no fixed agenda. Once you make any decision, it works around that decision. There is no right or wrong, only a series of possibilities that shift with each thought, feeling, and action that you experience. If this sounds too mystical, refer again to the body. Every significant vital sign—body temperature, heart rate, oxygen consumption, hormone level, brain activity, and so on—alters the moment you decide to do anything . . . Decisions are signals telling your body, mind, and environment to move in a certain direction."*
> —DEEPAK CHOPRA, *THE BOOK OF SECRETS: UNLOCKING THE HIDDEN DIMENSIONS OF YOUR LIFE*

The human spirit is indomitable. Accepting that some decisions about how you're going to live and behave and the commitment you make to those decisions which will ultimately shape your destiny is an absolute marvel. Most of the answers you seek in life are already within you, and you have the right to access your best choices. As my personal story at the beginning of this chapter points out, decisions have to be made on all kinds of matters; and we have to make them for ourselves. We should take whatever time we require making the best ones for ourselves and sometimes that process will include research and counsel. Will we always make the best ones? Some work out and some do not. You still have to make them with whatever information you've gathered, carefully and thoughtfully. Remember that you can always steer yourself in another direction if the first choice doesn't serve you best.

When it comes to personal improvement decisions, it's not enough to simply think that you would "just like to do something"—because thought, while fundamental and necessary, of course, is not enough for a committed decision. Decisions require the thought process to proceed to the level of commitment; and if you're stuck mulling over the idea that you'd just like to move in a certain direction, you haven't gone far enough. The key is to arrive at and firmly commit to a decision and then follow through with appropriate and timely action. For your decisions to make a positive and significant difference in your life, you *must* follow through with action—action which seals the deal.

Many people don't actually make committed decisions—they make excuses. Decisions require commitment. Commitment requires taking action. And action always results in change. Decisions dictate the action we take and the results for which we prepare, strive, and which we anticipate.

As I became more experienced in Sexual Assault Investigations and the understanding of human behavior and recovery, it occurred to me after meeting some victims on more than one occasion that some of them were hostaged into feeling like victims, as I mentioned in a previous chapter. They couldn't get past the evil that had been done to them or even accept that they weren't at fault for what had happened. Sometimes the best-meaning people can deliver the worst possible messages; and some people are just downright ignorant. All you have to do is access the Internet to read how so many men blame sexual assaults on the clothes a girl wears or the places she frequents. Many victims cannot cope with what has been done to them; and it affects their thoughts, their feelings, and their sense of self-worth, among other consequences. Of the victims whom I met and consoled, some had lost hope. They had misplaced their power and control. It had been captured and detained in another room of their mind.

To help un-hostage their power and control, and return it to where it belonged (that is, working *for* them) I decided to present two T-shirts. On one T-shirt was printed the word "Victim." On the second was printed the word "Survivor." I then asked them to choose one of the two T-shirts to take with them. I explained that if they chose the T-shirt that said "victim," so much of their lives, relationships and how they acted would be affected by the choice they made. If they chose the "victim" T-shirt, their relationships, behavior and the way in which they saw themselves and others would be reflected by it. Although they might choose not to wear the T-shirt, the message would still be there: "Hey, I'm a victim." Moreover, they would be granting the person who assaulted them continued control over their thoughts and behaviors. I told them that I was afraid that if they chose the victim T-Shirt they would suffer from that label long after they had left my office.

On the other hand, I offered the "survivor" T-shirt. By choosing this one I explained they would be making the choice to reclaim their power and not let the assault affect the way they lived their lives. They would be taking a huge step in restoring their strength, power and control to where it had been before the assault, and in quite possibly discovering they are even stronger because of it.

This choice between "victim" or "survivor" T-shirts would have an effect on their mood, happiness and behaviors. It's how we see ourselves that matters. Imagine for a moment how horrific it would be to be the victim of a sexual assault. Imagine for a moment how it would feel to be the victim of a rape. Imagine how it would be to live with the knowledge that someone had taken something so precious from you, and left you to live with it. I often left interview rooms with victims thinking that death would have been a welcome alternative to their suffering—in their minds, not mine.

The mind can be a very fragile thing, but it can also be our strongest advocate. It's up to us. I had presented victims with an option on how they could choose to see themselves. In the case of the victims of sex offenses, they had lost a sense of their value and worth and had come to see themselves as victims. They judged themselves. They had, in an unconscious way, allowed someone to make them feel less than who they really were/are. No one has the right to inflict this abuse—both physical and emotional—on another human being. Upon reflection, the victims who chose "survivor" were not simply survivors: they were the power survivors I referred to earlier. The T-Shirts ought to have read: "POWER SURVIVOR—I kicked evil in the teeth and won."

I'm not minimizing the traumatic reality anyone experiences when they are sexually abused, suffer severe loss, disability, or other hardships. Nor am I suggesting that in every person, simply saying to oneself that you'll be a "Power Survivor from this moment on" is the magic bean that will eliminate Post Traumatic Stress or some other very real psychological condition that might appear. What I am saying is to tell yourself that you are stronger than what has happened to you. Tell yourself that you are entitled to be a Power Survivor and that you can—and must—make choices to move beyond what has or is happening in your life. Tell yourself that you MUST make decisions and choices that best serve you and that WILL set you on a path of recovery, hope and happiness. You can condition yourself to overcome just about anything; and it begins with what you tell yourself and what you believe, one wonderful step at a time. The journey of a thousand miles begins with a single step after all. Facing your setbacks, traumas and sadness—head on—and dealing with them with purpose, passion, determination, and vision is essential to winning the battle overcoming them.

The problem with labels

Regrettably, we often label ourselves harshly and make decisions based on those labels or labels that others have given us. Labels can be as harmful to us as they can be constructive, depending on what label you choose to believe. For example, if you choose to label yourself as being "overweight," you'll feel a certain way and you'll make decisions based on that label. Furthermore, if you label yourself "stupid," you'll also feel and take actions which fit that label. I did. You will have accepted it for yourself. We tend to live up to the labels we give ourselves or sadly, which others attribute to us.

Along with labels are innate feelings, beliefs and behaviors associated to them; and depending what labels you accept, the resultant feelings can be both good or bad. Far too often we permit others to stick hurtful labels on us and we just accept them as fact. It's like someone coming up to you from behind with a "Post-it-Note," slapping it on your back, and having it stick. If you then choose to believe it and leave it there, others will also believe its message.

By accepting any self-destructive label placed on you or given to you by yourself or others, you alter your actions accordingly. Your actions and decisions will be influenced by each label; and if the labels are less than positive, the results will be reflected negatively in your feelings and behaviors—overtly or perhaps subtly. Have you or others labeled you as "ugly, stupid, fat, gross, unworthy, unlovable, hopeless, moron, loser, disabled, queer or inferior?" How will such a label affect how you see yourself, how you feel about yourself and how you will behave? How about this list: "Adorable, amazing, awesome, good-looking, charismatic, successful, confident, loveable, generous, kind, radiant and unlimited?" Which from these two lists would you prefer? If you see that you have some of the negative ones and want to change your labels, conduct a serious self-examination and get it done.

Our thoughts condition our beliefs and our beliefs result in the actions we take. "You are today where your thoughts have brought you; you will be tomorrow where your thoughts take you." (James Allen) Is it therefore not better to place rich, positive, and powerful labels on ourselves and strip away the bad ones we've put on ourselves or that others have imposed?

We each have seeds of greatness and potential within us

I believe that within each child, within each person from birth, there are seeds of greatness and potential. These seeds are different for everyone, but each of us has them. Seeds filled with the potential to love, feel joy, grow in happiness and be creative. Seeds of service— that is, a capacity for service, selflessness, kindness, confidence, gratitude, empathy, respect and understanding are all within us. Seeds that are begging to be nourished and to grow—to give and to give back to this world, making it a better place than when we first arrived. Seeds that when fed will blossom to their full potential and shout out, "I'm here, I'm alive, and I'm loving it!"

For these seeds to grow, however, like any living thing, they must be fed and nurtured. As children, if we are lucky enough, kind and supportive people will begin to feed those seeds with words of love, encouragement and support. But if we are not lucky, those seeds will be neglected; and the love they need for growth withheld. In fact, the harsh truth is that in some cases, not only is the love not given, someone tries to rip the seeds from the soil and drown them forever. But they can't. Those seeds are endless. They live, despite what anyone tries to do to them because they exist in every fibre of your will and body. They may be hidden but they are ever-present, waiting to develop to the point where each of them will turn to the sun and exclaim, "How does a single blade of grass thank the sun?"[32]

If you search within yourself, you'll find those seeds which may not have received the nourishment they needed. And if they haven't been fed, it will be up to you to feed them. It will be your responsibility to nurture and develop them. No one else can live your life for you and no one else can feed your potential better than you. Look deep inside yourself for those underdeveloped seeds and help them grow. With each of them that you care to develop will come new wonderful possibilities and rewards.

You may think that you're the only one . . . but you're not

Everyone goes through trials, difficulties and challenges. We wake up each day and begin our day with thoughts about ourselves, our lives and our destinations. Not one person has the perfect life. In fact, as

---

32. Doretta Lau; www.dorettalau.com.

a young police officer I remember driving down a busy street with houses on the left and the right. And I remember thinking that behind each of those doors were people who had problems and things going on in their own lives that were hard to deal with. Nobody is exempt from feeling pain, sorrow or hopelessness. But the fact is, although we all experience sorrow and setbacks in our lives, many people choose not to be discouraged and defeated by the bad things that happen to them. Successful and happy people have made the decision not to allow themselves to be dragged down by the negative things that happen to them—they choose thoughts that will move them past their setbacks and into a positive state of mind. Some people actually see problems as "opportunities in work clothes"; and it is these people that we see climbing the ladder of success. Don't get me wrong. I know that not all bad things are opportunities in work clothes. Some are just plain bad. But for a lot of setbacks, some choose to see them differently. And those individuals, well, they're no different than you and me on the outside. But their thought process is very different; and that's why they choose to look at setbacks differently.

I remember when I first started acting in film and television, one of my coworkers from the police station had seen one of the televised programs that I had been in. And he came to me and asked: "Why you? Why did they pick you to be on TV?" For a few moments, I didn't know how to answer. After some reflection, I gave this answer: "Why not me?" I had made a decision to pursue acting with a passion. Yes, I had a few lucky breaks but I pursued what I was passionate about. So why not me? Why not *you* with the goals you work toward achieving? When we make decisions to improve our circumstances or to pursue something that we are truly passionate about, why shouldn't we be the ones to achieve what we set out to achieve? The only person who is going to prevent you from getting what you want, is you. Ok, you may be thinking: I want a lead role in a Blockbuster Hollywood movie. Are you telling me that simply by pursuing that goal, I'm going to get it? Or that beautiful girl/handsome guy I've been dreaming of dating? Are you telling me that by pursuing her, she'll say "yes"? No—I'm not telling you that. But what I am saying is that if you don't try, you'll never know. If you don't give it your all, how can you expect to achieve or to gain anything? If you don't knock on the door, how can you expect it to be answered? And for those who do try . . . ? Some get that Blockbuster movie and some get the date. But *they* tried; and if you don't, you'll never know.

We are the authors of our own destiny; and once we accept the fact that we can create a future for ourselves that is meaningful, it's up to us to work our best at making it happen. And if we get a "no" for one thing, we find a way to turn it into a "yes," or we move onto something else that will please us just as much. Yes, you're limitless; but you'll only get the things you go for. You'll miss out on all the things you didn't go for. You'll only succeed at what you devote your passion to. It's amazing to think that we each have such great potential. Every human being has unlimited potential waiting to be accessed. And this potential is waiting to be tapped into and molded into success, providing we focus our minds and energy into achieving the results that we want to create for ourselves. Decisions are the first step to reaching the goals we imagine for ourselves.

Caring for your inner garden

Our thoughts and beliefs can be compared to a garden. With a garden, it's imperative that we nourish it and plant only those things that we want to see grow. But it's not enough to simply plant something and leave it unattended and unnourished. If we don't nourish the soil regularly, provide the proper amount of water and nutrients along with taking thoughtful, consistent care to ensure a healthy garden, the chances are slim that the seeds that we have sown will grow healthy and to their full potential. We reap what we sow. You just won't end up with a healthy garden if you do not nourish and tend it; and the results you envisioned and expected won't happen, because you neglected to care and to work at achieving the best garden you had set out to grow. On top of that, if you don't care for the garden on a regular basis, weeds will creep in and will often choke out your garden and kill the plants. That's what happens to us with great goals as well. If we neglect caring for them and tending to them regularly, the weeds of doubt and defeat will take over, and soon you'll abandon even trying. And as with each garden, there are seasons that may affect growth; and that's a reminder that despite a temporary lull in growth which we might experience, there is always tomorrow. Tomorrow brings new hope and a new season is ready to unfold for you.

Peter Sellers, a departed wonderful actor made his last film in 1979 called *Being There*. In the film, Sellers played Chance Gardener. His character was an actual gardener—a simple man who, through a series of unexpected events, ended up at the White House and being consulted by the President. But all poor Chance knew were gardens. His child-like simple brain didn't understand anything but that; amazingly, however, his advice to the President on economic growth made sense. The following is an excerpt from that film that makes absolute sense, no matter what your circumstances are:

PRESIDENT: Mr. Gardner, do you agree with Ben, or do you think that we can stimulate growth through temporary incentives?

[Long pause]

CHANCE THE GARDENER: As long as the roots are not severed, all is well. And all will be well in the garden.

PRESIDENT: In the garden.

CHANCE THE GARDENER: Yes. In the garden, growth has it seasons. First comes spring and summer, but then we have fall and winter. And then we get spring and summer again.

PRESIDENT: Spring and summer.

CHANCE THE GARDENER: Yes.

PRESIDENT: Then fall and winter.

CHANCE THE GARDENER: Yes.

BENJAMIN RAND: I think what our insightful young friend is saying is that we welcome the inevitable seasons of nature, but we're upset by the seasons of our economy.

CHANCE THE GARDENER: Yes! There will be growth in the spring!

BENJAMIN RAND: Hmm!

CHANCE THE GARDENER: Hmm!

PRESIDENT: Hmm. Well, Mr. Gardner, I must admit that is one of the most refreshing and optimistic statements I've heard in a very, very long time.

[Benjamin Rand applauds]

PRESIDENT: I admire your good, solid sense. That's precisely what we lack on Capitol Hill.

Planting a healthy garden requires the proper seeds, the proper soil, the proper environment and the proper care. Your choices and the action you subsequently take to grow the perfect garden will be compromised if you don't plan and research how to achieve the best results. And always take into account the seasons. But don't let that discourage you—if you experience stillness but have cared for your garden of life, all will be well.

Similarly, as I wrote earlier, if you own a car and neglect to properly service and care for it, eventually your vehicle will break down and you won't reach the destination you intended to reach. This will translate into frustration, cost and possible breakdowns. Taking care of the very vehicle you depend upon to take you places is an absolute must if you expect to get anywhere. I know you've heard it earlier—but some lessons need to be repeated. The lesson? Your body, mind and soul are the same as the garden, the vehicle and the bank account. Neglect them and they will break down and never give you what you most want and deserve. They'll become useless and possibly a burden. So how does this compare to the decisions we make in other aspects of our lives? It translates in this fashion: first, we need to begin with a rich, solid vision of what we want to achieve. We must have the "end in mind," our destination, when we set out to achieve our chosen goals.

With a clear image of what you want the results to be, you must then decide what the best method of achieving your goals is. This requires a map—a plan, and focused thought, effort and consistent action on your part. You need to steer the vehicle, otherwise you'll run off the road. If you aren't certain how to get to where you want to be, talk to people who have achieved the goals you're after. Mimic their behavior or read books, study, learn and research the Internet for the best methods of getting what you're after. Spend some time understanding the best methods of achieving your dream and put them into action. If your vision is unclear, then take the time to clarify it by researching and writing down your goals. The action of writing down your goals holds you psychologically accountable to them and serves as an excellent reminder of what you're really after. Set realistic goals and realistic timelines for achieving those goals; otherwise you will become discouraged if your goals and timelines are unmet. Monitor your progress and document your results. Determine if what you're doing is working or whether you need to modify your map and change direction and approach. If you're not seeing the results you want—change your approach. Find new ways. Don't keep doing the same things if they are not working for you. Remember what Einstein said about that? He told us to change it up. He observed that "Insanity is doing something over and over again and expecting different results."

The company you keep can help you reach your dreams

Surround yourself with positive people and supporters if you're able to, because positive people generally help us bring the best out of ourselves. Remember the statement, "garbage in, garbage out?" Without creating a good and positive environment and approach for ourselves, the likeliness of success is severely diminished. We need to have a clear vision of what we want. Then we have to determine the best way to reach that goal. Create the best vision that you possibly can for what it is that you so passionately want. Don't start with an unhealthy garden; start with one that promises a good crop. See yourself as having already achieved what it is that you have decided to do. For some people, they have decided to create "vision boards." Vision boards are simply a collection of pictures, stories and inspiration that goal-oriented individuals keep in a place where they can see it daily to remind themselves that this is what their goals look like.

Find the map you need to get you to the place you want to be

I needed a road map to get me to where I wanted to be; so I set out to find that map and then followed the best road to get me there. I had to modify my routines and sometimes I did things incorrectly. I didn't always have the best methods on how to get to where I wanted to get, but I learned. And kept trying. If you don't have the knowledge, it's up to you to get it. It's up to you to find the best map for yourself and that may mean asking others for direction. And if you set out on this journey and find yourself getting off track from time to time, remember your vision board. Post a picture of what you could look like when you reach your goal or what you could have by following your decision, and remind yourself to stick to it. This doesn't only apply to physical fitness and a healthier lifestyle. This applies to every decision that you make that will improve your life. Perhaps you want to study the guitar, or of just have a healthier mind-set. Post a picture of a healthy body on your vision board. Post a picture of a trip, a house, a love or an ideal job. It's your vision and your board— put what inspires you on it.

You may be asking yourself how to get there. Remember, "The journey of 1000 miles begins with a single step." Take it! The important thing is that you *take that first step* and keep moving forward. Envision yourself being successful at whatever it is that you have decided to pursue. Fill the garden of your mind with positive thoughts of success and an "end vision" of where you would like yourself to be, and follow through with the necessary action to get you there. Remain flexible. If your approach is not working, find a way to make it work. Change your map and follow the best directions to help get you there. Research what it is you want to achieve and change your methods if your current methods aren't working for you. Don't be afraid to experiment. Don't be afraid to learn. Don't be afraid to fail. Don't be discouraged from moving forward; because far too often, we give up right before we find what we're after. Discouragement can creep in for each and every one of us; but it's the decision of how you are going to treat that discouragement that will set you apart from those who never succeed. Successful people plan and move forward. Successful people also fail from time to time; but that failure does not result in discouragement to the point of defeat. Successful people have discovered that if one thing doesn't work, they'll be flexible enough to change their approach and make the next thing work. And if it takes a dozen tries, they understand that this is simply the cost of being successful.

One need only take a look at some of the most successful people in this world to see that most often they had been defeated by many challenges that they first endeavored to succeed at. Take, for example, Abraham Lincoln. In 1831, he lost his job. In 1832, he was defeated in the run for Illinois state legislator. In 1833 he failed in a business attempt. In 1836 he had a nervous breakdown, and in 1838 he was defeated in the run for Illinois House Speaker. In 1843 he was defeated in the run for the nomination for United States Congress. In 1846, he was elected to Congress. However, in 1848 he lost a renomination. In 1849, he was rejected for a land officer position. In 1854, he was defeated in the run for United States Senate. In 1856 he was defeated in a run for nomination for the position of Vice President. In 1858, he was again defeated in a run for the United States Senate. However, in 1860 he was elected President of the United States! And he left his mark on this world. This is just one of the many examples of people who have failed several times but were never discouraged to the point of giving up. Our history is filled with stories of successes such as this. Why them? Because they never gave up and they had a vision. Nor should we give up on our dreams.

Believe you can and you can

It is truly amazing to recognize that the person in charge of your success is you. Once you believe in yourself and set realistic goals, you can achieve just about anything you put your mind to. No doubt, on your journey to success in achieving your goals, you will encounter discouragement. You will encounter roadblocks and your internal monologue will from time to time change from one of "I can . . . " to "This is just too hard, I can't do it." But as we saw in the example of

Abraham Lincoln, if he had given up after the first or second attempt, he would never have achieved the ultimate satisfaction of being President of the United States. It's difficult to move forward when we find ourselves in a comfortable spot, remember? I've had a few friends who had goals and aspirations during their younger years and then found themselves during their high school years taking on a summer job that paid well. The job happened to be in an auto factory. The money was good but the work was hard. But because of the convenience of the paycheck and of the moment, some of my friends found themselves too comfortable and that's where they stayed for the next twenty-five to thirty years, only to regret it later on. Life is like that sometimes.

Sometimes you may find yourself in a semi-comfortable spot but one you don't particularly want to be in. And you're prepared to abandon your goals and your dreams simply because where you are in the moment is comfortable and you feel secure. To go outside that comfort zone would require you to feel temporarily uncomfortable and nervous, and we are creatures who associate pain to that feeling of insecurity. Because we are beings who try to avoid pain at almost any cost, many of us don't choose to live to our true potential and don't move out of our comfort zones and go for the goals and dreams we once had. To be truly successful, however, you need to step out of those comfort zones and go for what you want. You need to be determined enough to want something better for yourself and to simply "go for it." You need to visualize what your life would be like if you were to pursue your particular goal and to also imagine what it would be like NOT to go for it. If you don't try, you may as well do nothing more than wish upon a star. "Chance" does not amount to much in life. Action does.

Your dreams can become realities only through hard work and a determined mind. Thoughts are empowering. But only if followed by action. You have been blessed with the power of thought and you have also been blessed with the ability to put your thoughts into motion. But it is simply not enough to think of something you would like. True power and success comes to those who form their thoughts, make decisions, and then follow through by *doing* something about it.

The apple doesn't fall to far from the tree. Sometimes, you have to replant

In my days as a police officer in the youth division, I encountered young people who were truly remorseful for what they had done. They were good kids. Then there were others who came into my office and the first thing they would do is swear like sailors and call me every name they possibly could think of. Their attitudes were full of anger and disrespect for the police, authority, the property and feelings of others, as well as for the welfare of anyone but themselves. And when it came time to make that telephone call to their parents to come and pick their kid up, I would often imagine that I was likely going to meet a carbon copy of the same type of personality in the parent as I had met in the child. If the child was remorseful, polite, and overall a good kid, the likeliness of their parents being the same was very high. On the other hand, if I met a kid who had a foul mouth, a bad attitude, and a lack of respect for the law and for police, the chances that their parents would be the same was also very high. And I was usually right. The apple doesn't fall too far from the tree.

We can be influenced by our environment growing up; but as adults, we have decisions and choices to make. These choices can take us anywhere. And although we may have been brought up in a poor environment, that shouldn't dictate how we turn out. It's simply a starting point. We are responsible for the choices we make in our lives.

I remember working in the Detective Office in the late 80s, early 90s, and one of the spots my partner and I dropped by regularly to check on, was a strip joint often frequented by Outlaw Motorcycle Gang members. It was a great spot to get information or find someone wanted on a warrant. It was also a tough joint and it had its huge share of problems. As well, it had a waitress who had provided good information more than once to me on cases I'd actively worked on, and she appreciated the police "presence" when we made unannounced visits to the bar at night. It kept the bar tame—at least for the time we were there. We were in plain clothes detective attire—you know—suit, trench coat and badge attached to our belts so all could easily see it.

More than once when I dropped by, however, I saw one of our undercover police officers on duty associating with gang members. By this time in our police service, we had formed a dedicated biker squad. Now this officer had infiltrated the Outlaw Motorcycle Gang— or at least, he had been recruited by them; and his job was to hang around and gain their trust—live like them, talk like them, and later report back to his police handler with whatever intelligence he could gather on activities the gang was involved in and planning. He had been undercover for a couple of years and he was quite good at it. As part of his undercover operation, he treated us with the same kind of disrespect the other gang members did, and more than once he would be the cause of a fist fight with rivals in the bar.

Our police department was now devoted to fighting organized crime and gangs; but we were not in the habit of dropping an agent in and then simply leaving him there. That undercover detective wasn't living with the gang every moment of the day, 24/7. He still had a private life outside of work; but that's not easy to maintain, especially when you work undercover. And after two years of spending so much time with these men, he developed some of the same habits, bad attitudes and beliefs by which the gang the gang lived. It had embedded itself into his personality. His police friends and his family had noticed it. He'd been undercover too long—and had become the company he kept. Constantly exposed to sex, drugs and power— he fell into the lifestyle he had been fighting. It rubbed off on him; and this is a danger in undercover work. His supervisors pulled him out of his assignment; but by that time, the damage had been done. He'd become so much like them, it took a long while for him to get "de-programmed" and return to the lifestyle he once knew and had been part of. But he did it. He worked at it and he succeeded.

It comes down to who you choose to be at your core, what standards you adopt for yourself, and who you decide to associate with. Most importantly, you need to be your own "best friend." You need to be the one to tell yourself what you want out of this life. You have to determine what is most important to you; and you have to begin to feed yourself with the same kind of motivation that you see others using in this world in order to reach your desired goals. I've read several books on motivation and on personal power; and it is clear from these educated authors and their research as well as my own, that the most successful people in this world are people who believe in themselves and who choose the highest standards for themselves. They have created themselves and didn't leave it up to chance or environment. That's right, you create yourself. And you create your destiny. If the way in which you think at the moment is not getting you to where you want to be, you've got to start thinking and behaving differently. This may require talking to people who can help you get to where you want to be or to read literature that can assist you to reach your desired goals. It has to come from within yourself, and not from outside yourself. You can't let your external circumstances or your external environment dictate where you ought to be or who you are to become. That decision lies with each and every one of you. It's your responsibility and duty to yourself. That means changing your internal dialogue from one that keeps you where you are if where you are isn't good enough, to one that takes you where you want to be. That also means feeding yourself with a positive diet of positive thoughts and trusting that you can achieve whatever it is you set your mind to achieve. Sometimes people just let others or themselves talk them out of moving forward.

Being "limitless" requires work

Understanding yourself, your weaknesses and strengths, is essential to your success; and you must understand that some goals will be achieved more quickly than others. Being "limitless" may have its limitations at first! Remaining realistic in your goals is a key element to achieving success and as important as taking consistent action to reach those goals. Failure is NOT an option. But fail you will from time to time. It's simply part of life and part of the human experience when you take on new challenges. Nobody becomes an expert overnight. Sometimes you reach a limit and discover you need to develop a talent. You need to find that seed in yourself and help it to grow. Hard work, tenacity, and the desire to reach your goals will lead you on the path to achieving your desired outcome, despite obstacles you may encounter on the way. Theodore Roosevelt captured his life's philosophy in his "Citizenship in the Republic" speech by saying the following:

> *"It is not the critic who counts; not the man who points out how the strong man stumbles, or where the doer of deeds could have done them better. The credit belongs to the man who is actually in the arena, whose face is marred by dust and sweat and blood; who strives valiantly; who errs, who comes short again and again, because there is no effort without error and shortcoming; but who does actually strive to do the deeds; who knows great enthusiasms, the great devotions; who spends himself in a worthy cause; who at the best knows in the end the triumph of high achievement, and who at the worst, if he fails, at least fails while daring greatly, so that his place shall never be with those cold and timid souls who neither know victory nor defeat."[33]*

This is your present; and in mere seconds from every present moment, your future is waiting, unformed and ready for YOU to dictate it. It is up to you, and only you, to shape it into whatever you wish. Every passing minute is a chance to turn everything around. Stop waiting for things to happen; start making them happen. Choose a goal and picture it in your mind. Imagine what it would be like to touch it, feel it, experience it and enjoy it. Imagine having achieved it, as though it was already yours. Then move toward it. You are the one who has to create your own destiny, and you can't depend on your destiny to be created by anyone other than yourself. So once you make a choice to achieve a certain goal, make the decision to act on it. Remind yourself that you are able to do anything it is that you set your mind to do. Remind yourself that your past does not have to equal your future, and that past failures are just that: past failures. Whatever may have happened to you in the past has no hold on preventing you from reaching your goals now.

---

33. From Theodore Roosevelt's "Citizen in the Republic" speech, delivered at the Sorbonne in Paris, France, April 23, 1910.

You can't live in the past. You live in the moment, in the now. The past is past. Simple as that.

With a goal now in mind, and a firm decision to pursue it, determine the best route to take in order to reach the desired results you want. Write it down. Keep that journal. Begin by mapping it out and plan the best way for you to get there. Is there a role model you can follow? A set of guidelines you can benefit from by reading? Program your destination and the steps you'll take into your own navigation system—and if your maps are out-dated, get new ones. Research. Talk to people who have achieved these goals and learn from them. Mimic the behavior of others and adapt the attitude of a true warrior. Remind yourself, "I can!" Be realistic in your goals, taking into account any obstacle you may face while reminding yourself that despite whatever obstacles you do face, you can get by them. And start moving forward by taking action. Without action, there can be no results. Keep moving forward and remain flexible. If what you're doing is not giving you the results that you want, be prepared to modify the way in which you're doing it. Be prepared to learn better ways of reaching what it is you want. Flexibility is a very important component to success.

CHAPTER 10 SUMMARY

◆ Many people don't make committed decisions—they make excuses. Decisions require commitment. Commitment leads to action. And action results in change. Decisions dictate the action we take and the results we'll get. Whatever it is, decide. Think it through and get rid of any thoughts that keep you hostage and prevent you from taking the best action for yourself.

◆ Problems/roadblocks happen. Don't cry too long over it—give it only a few tears if you must, but then move on. Digging yourself deeper into pity, fear and discouragement won't help you get through it. Move on. It isn't going to change unless you change. Then everything changes.

◆ If you were a victim of abuse, and it's in the past, leave it there. Choose the T-Shirt that says "survivor" on it. Wear it without shame or fear. You are deserving and are worthy of overcoming anything. If you're still being victimized—get out of whatever it is that is keeping you there. There's help—trust me. Find it, call upon it, and leave it behind. Get the survivor t-shirt. I can send you one.

◆ Have you or others labeled you as, "Ugly, stupid, fat, gross, unworthy, unlovable, hopeless, moron, loser, disabled, queer or inferior?" How will that affect how you see yourself, how you feel about yourself and how you will react? How about this list instead: "Adorable, amazing, awesome, good-looking, charismatic, successful, confident, loveable, generous, kind, radiant and unlimited?" Makes for a happier life.

◆ There are seeds of greatness within you. It's your responsibility to nurture and help them grow. No one else can live your life for you and no one else can develop your potential better than you. Others can help you find and develop your gifts, but the work has to come from you. Feed your garden and they will grow.

◆ "Insanity is doing something over and over again and expecting different results."

◆ Successful people have discovered that if one thing doesn't work, they'll be flexible and willing enough to change their approach to make the next thing work. And if it takes a dozen tries, they understand that this is simply the cost of being successful. How about you try that instead of giving up next time?

◆ Your past does not have to equal your future, and your past failures are just that: past failures. Whatever has happened to you in the past has no hold on you. You can't live in the past. You live in the moment, in the now. The past is past. Simple as that.

CHAPTER 11

Action

"You are what you do, not what you say you'll do."
—C.G. JUNG

My confidence took a beating after my ex-wife announced her affair and her wishes for a divorce. It quickly occurred to me that my plans for my acting career and the financial security I had counted on were about to change drastically. So much of what I had planned on was inevitably going to change and I could do nothing about it.

For anyone who has experienced divorce, you'll appreciate that it is a very emotional time and a lot is at stake—for both parties. Decisions are often made under duress; and despite your lawyer giving you the best advice, you often don't hear it. It's an example of the "fight or flight" principle I discussed in an earlier chapter. The voices you hear are not always clear and coherent—as though your head were submerged in a pool of water a foot underneath the surface. You hear the sounds coming from the person's mouth but you don't hear the words.

I knew that I had some difficult decisions ahead of me and that those decisions would have to be followed by a thoughtful plan of action. Returning to the police service was not an option. My service had a practice to not rehire anyone who had left. I had been knocked off my course and my confidence suffered. I was faced with the need to make a number of critical decisions, each requiring specific action.

I soon discovered that the longer I put off some of those decisions, the more money it would cost me. It also created severe stress within me and a feeling of hopelessness. My friend Pat called me shortly after my separation to inform me that a job as an investigator was available with the Office of the Independent Police Review Director, also known as the OIPRD[34] in Toronto, Canada. This office provides a public service to people who report police misconduct; and at the time Pat first made me aware of the job vacancy, I declined, basing my decision upon advice with which my lawyer had provided me. Six months later I was almost out of money when Pat called again to inform me that another vacancy had opened in the OIPRD. I'm not generally one to overlook opportunities as I had done six months earlier, and so I applied. I worked there for 18 months on contract. The money was a blessing and it provided a much-needed and appreciated boost. I had a great deal of respect for the director of the OIPRD whose qualities of grace and dignity reminded me of Sydney Poitier. He was a respected and intelligent leader and a remarkable man. Leaving that office after the contract was not easy. But it also took me to other places I may never have reached.

The financial security provided by the OIPRD was now gone, and I found myself once again faced with decisions on how to earn a living and what steps to take to pursue my dreams. Sometimes finding yourself in times of trouble brings out the best in you. You must be willing to take chances and risks. Most people do not. They simply give up.

I incurred setbacks and disappointments; but I also realized that I was greater than my circumstances and that it was up to me to make everything work. No one was going to save me; and despite being shaken from the confidence I had developed throughout my life—starting back in grade 7, I now had to work to reclaim it. It was rightfully mine. A series of opportunities unfolded because I was willing to see them. Friends listened to and supported me when I needed it. A friend I had met reminded me that knocking twice

34. www.oiprd.on.ca/En/Pages/Home.aspx

for what you want in life is crucial and reaps tremendous rewards; and my family believed in me. But it came down to ME and what I wanted. I put down the shovel, stopped listening to those self-doubting voices in my head, and started climbing out of the hole. I moved upward and forward.

> *"Twenty years from now you will be more disappointed by the things that you didn't do than by the ones you did do. So throw off the bowlines. Sail away from the safe harbor. Catch the trade winds in your sails. Explore. Dream. Discover."*
> —H. JACKSON BROWN, JR.

We have now examined the first three necessary steps to success: your thoughts, your beliefs and the decisions you make. All three of these would be nothing without the following: action. Understanding your potential and creating a belief that you are certain that you will reach the goals you set out for yourself is crucial to your success and must be followed with planning and consistency. Keeping a journal and mapping out where you would like to be in a month, two months or even a year is a great motivator to document your progress.

I have asked a lot of people where they see themselves in two years—or five years. Even those who have told with me their dreams are often at a loss for a decent answer, opting to say, "I've never thought that far." Well, think about it. By now, you have made a decision to un-hostage yourself from what's kept you prisoner and you're going for what you want; so it's equally important that you think the way successful people think.

Envision your goals and believe you'll reach them. Know that the action you take and consistent effort you put into it is what will result in success. The three earlier steps are nothing without action. If you begin with the belief that you likely won't reach your goals, you will subsequently put little effort into the actions you take; and you will receive exactly what you put in—few results—if any. Successful people start with a strong belief in certainty; a certainty that they will achieve what it is that they set out to do; and they follow through with consistent daily action to get there. They're passionate about their goals. They march to the beat of their own drum. As you must! It is this belief in yourself and your ability to achieve your goals that will energize your actions and translate into your behaviors.

Never lower your expectations and always find the courage to move forward, despite the naysayers and despite whether at first you're not getting the results you had expected "right away." Don't be discouraged if at first you don't succeed. The familiar axiom, "If at first you don't succeed, try and try again . . . " is quite true when you set out to achieve your goals. You will need to change the way you're going about it if the results aren't what you expected at first. Consistent action with the flexibility to change the things that are not working for you will ultimately result in your success. And the more action you take and passion you create along with the willingness to learn from the things that are not working for you will put you on the surest path to getting it right, and achieving the success you desire.

Dreams often require sweat and work

I often browse the web for inspirational quotes and videos. Watching these helps me in times I need a boost. I came across one on YouTube called "Dreams," by Les Brown.[35] Les had the following to say:

> "I don't know what that dream is that you have. I don't care how disappointing it might have been, as you've been working toward that dream. But that you're holding in your mind that it's possible and some of you already know that it's hard. It's not easy. It's hard changing your life. That in the process of working on your dreams you are going to incur a lot of disappointment, a lot of failure, and a lot of pain. At moments when you're going to doubt yourself

---

35. Les Brown. www.youtube.com/watch?v=ykx9bxqAFn8

and say 'God, why is this happening to me? I'm just trying to take care of my children, my mother. I'm not trying to steal or rob from anybody. How does this have to happen to me?'

For those of you that have experienced some hardships, don't give up on your dream. The rough times are going to come, but they are not going to stay. They have come to pass. Greatness is not this wonderful, esoteric, elusive, god-like feature that only the special among us will ever taste. It's something that truly exists in all of us. It's very important for you to believe that you are capable of greatness.

Most people raise a family, they earn a living, and then they die. Somewhere along the way, they stop growing, they stop working on themselves, they stop stretching, and they stop pushing themselves. Then a lot of people like to complain but they don't want to do anything about their situation. And most people don't work on their dreams. Why? One reason is a fear of failure. What if things don't work out? Another is the fear of success: 'What if I succeed and I can't handle it?' These people are not risk-takers.

You spend so much time with other people; you spend so much time trying to get people to like you. You know other people more than you know yourself. You study them, you know about them, you want to hang out with them, and you want to be just like them. And you know that you've invested so much time in them, you don't know who you are. I challenge you to spend time by yourself. It's necessary that you get the losers out of your life, if you want to live your dream. But for people who are running toward their dreams, life has a special kind of meaning."

In the few paragraphs you've just read, Les Brown keys in on significant truths. Some goals are difficult to achieve and it is very possible and likely that you may encounter some failure at first try. It is not enough to simply have the desire to reach your goal, but consistent action is a necessary ingredient. And what does the word "consistent" mean? It means continual, unchanging in achievement, constantly adhering to the same principles and course of action. For example, if my goal is to improve my physical fitness and develop muscle and a toned body, making a decision to do it and then following through with research on how to do it is not enough. It also requires action. So, if I go to the gym and work out really hard for a week or two and then stop, I won't see very many results, if any. I'll get what I put into it: a week or two of training will equal a week or two of benefit. But it will not create a lasting change. Simply because I was not consistent in my behavior and my action.

Some goals are life-long commitments and require regular action for the rest of your days. They become lifestyles; and doing them repeatedly and continuously will become easier and easier as new habits are developed. You need only step into the gym and watch some of the committed trainers work out to see that they have dedicated a place for personal training in their lives. It becomes a personal challenge and a way of life. When I mentioned to you that in 2001 I made a decision to change my life by including fitness in my daily routine, I was working full-time, was married and had two children. I was teaching at a police college and wondered when I was ever going to find the time to actually fit my workouts into my busy schedule. I chose to rearrange my schedule, and make fitness part of my daily life. Sometimes that meant getting up an hour earlier than I normally did so that I could go to the gym before my workday began. Many people do this and it energizes them for the rest of the day. Other times it meant spending my lunch hour working out and eating my lunch at my desk. There were times where I scheduled it in my day as an appointment with myself. The point is: I made it part of my life and I scheduled it in to my day and eventually it became easy to do because it was one of the important things that I was doing for myself. It may be necessary for you to do the same thing with your goals.

Perhaps your goal will require an hour or two of your time a day to achieve. If that's the case, then you will need to schedule that time into your day-planner and have other things work around it. But you *will* need to fit it into your schedule and make it a priority. Otherwise that dream will never flourish into anything.

Don't allow yourself to fall, from time to time, into a false sense of belief that your goal won't be hard to reach. Depending on what it is that you're after, some goals will take more effort and more work to attain than others. Along with that, you'll need to face the reality that sometimes you'll be frustrated and sometimes you'll feel like giving up. That's human nature. Remember, we are conditioned to avoid pain and pain comes in many different forms. You may experience the pain of frustration, the pain of defeat and the pain of *temporary* hopelessness. By now, you know that you are the author of your own thoughts and that you can instantly change those thoughts to improve your immediate condition. There are no magical formulas in achieving success, but there are proven methods that work and work well. Understanding that some goals will be difficult to achieve will help you to face those difficulties when you reach them, and more importantly, to move past them. And with that attitude, you will achieve your goals. Weeds may arise to choke your efforts, and do not ignore them. Be a good gardener to yourself and deal with the weeds by removing them one by one. Don't allow them to multiply and take over the garden of your dreams and desires.

It's not work if you love what you do

Success is work and remaining successful requires work. However, for many successful people who pursue the passions of their lives, they don't call it "work." They call it different things, like challenges and opportunities for example. Their vocabulary doesn't allow negativity. They enjoy these gifts and look forward to new ones and new opportunities to keep them moving forward and prospering in relationships, health, personal wealth and everything else to which they put their minds. Successful people are dedicated, determined, and possess a consistent desire to achieve. Failure is not an option. They understand that commitment is a necessary ingredient to success; and at the end of each day they know that they have done everything within their power to fulfill their dream, and that there is was nothing more that day that they could have done. And that is the same passion that you need to develop in your own life in order to achieve your personal goals. Taking consistent action and moving forward one step at a time is a key component to success.

Why are some people more successful than others?

I mentioned earlier that our beliefs and how we react to our beliefs affects our success. Action affects outcome. Plain and simple. We also know that what happens to us can seriously shake our belief system. At times, it's far easier for us to avoid creating a new set of beliefs than holding onto the old ones because we are so accustomed to the old ones and we are afraid of change. It's important to remember that how we interpret events that happen to us has a significant impact on what we do—what action we take, or fail to take.

Great things are accomplished by great people. The moment you start to believe that you are one of the great people, you're on your way to reaching what you want in life. What one person does as a result of what happens to them isn't necessarily what you will choose to do. But if you examine people who are happy and successful in their lives, you can be certain that they have made it a habit to change their internal monologues and beliefs from self-defeating to self-improving. They make no excuses. I'll give you a simple example. If you tell yourself, "I'm good-looking/beautiful," but you don't sound convinced to yourself that you are, what happens is, you don't believe it. And consequently, doubt takes over. And if doubt takes over, you begin to tell yourself that you really are not good-looking or beautiful. Consequently, you will feel that way; and it will reflect on how you feel about yourself and what you project to others. People are drawn to people who are confident and self-assured. On the other hand, if you tell yourself that you are good-looking/beautiful and keep repeating it in your mind with total belief and passion, you will begin to believe it and will instantly enjoy how you feel about yourself. Your sense of self-worth will increase; and others will notice the change as well. You'll transmit a message to those around you that you have confidence in yourself, and that belief will follow the law of attraction and be accepted by others as being the truth. People are drawn to confidence. And confidence is something that can be learned. You can develop confidence in the beliefs that you choose to have about yourself.

Confidence—facing your fears and nervousness and moving forward in spite of them

"We gain strength, and courage, and confidence by each experience in which we really stop to look fear in the face . . . we must do that which we think we cannot."
—ELEANOR ROOSEVELT

Confidence is one of those precious keys to success we've been examining throughout this book. Without this key, you won't get far. You'll hop into that "hope mobile"; and without the key, you won't be able to move ahead. Hope without confidence bears little fruit, if any. You see, hope is like the fuel, and confidence is the starter that ignites it. Together, they galvanize you into action; and you then get to use all your tremendous abilities to move in the direction in which you wish to go.

If you don't have much confidence at the moment, it doesn't mean that you can't create and develop it. It may just mean that your confidence is being held hostage by yourself. Don't worry, if that is the case—we already know how to release it, don't we? And if you're starting with little or no confidence at all, then it is essential that you begin to change those beliefs about yourself which are keeping you from believing in yourself. True self-confidence is not an overnight acquisition. We are all worthy of having it, however; and one of the first steps to developing that confidence is to recognize what insecurities you may have about yourself, and why it is that you may not yet have attained it.

Let me clarify one thing before we go further. Arrogance cannot be mistaken for self-confidence. Some people do mistake the two. Arrogance is something completely different from self-confidence. Arrogance is the notion of being somewhat confident but which tends to lead toward elitism, bragging, being a show-off and even bullying. Confidence is not being belligerent or pushy. It's believing in oneself and one's ability, without having to brag or force anything onto anyone.

To begin a self-examination of your level of confidence, you can ask yourself what your internal monologues are telling you about yourself? Why is it that you may be feeling uncomfortable or less than proud of who you are, if indeed that's where you're at right now? If you are lacking in this vital area of being confident in who and what you are intrinsically, ask yourself a couple of questions: such as, "What has led me to feel this way about myself?"—and ask what others are doing to build their own self-confidence and how you can pattern that, if need be. Some of the thoughts that you have which prevent you from being confident might go back to a past trauma or negative experience, and that is keeping you hostaged, whether you realize it or not. We've all had those kinds of experiences; and some people have chosen not to allow past traumas or stale, defunct beliefs to stand in their way at building the confidence they deserve in order to be successful in all aspects of life. Is it worth holding on to a bad past experience or belief? No, it is not. Truly not. It won't get you anywhere . . . and certainly not to where you want to be. Your navigation system will need an update; and you'll need to refresh your internal map to get you there.

A Polygraph Story

When I was a polygraph examiner, a lot of suspects, who often lacked confidence and belief in themselves, attended my office for examinations. Many felt they were at the mercy of others. Now a polygraph instrument, or "lie-detector" as some call it, is designed to record the physiological changes that occur in a person's body when they are under the stress of being asked specific questions about their guilt or innocence in a crime under investigation. The instrument measures heartrate, respiration and GSR, (Galvanic Skin Responses), and sweat gland activity. It records base-line and stress responses. A comparison is then made to examine the changes that occurred when that subject was asked one series of questions as opposed to another. It registers changes in their physiological responses that inform the examiner what questions were most disturbing to them, and that directs the examiner to draw a conclusion. A determination can then be made to assist the examiner in evaluating truth from deception.

However, the polygraph instrument would be completely ineffective if not for the expertise of the examiner. It is imperative that the polygraph examiner understand his or her job thoroughly and be able to use the instrument the way it was designed and intended to be used in order to have it record accurate responses to enable the examiner to make a proper determination. The examiner spends a great deal of time getting to know the individual sitting across from him or her in advance of the actual test. As you might imagine, most people who come in for a polygraph examination are nervous; and it's the examiner's job to take the time to make the examinee feel comfortable to the point that the examiner can establish what is called a "base-line," a normal state free of most stress—a relaxed state, taking into account that some elevated stress will likely still be present, but not enough to affect the charts that will later be studied.

The "pre-test" phase takes place so that the polygraph examiner establishes rapport with the examinee. This means, for example, trying to find something you share in common and getting to know details about—for instance—where the person was born, where they were raised, and what their interests are—small talk to develop trust and comfort. I have examined people who were accused of everything from petty theft to murder. I've examined housewives, priests, bikers, gang members, business people, mothers, fathers and everyone in between. When the pre-test phase was completed and it was time for the actual polygraph examination (the in-test), the examinee had become much more relaxed, establishing that base-line because he/she understood the process and was comfortable with the examiner. In the majority of cases, there were no surprises in store for them and they now knew it. A sort of trust had been established. I had explained how the instrument worked, what it recorded, and what questions I was going to ask them. I had assured them that my job was not to judge them but to simply determine the truth. I told them that I was not there to find them guilty of anything and that they would be treated with dignity and respect. This was an essential step in gaining their trust and conducting a fair test.

Some people who took the test were innocent; whereas others were not. Once the examination was completed, I would already have a very good idea whether the person sitting across from me was being truthful or had been deceptive. The pre-test phase is one in which the polygraph examiner uses his or her ability and training to help detect deception. The extensive training teaches the polygraph examiner how to "read" people and what questions to ask that would help in the later determination of the truthfulness or lack thereof of the examinee's responses. We would evaluate their responses to questions scientifically designed to compare to the answers truthful people would likely give. It's a tool—not foolproof, but a quite reliable indicator of the truthfulness of responses. If, after I examined the polygraph results, I determined that my feeling and opinion about the person's guilt was corroborated by the charts I examined, it was now time to interrogate that suspect. Examining the charts was something we did outside of the interview room and could take anywhere from 10 minutes to half an hour or even longer, depending on the complexity of the charts. Keep in mind that the decision at which the polygraph examiner arrives regarding a person's guilt or innocence has a huge impact on the police investigation that may follow and on the consequences to the life of the person who is being accused of whatever felony. On more than one occasion, I returned to that interview room after examining the polygraph charts and accused someone of murder. Or sexual assault. My educated opinion held a lot of weight.

When I returned to the examination room with an opinion that the person sitting across from me was guilty of the crime of which they had been accused, I would then launch into an interrogation and use what is called a "positive confrontation." This simply meant informing the suspect that there was absolutely no doubt in my mind that he/she had committed the crime under investigation. For example, if the person sitting across from me had failed the polygraph examination and I had made the determination that he/she was guilty of murder, I would return to the room and the first thing I would tell him was, "John, after examining the polygraph charts, there is absolutely no doubt in my mind that you were the person who killed

Jane Doe." And that positive confrontation would be followed by the interrogation. One of the things that I had been trained to do was to use what is called a central theme; that is, integrating the polygraph examination into the subject of confidence. This "central theme" was nothing more than reassuring the person accused of the crime that I had no doubt they were a good person, despite what they had done. It was my job to reassure them (on more than one occasion) that I knew they were good—deep down inside; and that my job was to determine, not solely whether they committed the crime, but "why" they had. The point here is the central theme. Repeating to someone who has committed a serious and horrible crime, or a petty one, that they are still good, despite what they have done, is so important to determining the truth, their truth.

Even good people make mistakes. Even good people commit crimes. Not everyone that sat across from me in that polygraph chair was a bad person. In fact, most people who sat across from me and who were guilty were good people who had made bad mistakes. But we all make mistakes, some more serious than others. We also all get second chances. That central theme, "you are good" was an essential component of the interrogation because it reminded people of who they were, despite what they had done. And it was amazing how those few words would help the person sitting across from me to actually reconnect with that feeling of being good. When they had first arrived in my office some two and a half hours earlier, they had had no idea who I was. We were complete strangers. And if they had committed a crime, they certainly didn't want to tell me about it. If they confessed to the crime, there would be consequences. Those consequences might include shame, a criminal charge, and even jail. But the central theme—"you are a good person"—would often make the difference in whether they told me the truth as opposed to whether they would continue to deny it.

What I discovered from all this is that a lot of people are never told or reminded that there is good in them. Many, due to their circumstances, the people in their lives, and their environment, are never told that they are appreciated, loved, and worthy. They are never told that they are good. I saw grown men break down and cry because they had lost the belief that they were still good people. My interrogation would often include encouraging themes reminding them that, despite what had happened to them in the past, it did not have to equal their future. I would remind them that there is good in everybody and that they were destined for so much more, if they so choose. You might be asking yourself, "Why would a murderer confess to the crime?"—and the answer is somewhat complicated. On some occasions, they felt a great deal of regret and remorse for what they had done. They wanted to "get it off their chests." Others wanted people to know that they were good and that the crime they had committed was not a reflection of who they were essentially. On the one hand, people might see someone who has committed a murder as nothing more than a cold-blooded killer. But, from the felon's point of view: given the option to be seen as someone who is not a cold-blooded killer . . . that he/she may be viewed as someone who acted in the heat of the moment . . . the perpetrator is often motivated to confess. Whatever it was that resulted in their aligning with the truth and in their subsequent confession was something only they could answer. Some of them simply needed to be reminded that they were good people.

We need to remind ourselves on a regular basis that we are worthy of so much that life has to offer. You don't need to be sitting across from the polygraph examiner to remind yourself that you are worthy and that you are good. This is something you can and should do for yourself. Once you begin to believe in yourself and in your self-worth, you are on the road to finding the confidence you need. Reminding ourselves that we are good is something that we must do as often as we possibly can, especially when we start to doubt it. And if we tell ourselves often enough that we are good, we begin to believe it and our actions begin to show it. Reminding people that they have made mistakes as opposed to being complete failures gives them the courage needed to face whatever follows. At least, it is a beginning.

Sometimes we are beaten down so badly by what happens to us or by some of the things that we have done that we feel that there is little hope of a new beginning. We begin to doubt that our lives can be any different because of our past and the beliefs we have come to accept. That voice in our head, the internal monologue, defeats us.

But that voice is not the voice of truth. Whatever it is that we faced in the past is *in* the past. Reminding ourselves that we are still good despite whatever mistakes we have made helps us to believe in ourselves; and that goes a long way in building the pillars of self-esteem and self-confidence.

Changing beliefs to recondition ourselves: two kids in cages[36]

I remember a time I was working in the Sexual Assault and Child Abuse Unit. It was a Friday afternoon. I had worked the day shift. I had left the office and one of the young detectives I was training was working the afternoon shift. She was relatively new to investigations and I had instructed her that if any case should come in with which she needed help, that she should call me. She was also working that shift with a more experienced detective, but I had the most experience and was her go-to person. Not twenty minutes after I had left the office, I received her call. I remember her first words: "You are NOT going to believe this."

What I'm about to tell you sounds like a horror story. Something you might read about happening in some far-away place—but not in Canada. We usually don't experience incidents like this. It just doesn't happen in Canada, does it? Right. Let's keep telling ourselves that. The detective filled me in briefly as I returned to the office. She informed me that she had received a telephone call from the Children's Aid Society who was en route to the police station with three witnesses who were prepared to provide statements on how two young boys had been held captive in cages for years. That's right . . . in cages.

After I got back to the office, the Children's Aid Society (C.A.S.) workers arrived with the witnesses. One of the witnesses was the boys' grandfather (whom I shall refer to as Grandad for the sake of convenience), one was the boys' step-sister, and the third was a

36. www.durhamregion.com/news-story/3457526-years-later-victim-in-black-stock-abuse-case-speaks-out/

family relation as well. My instructions pre-interview to both the other investigators was to first issue a "caution" to the witnesses, simply and lawfully informing them that they were under a legal obligation to tell us the absolute truth; and that, if they didn't, there would be consequences and possibly criminal charges to face by misleading the police. The C.A.S. workers informed us that these boys, whose approximate ages at the time were twelve and fourteen, had been held captive in cages by their adoptive parents from the ages of approximately five and seven. I could tell in their voices that they were emotionally affected by what they had heard, and that they believed the stories. The witnesses had by now arrived and were waiting to be interviewed.

I decided to speak to the boys' grandfather, Grandad, the most senior of the three witnesses, and the one I thought could provide the most evidence. The other investigators were going to speak to the remaining two witnesses. We all made our way into our separate rooms to conduct the interviews that were being videotaped and audio-recorded. The grandfather was a very decent man. He had tears in his eyes as he told me the following story. He had experienced an ongoing and very strained relationship with his daughter for several years. Apparently, she was a very aggressive woman who often denied him access to see his two grandchildren; and when she did grant him a visit, she was very specific about how much time he could spend with the boys and where the visit would be. The visits always took place in her home and in her presence. They were never long in duration and when it was time for the boys to go to bed, the boys would make their own way upstairs and put themselves to bed. The grandfather would offer to go upstairs with them to say his final goodnight, but always under the strongest objection by his daughter.

The boys had now reached an age where they were about to enter high school; and Grandad's daughter had asked some family to attend her home one evening. Her plan was to convince them that they should support her in her mission to persuade school authorities that she was suitable to homeschool the boys. Up until then, the boys had been attending a grade school in a rural community northeast of where I was stationed. Grandad went on to tell me that he had seen the boys several times over the years, and that he always had a feeling that something wasn't quite right. Whenever he tried talking to his daughter about his feelings, she would hear nothing of it and stopped him in his tracks.

After attending the daughter's home for this meeting, the three witnesses left. At first, they were each going to head their separate ways to "think about it." There was little love between them; and that was largely due to some terrible gossip his daughter had managed to spread among the three over the years with the sole purpose of keeping them from connecting as a family because of what she had been doing to the boys. The grandfather did not believe that it was in the boys' best interest to be home-schooled; but earlier in the meeting his daughter had become very demanding in her direction to the family that they support her. They were told that when they were contacted by the authorities, they were to all agree that she was an excellent candidate to home-school the kids. The visit became an emotional one for the grandfather who had not seen his granddaughter for quite some time; and after the brief visit, as they were leaving, he suggested that they all go for coffee to catch up. They made their way to a coffee shop; and his granddaughter then broke down emotionally and told them a story that they had certainly never expected to hear. And would never forget. She was still living at home with her parents and her stepbrothers; and she was now a woman in her twenties, married with a small child of her own.

Now, the two boys in this case history were actually the children of Grandad's second daughter who had died of a drug overdose. When she, their natural mother, had passed away, they were only infants (who had, unfortunately, been born with fetal alcohol syndrome); and Grandad's other daughter, the boys' aunt, had decided that she would adopt the boys—an action which would provide her with a monthly income to care for them. As I discovered, however, she was not very interested in actually taking care of the boys. She was more interested in taking care of herself; and the monthly income would come in handy for her because she and her husband didn't draw much money monthly to survive on. So she adopted the boys. As the boys grew older, she quickly lost patience with them. She lost so much patience with these two young boys that she ruthlessly decided that her sleep was far more important than the welfare of the boys; and she thus decided to tie them to their beds at night.

At the time of the adoption and the subsequent onset of the pattern of abuse, this family resided outside of our jurisdiction in a farmhouse with dirt floors and stone walls in the basement where she put their beds. Every night, the boys would be tied to their "beds" and left on their own in the dark, damp isolated farmhouse basement until she decided to get up and untie them. This abuse went on for a couple of years; and the family then moved into our jurisdiction, into another remote farmhouse. When it was time for the boys to go to grade school, she noticed that the ropes she had been using to tie the boys down at night had been leaving burn marks on their wrists and their feet, and she knew that the marks would draw attention when they went to school. So she came up with an idea. She had a dog and the dog had a cage. It occurred to her that she could lock the boys in dog cages to secure them at night. And that is what she did. The boys went from being tied to a bed to being locked in dog cages. At night, she would put each of them in diapers and they were given firm instructions to hold their bowel movements until the next day or they would suffer beatings. Each morning, or afternoon—she got up whenever she felt like it—she would strip the boys down and check their diapers and rectums. If they had bowel movements during the night she would make them suffer. They received regular beatings.

The boys were also brought up believing in God and the Bible. The Bible was one book they were permitted to read and their "mother" would remind them what it said in the Bible: to honor your mother and father, as the good book instructed. She twisted the Good book to meet her deviant needs. She used that passage to mean that they were never to discuss what happened in the house with anyone else. They were brought up to keep everything to themselves and never to discuss what happened in the home with anyone. They were conditioned to obey and they knew nothing different.

These boys had been held captives all their lives, and they knew no other reality but this one. Day after day, the boys would go to school. At times, the boys would show up at school in their pyjamas.

And it was never questioned in depth by the school authorities. The boys were also being drugged as we discovered, "to help them sleep." As you may be aware, due to the fetal alcohol syndrome, the boys were a little "slow," and didn't have many friends. The other students felt that they were odd and some felt bad for them. But no one bothered to look into their lives in depth. And so they made their way through grade school; and although they did not grow as quickly as the other children, they did grow. The cages eventually became too small to "contain" them. Their stepsister, the mother's natural daughter, was never kept in a cage. She was treated "normally" and she eventually gave birth to a child of her own. A crib was purchased for her infant; and it occurred to the boys' adoptive mother that she could no longer keep the boys in the dog cages. She decided to get two additional baby cribs and used the sides off a third crib to form tops, converting the cribs into boxes. She then used chains and a padlock to secure the boys in these cribs at night. The cribs had mattresses; and the boys were again given instructions that they were not to have any bowel movements during the night. And every day, their mother would conduct her daily examination of their diapers and rectums. To avoid beatings, one of the boys would eat his feces at night in an effort to escape a beating. This was the life they knew. This was their existence.

When the boys' grandfather would visit, he was never made aware of what was going on. His daughter, their stepmother, had firm instructions for her father. As previously mentioned, the visits were to take place in her presence; and there were to be no outings. The visits were short and the boys behaved. They were instructed to, and they obeyed. The grandfather would leave unsatisfied, unsettled, and wondering what was going on that he could not fathom or comprehend. But his instincts continued to issue warnings that something was amiss. Now the boys' adoptive father (their uncle) was not as mean to the boys as their adoptive mother (their aunt). From time to time, he would get up early and unlock the boys from their cribs to take them fishing. But he too was under the control of his wife. I remember them comparing her to a "mob boss" that nobody would dare cross. If they crossed her, there were severe consequences to be had.

One of the boys tried escaping one night and ran from the farmhouse, during a thunderstorm, toward a nearby highway. He didn't get too far and was kept outside for the night in the storm as his punishment. These boys had been conditioned to believe that they were no good and that they were under the complete authority and control of their mother. They had no idea that their mother was actually their aunt either. As the boys grew older, their environment and situation did not improve. Their stepmother was a very heavy woman. Alright, I'll say it: she was downright obese. And she kept her fridge stocked full of good food. But the boys would seldom get to enjoy any of the good food because they were fed much less than she, her husband and her daughter. From time to time, they would go out to a restaurant where the mother would have a wonderful meal, but the boys would share a plate of French fries. How I came to know all these details was as a result of the interviews I later conducted with the boys once they learned to trust me. I'll talk more about that in a moment.

Now let's fast-forward to the time the boys were about to graduate from grade school to high school. The "mob boss" (their stepmother) was concerned that if the boys went to high school they would likely meet other students and teachers who would ask more questions. It would be high school after all. And there was always a possibility that the boys might start talking now that they were older. And she couldn't risk any of that. Which is why she drew the family together on that fateful evening to discuss her plans to homeschool them and keep her evil secret from being discovered. In that way, she could continue to receive her monthly checks, and the boys would be under her absolute control.

But that did not sit well with the boys' grandfather or their sister, and the truth came out. On that Friday night following the interviews of our witnesses, the other two investigators and I compared notes. All the stories were the same. I then directed Detectives and the Children's Aid to the boys' home where the boys were found—one already locked in his crib. The accounts were true. The boys would lock themselves in their cribs each night as they had become conditioned to do. It was a horrific reality, and we were just the observers. Those two boys were real victims. They were rescued that night; and it was now our job as investigators to encourage them to disclose the details of what had happened to them over so many years. I was especially grateful on that investigation for the communication skills I had developed over the course of my career at that point, as getting people to talk is essential; and getting these boys to talk would be, I conjectured, no easy task, following their lifetime of severe abuse thus far. Nevertheless, in the days that followed, I established a very good rapport with the two boys; and they opened up and provided us with countless details from their past. It was heartbreaking, to say the least.

Sitting in the office one night with the investigator who had first received the call, I asked her what she thought about us giving the boys a comic book type Bible. I had seen one in a Christian bookstore that had all the stories of the Bible in animated form and I thought it would be a nice gift for two boys who believed in the good word. So we bought them each one of these Bibles and made sure they got them in the homes in which they had now been placed. When news of what had happened spread, there was a tremendous outpouring of good-hearted people from across the country who wanted to help these boys. They sent money, gifts and good wishes. Although these boys received bicycles, toys and other great stuff, the gifts they were drawn to the most were those two comic book Bibles. I kept in touch with them regularly following their rescue, and discovered that one of them had a dream. His dream was to become a police officer one day. Although I knew that that would not happen for him because of his delayed mental development, I encouraged him to explore other possibilities of helping people and reaching his personal goals by telling him that there was so much that he could do. We spoke regularly; and when he became a young man, he would drop by my office often for a visit. His past had held nothing but hopelessness. He was conditioned to believe that this was going to be his life for the rest of his days; and now that someone had provided him with a way out and a new opportunity, he began to dream, and he began to believe in himself. Even after the trial and the guilty verdict of his "parents," we kept in touch.

Eventually, this boy became a young man and an advocate for victims of crime! He joined an organization in support of Victims of Crime and began to share his remarkable story as he continually grew confident in himself and in his future. He chose to take control of his life and not to live in the past. He faced his future with a certainty that did not have to equal his past; and he took action to reach out to other victims of crime and encourage them not to give up.

This young man is a true example of how, despite what our pasts have been, there are always, always, opportunities for us to create a greater future for ourselves. There is always hope for new beginnings and new chapters to be written in our lives. How is that for a story of success and strength?

Tapping into our internal gifts

Each of us has the same ability: to take control of our lives by not living in the past—to tap into the internal gifts with which we have been blessed and find new opportunities for happiness and success. Sometimes it takes a story like this young man's to remind us that if they—abused beyond belief—could do it, we can too! The only one preventing us from getting out of a current undesirable state to a state of peace, contentment, and happiness, is ourselves. We create the happiness we experience by choosing to create it. No one gives it to us. No one takes it from us.

And this is a lesson for each and every one of us. Despite what our pasts have brought us, there is always hope for a new beginning. And once we begin to believe in ourselves and build confidence, we can accomplish just about anything. The choices that this young man made and the decisions that followed in his life resulted in the action he took to improve his life and to find happiness . . . which is what he found. Each and every one of us has a past. Some have had terrible things happen, and at times may have even lost hope. But our past does not have to equal our future. Past is past, and must remain there. We can take control of our present and turn it into something incredible simply by replacing negative thoughts and beliefs with positive ones. The secret is having confidence in yourself and believing in yourself to the point where you are prepared to make the necessary changes in the way that you think and in the actions that you take to achieve your goals. Once we begin to believe that we are strong, that we are worthy, and that we are able—then great things will follow— provided we take the necessary action to move forward with those goals. And the fact that, from time to time, we will fail on our initial attempts, need not be a deterrent to continuing to take action.

Failure does not have to be permanent

But that failure does not have to remain permanent. Any failure that we experience provides us with a new opportunity to get up and try again. We are all capable of achieving so much. Believing in yourself and believing in your future is a key to achieving your success. I've been talking about success, and I haven't asked you what associations the word brings to mind for you. But I ask you now to consider your own definition of success. As I see it, success is reaching personal and spiritual goals with happiness and abundance in love, joy and relationships to name a few; to find and live the life that you deserve. Success means different things to different people, but success always involves self-improvement on one level or another. And if we take consistent daily action to improve ourselves, then we are guaranteed to find the successes we are looking for. Success takes work. But the work does not have to feel like "work." It can feel like opportunity. We must remind ourselves every day that we are not bound by our past and our past does not have to define who and what we are today, or who we will be tomorrow. That chapter of your life has not yet been written. You are the author of your book of life; and it is potentially full of chapters that are just waiting for you to write. Write them! Begin by believing in yourself. What a wonderful way to begin a new chapter! Begin by seeing new opportunities for yourself and taking chances. Turn a fresh new page and dare to believe. The words will come, and the chapters will be written as you live them. Try a road less traveled. You'll get accustomed to the terrain and its beauty soon enough. But just do it!

Remember what makes some people more successful than others? Their beliefs, their choices, their actions, their confidence in believing that they can achieve whatever it is that they set their minds to, and the chapters they choose to write in their book of life. They write in pencil and use an eraser to erase past mistakes and setbacks so that they can write new goals and maps. That's what makes some people more successful than others.

CHAPTER 11 SUMMARY

◆ Your thoughts, your beliefs, and the decisions you make are nothing without action.

◆ Despite setbacks and disappointments, realize that you are greater than your circumstances and that it is up to you to make your life abundant.

◆ Successful people begin with a belief of certainty—a certainty that they will achieve what it is that they set out to achieve; and they follow through with consistent, daily action to get it.

◆ You are the author of your own thoughts and you can instantly change those thoughts to improve your immediate condition.

◆ Hope is the fuel, and confidence is the starter that ignites it. Together they galvanize you into action and propel you in the direction you need to follow.

◆ In spite of our past, there is always hope for new beginnings. And once we begin to believe in ourselves we can accomplish just about anything.

CHAPTER 12

Navigating Through It All

Iremember investigating a series of armed robberies in the late 1980s. The armed gunman we were after had been wearing a disguise in each of the convenience store and gas station robberies. Each robbery occurred at almost the same time of the evening and the robber made the same demands in each case. He used the same words. Enough similarities existed to tie this robber to five armed robberies. My partner at the time wasn't that interested in the case and I found myself doing most of the work on it myself. I finally caught a break in the case after a witness saw the robber flee from a convenience store after a robbery, take his disguise off and hide under a wooden boat. The witness was able to lead me to where the robber had hidden; and thank goodness for stupid criminals, this guy dropped his wallet which contained his photo I.D. I'm not kidding. My witness was quick to volunteer that the image on the driver's license was in fact a true likeness of the suspect because the witness saw the mask come off. We even had an address. Does it get much better than this?

The suspect must have realized his wallet was missing and that his luck had run out because he fled the jurisdiction in a hurry, leaving no forwarding address. Darn—really? That would have been just too easy. I had enough evidence now to apply for an arrest warrant, charging the suspect with five counts of armed robbery. Given his past record and that he had travelled to several jurisdictions and provinces within Canada over the years, it allowed me to apply for a Canada–wide warrant. Three weeks later I received a call from the Quebec police informing me that they had arrested our suspect on our warrant and he was ours to pick up. My partner, a more senior Detective than I, had a fear of flying; and I didn't particularly want to drive there and back with him and our suspect. It felt like it was going to be torture. The car trip actually took eight and a half hours each way . . . and he drove all the way to Quebec while I had to listen to his country and western tunes . . . At least if I had been driving it wouldn't have been so terrible.

After taking custody of the suspect from a Quebec jail, we placed him in the back seat of our un-marked police car, gave him his rights-to-counsel, and cautioned about making statements. This "caution" is a warning, advising him that if he made any incriminating statements, those statements could be used against him in court. The suspect understood his level of jeopardy, and he was only too happy to be leaving Quebec, describing how a police helicopter had chased him into a densely wooded area; and from overhead he thought he could hear the laughing French policemen as they fired several shots from high-powered rifles at him. The bullets zipped passed him ricocheting off the rocks, but they kept firing until he stopped running, which he did.

The trip back was just as long as the trip there, but it didn't seem as long. My partner was a man of few words whereas my suspect couldn't stop talking. He talked about girls, food, parties and whatever else came to his mind. I decided not to talk about the case because the rapport we were building was well worth the wait. My partner didn't say a word, but our suspect and I sure talked up a storm. He even asked a coffee clerk out on a date at a drive-through, hands cuffed behind his back and all. Finally, as we were about an hour from our destination, the suspect asked me, "Aren't you going to ask me if I committed those robberies?" I answered, "Sure, did you?" He replied, "I sure did, and there's two others you haven't discovered!" One of the easiest confessions I've ever received to seven armed robberies. He pleaded guilty the next day.

Sometimes a detour can be a blessing

What had at first seemed to me to be a long and unnecessary trip to pick up one suspect turned out to be an unexpected road trip to a successful resolution and confession on seven armed robberies. As you may have guessed, losing out to my partner's wishes about what mode of transportation we should use to pick up our suspect didn't leave me very happy at first. It took longer to get there; but, as it turned out, the developments that resulted from that "detour" were much richer than I could have imagined. So it is with some of the paths we take in our efforts to reach our goals. Some goals take longer than others to attain, and some people might get there quicker than you. Your roadmaps or your navigation system may take you in a different direction or a direction you had not planned on taking in the first place. The important thing to remember is that despite how long it may take you, the trip is always worth taking providing you keep your goal in mind and remain focused. By doing this, the rewards are often greater than you imagine.

The Navigation system you might not have thought you had

I used to think the word "ignorance" was a bad word. But it's not. It simply means you don't quite know it all. Get yourself into a place of understanding and discovery if you want to move forward with a thought or idea that's new to you. I spent my first ten years of formal education in French schools, being bussed anywhere from half an hour to an hour and a half each way. French was the language my father demanded we speak at home; so every once in a while, after finally making it to an English school, I'd get confused by an English word or two. It wasn't that I was dumb. I just occasionally lacked knowledge, understanding or familiarity with certain words. Once it had been explained to me (after enduring many laughs from my so-called friends at the time), I understood it. I could then use my newly-discovered word in a sentence; and the more I used it, the easier it became to use. I stored the word as a "point of interest" in my navigation system—my mind—and each time I wanted to visit the word, it was there. All I had to do was access it.

Accessing your internal navigation system

Accessing your internal navigation system is accessing what you know, as well as your thoughts and beliefs. It's those thoughts and beliefs that provide you with direction. If you know how to get to where you want to go, than it's simply a matter of movement—the action I've spoken so much about. Taking action and going for it. If you don't know how to get there, then you need to get yourself the right instructions and find out how to get where you want to be. You need to develop the KSA'S: remember? The knowledge, skills and the ability to help you reach your destination may require some new input into your navigation system. At times, you may not end up where you first set out to be. You might take a detour, or an off-road route that will take you longer than you anticipated to reach your destination. But that doesn't mean it's a bad route. Often, the lessons we learn and the opportunities we have along the way make our destination that much sweeter to reach.

Discouragement

Discouragement often sets in when we don't see immediate results. But depending on the goal that we are trying to achieve, it is often impossible to get immediate results. One of the roadblocks is the inner chatter that often first arises to try to hostage us from even trying. Imagine your goal in this way: it's not much different than a destination that you may map out for yourself when you decide to take a trip.

If the destination that you have in mind to travel to is a long distance away, then it's only logical to understand it's going to take you longer to get there. If, however, you're going to be traveling a short distance, then accordingly, it won't take you that much time to get there under normal circumstances. The more complicated or difficult your goal, the more time it will take you to attain it. Simple logic. The idea is not to expect to see complete results immediately. Be prepared to experience small results at first that will, providing you stick to the map, get bigger over time. In other words, be realistic.

And for some people, despite the fact that their goal is huge, they get there a lot quicker than they anticipated. This may simply be attributed to knowing how to get what they want, prior experience, past mistakes that have been adjusted; or they may have studied and developed the essential KSAs. The point is to keep chipping away at your goals to the point where you breathe them. Whether it's a new job, a new relationship, repairing a fractured relationship or entering into a new fitness program—consistent action is the key. That and a good navigation system which you may already have or can easily develop. Whatever it is that you want to achieve, be prepared to put the work into it and don't get discouraged if you don't see immediate results. Many people give up on their dreams right before they are poised to reach them. I'm reminded of a cartoon I once saw in which two men were in a diamond mine. Both were underground, and one was a few feet below the other. The man on the top was chipping away at the stone and the diamonds were nowhere to be seen ahead of him. As for the second man, he was walking away from his goal with a look at discouragement and abandonment on his face and his pick over his shoulder. But we could see by the image that he was only inches away from the diamonds! He gave up right before he was about to hit the jackpot. Don't let that be you.

Sometimes, some of our best-made plans just don't turn out the way that we expected them to. For whatever reason, we sometimes find ourselves going in a totally different direction from that originally intended. It might be that we turned left instead of right. We went East instead of West. We hopped the wrong train and found ourselves going in a totally different direction. Any number of things can happen to twist our plans around. Then we come to the false realization that where we intended to be just isn't going to happen for us—at least not at this moment. We still have our goal in mind, but we may not be reaching it quite the way we planned. Discouragement sets in. And if we still want to end up where we had planned to be, we have to change direction and modify our plans. I've had a number of those detours and roadblocks in my years—circumstances and situations that I had not counted on happening. I'm reminded of Jamie

Foxx's line in the movie *Collateral:* "Sometimes you've gotta roll with the punches . . . eat chain."

These unexpected twists and turns are not always easy for us to deal with. As I thought about a few of my own, I wondered whether those unexpected events occurred for a reason. Was it fate's intention for me to take a wrong turn, or have someone announce to me that my life was about to significantly change? Was it fate or design that had me looking for a job after retirement because I had lost the financial security I once had? Were these tests to see if I was paying attention to life, or was the path I was on the wrong one for me to be on? Or was it just a bad hand of cards I'd been dealt? I suppose I'll never really know the answer to those questions, nor may you with yours. Despite the bad hand of cards, so many wonderful things and wonderful people entered my life; and it is because of them that I have to believe that somehow, some of this was meant to be. I didn't hostage myself to my circumstances. I created new opportunities. On hindsight, many of these detours led me to wonderful experiences I never would have otherwise experienced. They were blessings. Yours may be too.

Our lives would be very different if we had every one of our plans turn out exactly the way that we had intended them to. If everything turned out according to your plan, perhaps you wouldn't have met some very special people who are now in your life. Or maybe you wouldn't have grown quite as strong as you are right now. On the other hand, if you had the same old thing day in and day out without feeling challenged and alive, maybe your life would simply unfold in the same way that it has always unfolded—with no variety and no excitement. You would expect—and get—the same old thing. Nothing new, nothing different, nothing exciting, nothing unexpected. So maybe those unexpected turns and delays are actually blessings in disguise.

That's not to say that we haven't imagined a special ending in our own minds for our "best-made plans." Of course we have! We are, after all, the creators of those plans. So they'd better have a great ending in our own imagination. And as the artist of our own life, I'm certain we each paint the most beautiful painting for ourselves. It starts with our thoughts.

But what about when we do take those wrong turns or those unexpected things happen? Maybe someone else comes into our lives with a brand-new brush and new colors to add to our canvases. And we find ourselves experiencing something delightfully new and different. We begin to see a new painting unfold in front of our eyes, rich in color and beauty. But only if we have the eyes to see it. That has certainly been my experience. And we can only appreciate those new experiences if our eyes and hearts are open and willing to see the beauty in tough times. So it is our duty to ask ourselves: "Why did this happen? What can I learn from it, and how can I make this work for me? What is life trying to tell me here? Am I missing something? Does something need to be adjusted here? What can I do to improve this for myself? What do I need to change in order to reach my goal? What can I see now that I can appreciate as beautiful?"

It's not enough to just let things happen. That unexpected event, bad hand of cards, or the failure to reach your goals as quickly as you had hoped will work out far better for you if you ask yourself the right questions, challenge yourself to move beyond setbacks and encourage yourself to be stronger than the kick life has just given you. Remember, you are the author of your own destiny, the Captain of your own ship. If you began with a particular end in mind, then regardless of the obstacles and roadblocks, you still have a choice and the opportunity to adjust yourself and your direction to reach those goals. Make it work for you.

Discouragement will only lead to depression—that dark tunnel behind the door that hostages you. And depression will lead to withdrawal, perhaps substance abuse, feelings of inadequacy and hopelessness. I could go on. Despite what happens to you, you must struggle to find the good in those unplanned setbacks and accept the fact that life does sometimes just happen, that it isn't always fair or right, and remind yourself that you do have the ability to shape it to where you want it to be. We must remind ourselves that we have the strength to take ourselves to where we need and want to be and to make the best of it. We need to stay strong. It may not always seem like the right things are happening in your life, and you might feel discouraged by those unexpected bumps in the road. But how you choose to deal with them will affect the overall outcome to your realities and will also define and mold your very own character in the process. And you mustn't forget to be grateful for what you *do* have, despite any setbacks you may experience.

We have to believe that the stars are aligning for us each day of our lives, because far too few people will tell us that they are. Life is not going to write out that "everything is going to be awesome!" on a tableau for you to check out each day as you're leaving the house in the morning. So you must write it out yourself, believe it, and make it so. We all have to believe in our hearts that there is something great happening in this instant, and something even greater lies right around the corner for us. Because if we believe it that much, we'll make it happen or we'll see it when it appears.

A wrong turn can "turn" out just fine

Once I was at Union Station in Toronto and I got turned around. I'd lost my sense of East and West and I ended up hopping on the wrong train! I don't know why fate chose for me to do that, and why it was destined that I didn't end up where I wanted to be as early as I had planned. Fact is, it wasn't "fate"; it was my mistake. I had been careless. Maybe there was a particular reason that it happened. Or maybe there wasn't . . . Who really knows? Did I figure out the reason for it? No, I didn't. I simply carried on. And so it is with your setbacks. You may not always understand why things happen the way they do in your life. But the night I hopped on that wrong train, I did end up having a pleasant and intense chat with a young woman who desperately needed to hear encouraging words. Perhaps that was the reason for my wrong turn. Maybe what I told her were the precise words she needed to hear that night. Maybe my being there at that time really wasn't an event specifically contributing to my needs, but it was helpful to the young woman.

I remember walking the beat one night as a uniformed patrolman. I'd only been on the job for a couple of years; and on that particular night I was working the midnight shift. It was about 4 o'clock in the morning and I was walking in the downtown area of Oshawa, Ontario. The bars had now closed; and very few people were typically out and about in this small town at that time of the morning thirty years ago. As I was walking along one of the main streets I saw a young man sitting on a curb. He didn't see me as I approached him from behind; but when he did notice me he was startled, to say the least. He just about jumped out of his skin. He was terribly upset and wasn't sure what to make of me—a uniformed cop, at 4 AM seemingly creeping up on him. He had been drinking but wasn't drunk. I can imagine that the thought he had at the moment was whether or not I was going to give him a hard time about it. But I didn't. I sat down beside him and started to talk about nothing in particular. Just small talk.

He didn't expect a nice conversation from a cop at that hour; and he started to open up. About fifteen to twenty minutes into our conversation, it got pretty deep. I guess the words I had been telling him had an effect on him and he began to cry. He confessed to me that he was contemplating suicide and was just deciding where to do it when I had arrived. We talked a lot more and I reminded him that whatever happened to him in the past did not have to amount to his future. I reminded him that there was always hope; and that, despite how he might feel about himself at the moment, tomorrow was a new day and there were always people out there who were willing to help him get through it. I gave him one of my business cards and told him that I was one of those people; and by that time he had a beam of hope to give his life another try. I called for a police cruiser and then accompanied him to his home and made sure his parents knew what was going on. The four of us had a good talk; and I left this young man with hope and a smile. That and a supportive family. Sometimes it's not about us and sometimes when we least expect it, something wonderful happens. Or someone wonderful happens. Life's unexpected turns can be blessings in disguise.

CHAPTER 12 SUMMARY

◆ Accessing your internal navigation system is accessing what you already know as well as what your thoughts and beliefs are. It's those thoughts and beliefs that provide you with direction, so make certain that you have the right maps and destinations in mind.

◆ Some goals take longer than others to achieve. Some people get there quicker than others. The important thing to remember is that despite how long it may take you, the trip is always worth taking, providing you keep your goal in mind, remain focused, and keep moving forward.

◆ Regardless of the obstacles that roadblock you, you still have a choice and the opportunity to adjust your direction to reach your goals—to make it work for you.

◆ Life is not going to write "everything is going to be awesome!" on a tableau for us to check out each day as we're leaving the house. So we must write it out ourselves, believe it, and then make it so. We all have to believe in our hearts that there is something great happening right now and something even greater right around the corner.

CHAPTER 13

Everyone Needs TLCs

My family and I paid a price because of my father's alcoholism. My older brother paid the price at the age of 16 for being a normal teenager with long hair growing up in the 60s. He had to leave the house because of my father and he never returned home. My older sister was sent to a convent in her early teen years; and because I somehow became my father's favorite, I remained at home. I played the role of the "good son" whenever I could. Always being a perfect child was not possible; and needless to say, I messed up more than once and got a beating for it, in spite of being the "favorite." My father was a tall, muscular man; and his beating tool of choice was a worn-out barber's belt. Sometimes my father would pause during a strapping to catch his breath before picking me up and carrying on.

Once when I was about six years old, he decided to shatter one of my childhood beliefs. It was Christmas time. We were all excited for Christmas, and I couldn't wait for Santa Claus to arrive. A week or so before Christmas that year, my brother and I were standing in the stairwell a few steps from the front door when my father walked in with his .22 rifle, looked up at us, and coldly announced that he had just killed Santa Claus. He then walked calmly to the basement to put his rifle away as my brother and I stood on the stairwell crying our hearts out. Santa Claus was dead.

On another occasion when I was between the ages of six and eight, I accompanied my father as he drove to a rundown country farmhouse just outside of the city. He had me tag along as he often did; and after we arrived at the place, he had me follow him up a path. I wish I could say that it looked like Norman Bates' house, but it didn't. It was a run-down country bungalow; and as I followed him, I heard the squawk of a hideous caged bird in the front yard that startled the hell out of me. The bird's cries were soon drowned out by what sounded like babies crying. Fear then set in even deeper and my heart was beating hard. I was terrified, but I followed. We walked past the house toward a large cement building in the back where the cries got louder. As we approached the door, the sounds of the crying infants got louder; and I obediently followed as my father opened the door leading into the building. We stepped in, and there I discovered what it was that I'd heard crying and the cause of my fear. Hanging from hooks above us were pigs being slaughtered; and the next thing I saw was a man plunging a knife into a squealing pig and tearing it open as blood and guts spilled out onto the floor by his feet. My father had taken me to a slaughterhouse where I got a bird's eye view and an image I'll never forget. My father killed himself when I was 17. I found him the first time he attempted it—with that same .22 rifle he had used to kill Santa Claus when I was a kid. Nobody was there the second time.

I know now, after all these years, that living in that environment actually helped shape me into being the person that I am today because of the choices I made at an early age and the lessons I've come to learn through them. With very little good guidance from my father, I had to discover how to grow and communicate effectively on my own and how to fend for myself. I also became a "protector" for others. It was those experiences and the ones of helplessness to protect my mother and siblings that helped me decide to be a cop—to serve and protect others. God bless my mother for trying her best; but understandably, she had her hands full taking care of five children, a household, tenants in the basement and an abusive husband. My self-taught, gradual lessons and experiences have served me well over the years. And I am constantly striving to discover more. This includes reading positive material and listening to positive people. Surrounding myself with good people (we are the company we keep) and taking personal growth courses and seminars, working on understanding myself, my strengths and weaknesses, and then building on those strengths and minimizing my weaknesses. Tending to my primary human needs and trying to nurture each of them. As children, we have little control over our primary needs; but as adults, we have full control over how to modify and shape those needs. Tending to them and putting thoughts, decisions, and choices all into account propels us to the successful lives we deserve.

When I was a police officer, I hated hearing a defense attorney plead to the court that his or her client acted criminally because of their backgrounds or upbringings. I'd sit in court and listen to the rants of the defense as they blamed the accused's behavior on something or someone else, other than him or her. "Their needs weren't being met;" or someone had abandoned or abused them. It was an easy "cop-out" to blame others for their criminal behavior.

So many people do it. They refuse to take responsibility for their actions and consequently live very unfulfilled and sad lives, blaming others for their unhappiness. These folks fail to grasp the concept that whatever has happened to them in the past does not have to hold them hostage. At some point in each of our lives we have to be responsible. By blaming others for the way we're turning out or for the way our lives turned out is letting ourselves down. Accountability begins with us.

You decide how your past will shape you.

Our Primal Needs

According to human needs psychology, our behaviors are motivated by the desire to meet one or more of our primary needs: the need for stability, variety, significance, love and connection, growth, and contribution. Tony Robbins, in his book *Inner Strength,* describes it much like this. We need:

1. **Stability**: We all have a desire for stability, safety, and comfort in our lives. Even though certainty—or stability—may ultimately be an illusion, in order to feel confident in our lives, we need to believe that: our homes will be waiting for us when we return to them, providing us with the shelter we need; our partners will stand by us when things get tough; our jobs aren't in jeopardy; we

will continue to receive an income; and there will be food to eat. Without a healthy dose of "certainty," uncertainty sets in and influences how we feel about our security and our survival. Having said this, a certain amount of uncertainty is also essential to our overall happiness. If everything were certain and predictable, our lives would be boring and stale. We need variety and spice—an occasional pleasant surprise, some challenge and excitement! Balance is essential—but certainty in the most important matters is essential and stabilizes us.

2. **Variety**: The need for stimulus and change. Variety is, as they say, "the spice of life!" Without variety, life wouldn't really be worth living. Imagine a steady diet of steak. Meal after meal after meal; day after day; month after month; and year after year. If you're a steak lover, the first "few days" would be great. But after a while, your taste for steak would diminish; and after a while longer, you'd grow to hate steak. It's human nature. We need variety. We need spice.

3. **Significance**: The need to feel special and worthy of attention. We all want to feel like we make a difference on earth and that our existence matters. We want to be noticed and acknowledged, if not by everyone, at least by someone—even if that someone is simply ourselves. Each day we should repeat a Mantra to ourselves that boasts: "I matter!" "I'm someone!" "I make a great difference." Mantras work.

4. **Love & Connection**: The need to connect with others and ultimately to love and be loved. Without love or connection—we die. It's been scientifically proven that infants need to be touched and loved to live. The radio and our libraries of music sing to our need to be loved, touched, and to feel connected. We were never meant to be alone and will go to great lengths to connect with others and find love.

5. **Growth**: The need to develop and expand. Whether it's guitar lessons, yoga, cooking classes or studying a foreign language, we all have a need to grow and personally develop. To learn something

new, always. It challenges us and keeps us alert. Without it, we deteriorate and distract ourselves with a variety of substitutes— different addictions designed for instant gratification that replace the void left from not growing. Things like TV, sex, shopping (not that any of these are a bad thing in moderation), gossip, constant complaining, depression, etc. They can all become substitutes for not moving forward and personally developing one of the many talents with which we are all endowed. If your life lacks luster and fulfillment, check this area and take up a new hobby or develop a latent talent.

6. **Contribution**: The need to give beyond yourself. One of my most treasured experiences was my mission to the Middle East in 2005 where I worked at the Jordanian International Police Training Center, teaching police cadets at first, and later becoming an advocate and counsellor for them. I felt a spark of life I'd never felt quite as intensely before; and it still lives on today. We all need to contribute to something to fulfill one of our basic needs. So, make it a mission of yours to contribute to your life by contributing to the lives of others. When you're feeling down about how things are going in your own life, find someone and make a difference in theirs; it will make you feel good in the process. You'll feel a satisfaction of having enriched someone else's life and, consequently, your own. It's just the way we were made—our internal make-up. So these are our Six Basic Human needs.

What does this all mean? Most of us don't nurture each of our needs nearly enough. For some, and most, we might focus on two or three of these needs and ignore the others, to our detriment. Furthermore, the ones we tend to focus on are typically the ones that keep us dissatisfied with our lives. We're often so unaware of why we do what we do, and therefore ignorant about what the consequences of living an unbalanced life brings. Ignorance about which needs we most require to fulfill us can cost us the things we truly deeply desire: joy, happiness, fulfillment, connection, and love. Being aware of these six needs and nourishing them is like tending to a garden. Our gardens require constant attention and we reap what we sow. Too much water, not enough sun, neglect and inattentiveness can lead to the death of our plants; and in the case of our personal garden of emotion, a constant lack of fulfillment. Knowledge is power. Personal power amounts to success. Awareness is a gift you give yourself. Now that you're aware of your primary needs, tend to your inner garden more often and strive to cultivate each of these needs. Once you do that, you can move on to shaping your thoughts, choices, decisions and actions more effectively. That will help prevent you from being taken hostage.

The TLCs: Therapeutic Lifestyle Changes

So far we've examined how our thoughts can hostage us, the importance of the "STEP" principle, how our thoughts, decisions and choices can greatly affect the outcome of our happiness and the importance of taking positive action. We have just examined our primal needs and how tending to them can contribute to the quality of our lives. Now let's take a look at Therapeutic Lifestyle Changes.

In an article written in *American Psychologist* in 2011, author Roger Walsh[38] points out that "mental health professionals have significantly underestimated the importance of lifestyle factors as contributors and treatments for multiple-cycle pathologies, for fostering individual and social well-being, and for preserving and optimizing cognitive functions." He goes on to describe how TLCs are under-utilized despite a considerable amount of evidence as to their effectiveness in improving quality of life. The article said the TLCs can ameliorate prostate cancer, reverse coronary arteriosclerosis, and be as effective as psychotherapy or medication for treating depressive disorders.

What are the TLCs we should strive to enhance in our lives? First there is exercise. And I have mentioned the importance of exercise earlier in this book, but it is one of the TLCs. Exercise offers physical

---

38. Lifestyle and Mental Health. Roger Walsh https://apa.org/pubs/journals/releases/amp-66-7-579.pdf

benefits that can prolong your life and the quality of your life and help eliminate many medical conditions. Exercise offers both preventative and therapeutic psychological benefits and is inexpensive to boot! To quote the author of the article: "In terms of therapeutic benefits, responsive disorders include depression, anxiety, eating, addictive, and body dysmorphic disorders. Exercise also reduces chronic pain, age-related cognitive decline, the severity of Alzheimer's disease, and some symptoms of schizophrenia."

Next let us look at Nutrition and Diet. We don't have to look too hard to see how poor nutrition is affecting a large portion of the world population of these days. Since the popularity and consumption of fast food has increased so dramatically, so have obesity and other physical disorders related to poor nutrition. Our bodies were designed to eat natural foods; and the consumption of preservatives and pesticides does nothing but harm the Temple of the body that was meant to heal itself. Choosing to have a diet that consists predominantly of a large variety of colors of fruits and vegetables, also known as a "rainbow diet," fish, protein and natural foods will not only make you feel better, but it will make you look better.

Next in the TLCs we look at Supplements. There is growing evidence that suggests that food supplements offer valuable prophylactic and therapeutic benefits for mental health according to the article. For example, fish and fish oil are especially important for mental health and supply the body's need for the essential omega-3 fatty acids. Educating yourself about what supplements are best for the body would be a good investment of time.

Spending time in Nature has many therapeutic benefits as well. Sometimes all it takes to get rid of some of those negative thoughts that go through our heads is a nice walk in a natural setting. There is beauty all around us; and it is up to us to take advantage of it and look upon it as a way to de-stress.

Next we have relationships, recreation and enjoyable activities, relaxation and stress management. Religious or Spiritual Involvement is also part of the TLCs as is Contribution and Service to your community and others. All of these TLCs are worthy of examination and of implementation in order to live a full and happy life and as a means to free ourselves from our hostaged thoughts. Although I won't be spending much time on in-depth details vis-à-vis these latter TLCs, I wanted to mention them because they are consistent with nurturing your primal needs.

CHAPTER 13 SUMMARY

◆ At some point we have to be responsible for our own destinies. Blaming others for the way we've turned out is letting ourselves down by not reaching our full potential.

◆ Our Primal Needs are for: stability, variety, significance, love and connection, growth, and contribution.[39] We must ensure that we meet these needs.

◆ Exercise, eat well, supplement your diet and get back to nature. These TLCs will help you live well and fight off the attackers. Guaranteed.

---

39. *Inner Strength: Harnessing the Power of Your Six Primal Needs,* Copyright 2005, Tony Robbins, Simon & Schuster Ltd.

CHAPTER 14

Gratitude

*"Let gratitude be the pillow upon which you kneel
to say your nightly prayer. And let faith be the bridge
you build to overcome evil and welcome good."*
—MAYA ANGELOU,
CELEBRATIONS: RITUALS OF PEACE AND PRAYER

In our journey to free ourselves from those voices within that may prevent us from releasing our hostaged selves, it is important to examine the blessings gratitude can bring. Gratitude is a feeling and an attitude that we internalize and externalize in ways that help us appreciate those things we already have in our lives or those things we are about to receive. It is an affirmation of the good things we have; and it creates a sense within us that we are blessed despite whatever else may not be going quite as well as we had planned. This appreciation helps to balance our perspective on our lot, and may even tip the scale from one of prior dissatisfaction with that which we feel our lives to be missing to one of satisfaction with the actual abundance in our lives. Gratitude helps to encourage us and helps change any negative dialogue we have with ourselves to a more positive one; and the more we look for things for which to be grateful, the better our internal monologues and overall health will be.

The many benefits of gratefulness

*"Gratitude unlocks the fullness of life. It turns what we have
into enough, and more. It turns denial into acceptance, chaos
to order, confusion to clarity. It can turn a meal into a feast,
a house into a home, a stranger into a friend."*
—MELODY BEATTIE

There are so many social, physical, and psychological benefits to gratitude—even in the midst of adversity. Anyone who practices gratitude can attest to the benefits gratitude brings to their lives. Practicing gratitude will provide us with happiness and is a proven way to boost feelings of optimism, joy, enthusiasm, pleasure and other positive emotions. By supplementing positive emotions we effectively push negative ones aside. Some people practice by making entries into "gratitude journals," and benefit from their constant entries. Simply by practicing gratitude, we can improve our physical, social and psychological well-being, which translates into more success in every aspect of our life. Imagine, by looking for the many things for which to be grateful, you can improve your overall health and release your hostaged thoughts even further . . .

You may be wondering how exercising an attitude of gratitude can make such a significantly positive difference in your life. It has been scientifically proven over the last several years that people who practice gratitude have reported feeling more physically energetic, more internally and externally happy, healthier—experiencing a reduction in blood pressure, and far more optimistic. They find themselves more forgiving of others and of themselves, and often report feeling less lonely and isolated. Furthermore, in our journey throughout this book—that of examining our "hostaged" selves, in which we've been talking about being victim to thoughts that bring us down and prevent us from moving forward, being grateful and practicing gratitude certainly ranks as one of the key soldiers you may include in your life to help free you and promote your happiness.

By practicing gratitude on a regular—even daily—basis, you will be taking time out of your day to look at the all things that you're grateful for. And that can only result in feeling better about life. For example: one of the first things you can be grateful for is the fact that you woke up this morning. You did. Think about how many people didn't make it through the night due to health problems or accidents, and never got to see the light of this day. And having awoken this morning, are you one of the fortunate people who is enjoying good health? Are you able to breathe without the assistance of a machine and walk without the assistance of an electrical device? Are you bed-ridden or immobilized? And if you are, what are all the things that you *do* have going on in your life that you should be grateful for? Can you see the wonderful colors of the sky or smell the aroma of a per-fect meal? Find those things that are blessing your life and feel grat-itude for them. God knows they may not last forever. Anything can be taken from you—especially if you take them for granted.

Gratitude is an affirmation of the goodness that surrounds you

Gratitude is an affirmation of the blessings we each have. We affirm that there are wonderful things in our lives, gifts we've been blessed with, and benefits we've received. We may have our health, a secure job, an income, a roof over our heads, clothes to wear and food to eat. We may have eyes to see with and ears to help us hear and appreci-ate music. We may smell and taste, even something as simple as the first morning coffee. We may have someone in our life who cares about us and loves us, and whom we care about and love. Gratitude helps us see the better things in life. This doesn't mean that we need to see life as completely perfect, because life isn't perfect. We cannot ignore our burdens and challenges. But gratitude helps us to look at life through a brighter lens and helps us appreciate the wonderful things we *do* have. Gratitude encourages us to identify some amount of good-ness in our life; and when we do that, we can't help but feel better.

To increase our sense and practice of gratitude, our appreciation of the positives in our lives, we need simply identify and examine its sources. In doing so, we discover that the sources of that for which we are grateful come to us most often from outside of ourselves. We acknowledge that other people—or even higher powers, if you're open to this mindset—provide us with an abundance of gifts, helping us create happiness by providing for us. This simple exercise of finding sources for which to be thankful can also lead us to be grateful on an even deeper level: grateful for a friend who helped you; grateful for a kind word, a piece of art, a new song, the warmth of a heated subway car. Even for the job you have. Instead of saying, "I have to go to work tomorrow," try saying, "I get to go to work tomorrow!" You can find a plethora of reasons to be grateful for so many things around you. Remember that things can be taken away from us in a split second. Appreciate them now and be grateful for them. Doing this can actually help you hold onto them for even longer—if not forever. Taking things for granted can result in you losing them; and how many times have we heard people complain that it wasn't until they lost something that they realized just what they had?

Conditioning ourselves to have a spirit of gratitude for what we currently have is a key to finding the happiness that is directly within our reach. The physical, mental, social and spiritual benefits which gratitude brings to our overall well-being cannot be ignored; nor can it be overstated. Too many people take what they have for granted without stopping for a moment to experience and appreciate what makes them truly rich and blessed in this life. Is being financially wealthy the key to happiness? Absolutely not. It certainly can help make life easier in some ways; but it can also prevent you from experiencing happiness. Let me explain. When money and materialistic possessions become your god, your focus is redirected from what is truly meaningful in life to what can be truly life-defeating. How many people on their death-beds will look over their lives and wish they had spent more time working? Even Ebenezer Scrooge came to understand that all the money in the world had turned his heart into stone; and once he realized that, he experienced the beauty of giving, loving and gratitude. He released his past and the chains that bound him to an unhappy and unfulfilled life. He set himself free and put himself onto another path—a path that ultimately saved him from misery.

As a man thinketh, so shall he be

Published in 1902, James Allen's book *As a Man Thinketh* is packed with wisdom and thought-provoking philosophies. Concerning our thoughts, Allen writes, "As he thinks, so he is; as he continues to think, so he remains." If our thoughts are always focused on sadness, hopelessness, doubt and confusion then this is what we "will be." We will be sad, hopeless, doubtful and confused. We become the product of what we continually think and focus upon. Allen also writes, "All that a man achieves and all that he fails to achieve is the direct result of his own thoughts." Again, we are reminded that our thoughts help create and set us on the path to success and achievement. To be truly grateful is to practice an unwavering spirit of gratitude that looks at the blessings in our lives and not at the things we don't have. It doesn't mean we stop planning for greater success. It simply means we don't dwell on the bad; we dwell on the good and exercise an attitude of gratitude. Each and every day. Get in the habit of keeping a journal and document the many things for which you are grateful. Watch as it takes on a life of its own and helps you experience even more reasons to be grateful. I'm seeing a trend on one of the most popular social media sites of people taking on "gratefulness" challenges and documenting at least a few each day over a set period of days; and I can't help but notice that the authors are getting better at being more thankful! It's great to see.

CHAPTER 14 SUMMARY

◆ Practicing gratitude daily will provide you with happiness and is a proven way to boost feelings of optimism, joy, enthusiasm, pleasure and other positive emotions.

◆ Gratitude is an affirmation. It affirms blessings we each have. Take time to see the many blessings in your life.

CHAPTER 15

Faith

"I am fundamentally an optimist. Whether that comes from nature or nurture, I cannot say. Part of being optimistic is keeping one's head pointed toward the sun, one's feet moving forward. There were many dark moments when my faith in humanity was sorely tested, but I would not and could not give myself up to despair. That way lays defeat and death."
—NELSON MANDELA

We all have faith in something. Whether it's faith in God, science, ideologies or our own ideas about life. Faith is often seen as something religious; but it isn't exclusive to religion. Nor should it be understood to be so. Faith means different things to different people, but having it brings each of us hope.

Faith isn't always easy to have, but it is essential to embrace. Most of us don't wake up and suddenly find it. Rather, it is a practice, a habit, a discipline, like many other things that each of us desire to have, to develop, and to perfect. Faith requires us to place our trust in the knowledge that something much bigger than simply ourselves can play a role in our destinies; and that along with our own efforts, something wonderful is going to happen. Faith is accepting and admitting that no one person or one thing is completely in control of all the things that go on around us; and that at any time, life can take a remarkable turn for the better. Faith is believing that maybe today is the day that changes everything! Maybe this moment is the one you've been plotting and wishing for.

Simply having faith without putting in work isn't enough, however. Along with faith, you also have to take action. Sometimes you even have to act without knowing where that will lead you. But it's that belief that good things will come to you along with the effort you put into it that makes up what faith is really about. It's having a positive dialogue with yourself and telling yourself that good things are coming because you'll make them come. It's stepping into the often unknown world—believing that by having taken that step and action, good things will come to you. That's what faith is about.

Nevertheless, faith can sometimes be disappointing, especially when we experience difficulties, challenges and uncertainties. But it is exactly when we experience those things that we need faith the most. If we understand nothing else about faith, let's understand that faith is often the hardest thing to hold onto when we need it the very most. Faith can be that gift that pulls us through the most difficult times simply because we believe that it will. Faith can help get us to the next stage and help us reach a point of gratitude and understanding where we begin to see the bigger picture and trust that our hard work will pay off. By losing faith, we lose hope. When we lose hope, our monologues and dialogues begin to fill our heads with those very things that keep us hostage to ourselves and keep us from moving forward. Faith can help unbind our chains and free us to move forward in spite of circumstances. Faith is that one thing that can keep a person going no matter what they are faced with. But again, it's important to understand that faith cannot be blind. Faith must be accompanied by work. Faith cannot be seen nor can it be touched. It can only be felt and experienced. In those who possess an abundance of it, their quality of life is richly improved. Even though their days may be filled with situations of discouragement, they believe in something bigger than themselves; and that keeps them moving forward and looking within themselves and outside of themselves for reasons to feel gratitude and hope. Yes, faith is also being optimistic. And optimism is not a bad thing.

CHAPTER 15 SUMMARY

◆ We need faith the most when we experience difficulties, challenges, and uncertainties. Faith can be that gift that pulls us through the most difficult times simply because we believe that it will.

Conclusion

You become a hostage to yourself when you allow sabotaging thoughts to come into your head and give them a place to stay. Once you've shown them to a room in your mind, you will feed them. When you're the perfect host or hostess, those thoughts will enjoy the stay until you decide to evict them.

Our negative self-talk—that chatter in our heads—affects our state of mind and, subsequently, our actions. When the head turns, the body follows. It's a simple principle. By allowing any self-doubt, put-down or disempowering thought to take root in your mind, your body will react with increased stress and your actions will be affected. This kind of corrupted thinking has no place in a healthy mind and it really is up to you to stay healthy in mind, body and spirit. You have a defense system available to you and you need only to implement it the moment one of those thoughts makes an appearance. You are not a hostage to anything unless you choose to be. Recognizing when you're hostaged or about to be hostaged by your thoughts is a start. Developing the skills and strength to redirect your thought patterns from defeat to victory takes practice but with time and practice becomes effortless. You develop the mental muscle to program yourself for success.

To help defend yourself from being taken hostage in the first place, it's important to build yourself a strong life foundation. In a home, a strong foundation will help keep the building from collapsing. In you, a foundation also helps to keep you strong; and a personal foundation takes many shapes: surrounding yourself with positive people, reading uplifting material, exercising regularly and mediation, to name just a few. When you find yourself in a toxic relationship or surrounded by toxic people—remove yourself. Whatever cancer you keep yourself exposed to will affect you. Be more aware of what you allow into your head and your life—and who. You are the captain of your ship and no one will rescue you from being taken hostage by yourself *except* yourself.

We all understand that life presents us with challenges and opportunities. It's up to us to find the opportunities in the challenges that we are gifted with and to live the life that we want to live. No one else is going to live that life for us. No one else is going to create a wonderful life for us other than ourselves; and relying on others for our happiness will only disappoint in the end.

Acknowledging that life is not always fair helps us to accept that it isn't; and as strange as that sounds, it helps us cope with setbacks and face them with much needed determination to change our circumstances. Recognizing that life can knock us down from time to time and that we have the power to get back up is one of the many ways to achieve personal happiness.

Successful people often approach things differently than the mainstream. Mimicking their behavior will help you reach the places you want to be. It's our duty to change the negative chatter in our heads to positive ones. That begins with a positive thought, a choice, a decision, and action. In each situation in which you find yourself, you have a choice to "S.T.E.P." into it by first Stopping for a moment, Thinking about it, Evaluating your choices and then Proceeding with your best option. Remember that you're not stuck if at first your choice wasn't the best.

Beginning your day with positive thoughts and affirmations and reminding yourself that you are worthy of happiness and success is the best way to start your day. Choose your daily attitude and greet the day with a heart filled with love, hope, passion and drive. Having a spirit of gratitude and faith will lead you on your journey to happiness.

◆ Be aware that we can each be taken hostage by a thought, doubt, uncertainty, and even loneliness. There are many potential attackers ready to chatter up a storm in your head to lead you to hostage yourself. Follow these steps to prevent that from being so. . . .

◆ Be aware of that inner chatter in your mind and eavesdrop in on the content of your thoughts. If you discover that your inner monologues are harmful and hostaging, change the channel immediately.

◆ Call upon your inner defense system to help.

You are no longer a Hostage to Yourself. I believe in affirmations and suggest you review the following ones and repeat those which you feel apply to your life and circumstances. You'll be amazed by the results. Repeat them, believe them, and make them your own.

◆ I am not a hostage to self-doubt.

◆ I am not a hostage to him.

◆ I am not a hostage to her.

◆ I am not a hostage to this piece of cake or that next drink.

◆ I am not a hostage to this toxic relationship.

◆ I am not a hostage to that comment or that opinion.

◆ I am not a hostage to this setback.

◆ I am not a hostage to what you think of me.

◆ I am not a hostage to my current state of un-healthiness.

◆ I am not a hostage to my past.

◆ I am not a hostage to this addiction.

◆ I am not a hostage to any self-defeating mind chatter that pops into my head.

◆ I am powerful.

◆ I am worthy.

◆ I am unique.

◆ I am me and I'm proud of it.

◆ I am beautiful.

◆ I am strong.

◆ I am capable.

◆ I can.

◆ I will.

◆ I deserve.

◆ I am limitless.

◆ I _____.

You fill in the many blanks of what you're not hostage to. Your script can only be written by you. You have the director's approval to write the best one for yourself; and no one can write the perfect life for yourself but you.

I leave you with this timeless thought:

"God grant me the serenity to accept the things I cannot change, the courage to change the things I can, and the wisdom to know the difference."[40]
—REINHOLD NIEBUHR

You are not a hostage
Stay Strong

---

40. Reinhold Neibuhr. www.brainyquote.com/quotes/quotes/r/reinholdni 100884.html

APPENDIX A

Virtues Exercise

In this appendix, we revisit the earlier list of virtues found in Chapter 2. You may already possess most of these virtues and not all of them will need to be examined. You choose the ones that you'd like to work on. Keep in mind that the questions I ask are limited, and that you are unlimited. Take your time to think of questions that serve you best. You may wish to record your answers in a separate journal or notepad.

Acceptance: the act of receiving someone or something with contentment, understanding and forgiveness. Is there some area in your life that requires you to work on your ability to accept others and yourself more completely? What are your thoughts telling you about contentment, understanding and forgiveness of others AND yourself?

_____

_____

_____

Assertiveness: the act of finding your confidence and courage as opposed to dwelling on your self-doubt or shyness. Behaving with purpose and direction will help you find the happiness and success that you're looking for. Being assertive will also help prevent you from being taken hostage by any thoughts that are sabotaging in nature. People respect those who are assertive without being arrogant. Do you stand up for yourself? Do you ask for what you want?

Where can you improve on becoming more assertive? What are your thoughts telling you about your assertive self?

_____

_____

_____

Authenticity: the act being true to yourself, your personality, your spirit and your character. Being honest and living your life with integrity. Replacing low self-esteem in favor of high self-esteem and being yourself as opposed to simply a copy of someone else. Being different is not a bad thing—imagine a life without spice. When you see someone who is authentic and unique, that's worth taking a second look. Are you living to satisfy others rather than yourself and if so, how is that making you feel? How can you become more authentic?

_____

_____

_____

Beauty: the act of finding attractiveness within yourself and others will bring you joyfulness and peace as opposed to looking for the ugliness in life and others. Recognizing that beauty is truly in the eye of the beholder and asking yourself if your inner beauty matches your outer beauty. Everyone has their own unique beauty. I know you do. Does it really matter what others think of you? What makes you beautiful and what are your thoughts telling you about your inner and outer beauty? How can you improve your thoughts in this important area of your life?

_____

_____

_____

Caring: the act of feeling and demonstrating genuine concern for others and the world around you. Showing compassion and kindness as opposed to cruelty and insensitivity. Are there areas that, or people who, require more attention in your life? If so, who? And how can you begin today to show them that you really care? Are you genuinely concerned for the well-being of others?

_____

_____

_____

Cleanliness: the act of keeping yourself and your environment uncontaminated, orderly and pure. Rejecting dirtiness and impurity in both environment and thought. Having a clean mind, clean body and clean environment you become that much more prepared to resist intrusive thoughts from finding their way into your thoughts and taking you hostage. How organized is your life? Where can you improve? How are your thoughts doing? Any ones you should clean up?

_____

_____

_____

Commitment: the act of promising to live a hostage-free life and to reach the goals you've set for yourself by persevering. Pledging yourself to finding direction in your life and being loyal to yourself and to others. Pledging yourself to succeed and to ridding yourself of any hostaged thoughts that have managed to make their way into your head. Are you committed to self-improvement? Are your goals SMART? (That is, are they Specific, Measurable, Achievable, Realistic and Time-sensitive?) What are some of the goals you've committed to achieving this year? What are your hostaged thoughts telling you here and are you committed to changing them?

_____

_____

_____

Compassion: the act of demonstrating kindness to your fellow man, conscious of their distress along with a desire to be truly helpful, caring and understanding. Eliminating hostility and judgment. Are you a compassionate person? In what areas can you show more compassion to others?

_____

_____

_____

Confidence: the act of examining yourself to uncover feelings and beliefs in yourself that you can do so much more—and do it well. Believing that you can succeed at whatever you put your mind to. You are assertive and courageous. You pledge to get rid of self-doubt and uncertainty. Do you have the confidence you need to succeed? In what areas can you improve your self-confidence and what steps can you take to so do? What are your hostaged thoughts telling you about your confidence?

_____

_____

_____

Consideration: the act of thinking carefully before you leap. You **Stop** to consider carefully your next move and you don't simply "react" to what happens in your life. In consideration of others: You will show compassion and a caring nature. Ridding yourself of selfishness. Do you jump in to things too quickly without considering the consequences? If so, what can and should you do about that? And when it comes to others: Are you as considerate of them as you should be? If not, what can you begin to do right now to show more consideration for them?

_____

_____

_____

Contentment: the act of being happy and satisfied with the blessings you already have in your life. It is a fulfillment and joy with what you have now as opposed to a dissatisfaction and restlessness for what you don't have. You understand that all that you have can be taken from you in a mere moment. You pledge to take inventory of what blessings you currently have and you're grateful for all of them. Are you content with your life and the blessings you have at this moment? List what you're happy and satisfied with—or what you should be happy and satisfied with.

_____

_____

_____

Cooperation: the act of working well with others. It's about teamwork and unity, as opposed to defiance and resentment. Are you a cooperative person who works well with others? Where and how can you improve in this area?

_____

_____

_____

Courage: the act of persevering and facing your fears or setbacks. Being bold and confident, as opposed to hanging on to fear and self-doubt. Courage means moving forward despite the fact that you may

be fearful. Are you courageous? If not, how can you become courageous and what are the advantages in your personal world to become
fear free?

_____

_____

_____

Creativity: the act of finding your gifts and abilities and discovering
new ideas, new talents and new opportunities. For those you don't
currently have but want, you'll develop them. You'll find purpose and
detach yourself from what is simply normal. You're going to stand
out from the pack. What are your creative strengths? Is there an area
you'd like to develop? A new challenge you'd like to undertake?

_____

_____

_____

Determination: the act of finding the strength and focus needed to
continue your efforts to succeed and achieve something you're after
despite how difficult it may seem to you in the moment. You're committed and tenacious. You won't give in to complacency. Are you lacking in determination and commitment? If so, what's holding you
back—and just as importantly, what are you prepared to do about it?

_____

_____

_____

Dignity: the act of facing and behaving and conducting yourself with
self—respect. It's about exercising self-control, honor and respect
and rejecting egoism and selfishness. Do you conduct yourself with
dignity? Do you respect yourself completely? How can you improve

in this area of you feel you're not treating yourself with dignity—or treating others for that matter?

_____

_____

_____

Encouragement: the act of finding hopefulness and confidence from within yourself. Replacing your self-defeating thoughts and negative internal mind chatter with thoughts and chatter that makes you want to beat any setbacks down. It's about keeping your head up high and imagining that whatever failures or setbacks you've faced in your past only served to prepare you for this moment to forge ahead with confidence. Are you encouraged about life? What negative self-talk is keeping you from being as encouraged and confident as you should be? How can you turn that dark chatter into bright chatter? What should you be telling yourself?

_____

_____

_____

Enthusiasm: the act of being excited and truly interested in something you want! An active and passionate energy and desire. It's about being motivated as opposed to indifferent, bored and unexcited. Are you an enthusiastic individual, ready to take on the world and go for what you want with passion and determination? If not, what's holding you back and what can you do to un-hostage and unchain yourself from that lack of enthusiasm?

_____

_____

_____

Ethical: the act of following an accepted and right set of rules, which are morally correct and good. It's about exercising fairness and respect as opposed to being immoral and unprincipled. Are you as ethical as you can be or do you select the occasions to be ethical in? If you are unethical in some areas of your life, what are they and why do you choose to turn a blind eye in those areas? What can you do to improve in that area?

_____

_____

_____

Excellence: the act of finding distinction and quality in yourself and others. Pledging to strive to reach the very best you can in everything you do. Setting realistic and high standards for yourself and then reaching them with dignity, honor, passion, integrity and respect. Never being willing to ever settle for being mediocre. Do you strive for excellence in all aspects of your life? In what areas are you excelling in and in what areas are you not? How can you make improvements and what are the rewards you will reap by doing so?

_____

_____

_____

Fairness: the act of understanding equality and treating everyone in a way that doesn't favor one person or group over others. It's about practicing equality and justice instead of finding reasons for grievances and injustice. Are you treating others and yourself fairly? Do you value fairness—and if not, why?

_____

_____

_____

Faith: the act of putting your trust in something or someone you believe in (whether it be a program, a person or God). Finding confidence, hope and trust as opposed to apprehension and doubt. Believing that something will happen simply "because you wish it to." Do you have faith? Do you believe that today can turn out to be the best day of your life? What can you put your faith into that will bring you the best rewards?

_____

_____

_____

Flexibility: the act of being prepared and willing to make the changes you need to make and try new things. Listening and learning through understanding and detaching yourself from your old ways and thoughts. Letting go of stubbornness. Being prepared to go with the flow if the flow is headed in the right direction as opposed to paddling in the opposite direction and learn new things whenever possible. Are you flexible with others? Are you open to listening and learning? In what areas can you become more flexible in?

_____

_____

_____

Forgiveness: the act of letting go of something you hold against yourself or someone else. Here you should take a few moments to examine your life to determine your ability to forgive something or someone that has hurt or wronged you. You pledge to also learn to forgive yourself as well. By doing so, you'll help free yourself from your hostaged state and find peace. You'll release that anger and bitterness that kept you shackled. Is there an area in your life—a circumstance, a person or an act you need to forgive in? Do you need to forgive yourself? How will it make you feel by truly forgiving yourself and others?

_____

_____

_____

Friendliness: the act of examining your ability to extend the hand of true friendship and respect to others. Discovering who your real friends are and how to be a true friend to others. Pledging to be an example of kindness, helpfulness and love. Being selective when choosing your friends: you are the company you keep, after all. Ridding of shyness and surrounding yourself with friends of worth and value. Making the effort to be a sincere and true friend to yourself and those you choose to surround yourself with. Are you friendly? Do you accept others as they are? Are you approachable and a true friend to those you've let into your life? How can you be a better friend?

_____

_____

_____

Generosity: the act of being kind, understanding and selfless. Being a helping hand prepared to serve and help others as opposed to being self-centered and stingy. Are you generous with your time, money and love? Where can you improve in your generosity to others?

_____

_____

_____

Gentleness: the act of having a kind and quiet nature as opposed to one that's harsh and violent. You understand that this is not a sign of weakness, but one of great strength. Is your spirit gentle? Do you have a gentle disposition or are you easily provoked? How can you show your gentleness to others? To yourself?

Graciousness: the act of being polite in a way that shows respect. Acting with dignity and tact as opposed to rudeness and disrespect. Are you gracious in your behavior to others? Where, if anywhere, do you need to become more gracious?

Gratitude: the act of finding a spirit of appreciation and thanks for what you have, what others give you and for life in general. Finding happiness, joy, peace and contentment in the "now" as opposed to being disappointed with what you have or how things are in the present moment. Despite how bad your situation may appear, you recognize it can always get worse and everything can be taken from you in a moment—without notice. Do you thank God, the universe? Why not list at least a dozen things your grateful for?

Helpfulness: the act of giving assistance to those in need—without being asked. And when asked, giving that help with graciousness and service. Are you a helpful individual or do you need to reexamine areas you can become more helpful in? How are you helpful? How can you become more helpful and what will the rewards be for becoming more helpful to others?

_____

_____

_____

Honesty: the act of being fair and truthful to others as well as to yourself. Choosing integrity and truthfulness by avoiding deceitfulness. How honest are you? Are you selective with your honesty and if so, why?

_____

_____

_____

Hope: the act of understanding that hope is believing and expecting that something is going to happen or change for the best, and believing in your future even though it has yet to be written. Do you believe that today could be the day everything changes for the better? Are you a hopeful person? What are you hopeful for and how can you help that hope become reality?

_____

_____

_____

Humility: the act of seeing yourself as not being above others. Being modest and equal to others. Not displaying arrogance and pride. Are you a humble person? Are there areas you can improve on?

_____

_____

_____

Integrity: the act of being true to yourself and being honest; having strong moral principles, and extending these to others. Are you a man or woman of integrity? If not, what must be changed to make it so that you are?

_____

_____

_____

Imagination: the act of being imaginative is finding new and interesting ideas and having or showing creativity. Not allowing yourself to fall into the "ordinary." Not always settling for rationalism. Thinking outside the box and having fun doing it. Do you have a good imagination? What are the benefits associated in having a great imagination?

_____

_____

_____

Joyfulness: the act of feeling, causing or showing great happiness and finding it within yourself. Finding hope, peace and love as opposed to a disconnect and suffering. Are you a joyful person? Is your life filled with joy? How can you add joy to your life right now?

_____

_____

_____

Kindness: the act of being thoughtful, caring and compassionate as opposed to being cruel and selfish. When was the last time you acted kindly toward another? Have you "paid it forward" lately?

_____

_____

_____

Love: the act of feeling a strong and constant affection for someone else. Possessing a caring and selfless attitude toward others; exercising forgiveness and unity. Why not list who you love and WHY you love them? Then, go tell them so!

_____

_____

_____

Loyalty: the act of being faithful, honest and trustworthy as opposed to having a nature that betrays others or an organization, thought or principle. Are you loyal? If you lack in this area, where exactly and why? What can you do to become more loyal?

_____

_____

_____

Moderation: the act of being reasonable and avoiding behavior, speech and anything else that is extreme or that goes beyond what is normal and acceptable. Exercising diligence and responsibility as opposed to being obsessive and overindulgent. Do you live a life of moderation or do you overindulge in some areas? What do you overindulge in and what can you do to bring yourself back on track?

_____

_____

_____

Modesty: that act of not being too proud or cocky about yourself or your abilities. Showing humility when appropriate as opposed to pushing self-confidence in everybody's face. Are you a modest person? Are you pushy or cocky? If so, in what areas and how can you address that area of your life to self-improve?

_____

_____

_____

Optimism: the act of showing hope and trust in the future. Expecting that good things can happen. Seeing the glass as half-full as opposed to seeing it as half-empty. Exercising hopefulness and joyfulness as opposed to pessimism. List a few things you're optimistic about and if you can't, why can't you? What chatter needs to change in your mind to help you become more optimistic?

_____

_____

_____

Orderliness: the act of finding ways to arrange and organize your life in a logical and regular way. Being organized as opposed to living in chaos. How organized are you? What needs to be addressed here and list the ways you'll go about addressing them. Then do it.

_____

_____

_____

Passion: the act of having, showing and expressing intense emotions and desire in or for something, someone and myself. Showing enthusiasm and purposefulness as opposed to indifference. Are you passionate about your life? List a few things you're passionate about and a few things you're not passionate about. How can you become more passionate about the things you've go on your "I'm not passionate about . . . " list?

_____

_____

_____

Patience: the act of waiting for a long period of time without becoming annoyed or upset. Being determined and at peace with waiting. Working toward what you're focused on without expecting results immediately. Exercising patience with yourself and with others. How patient are you? Do you need to become more patient in some areas of your life? Is there something you can do to help things along? And if not, why are you fretting over something you may have no control over?

_____

_____

_____

Peace: the act of finding your state of tranquility and quietness. Express love, serenity and unity as opposed to anger and cruelty. Are you a peaceful person and surround yourself with like-minded peaceful people? If not, what steps can you take to bring about more peace and harmony in your life?

_____

_____

_____

Perseverance: the act of remaining focused and on track with your efforts to complete or achieve something despite whatever difficulties, failures or opposition is in your way. Being truly committed, determined and resilient. Abandoning laziness. How determined to succeed are you? Are you willing to go the distance? Are you willing to put the effort into it? What can you do to stay committed and keep moving forward?

_____

_____

_____

Preparedness: the act of being ready. Organizing yourself and taking pride in excellence and orderliness. Getting rid of complacency. Are you ready? Are you organized? What do you need to get ready?

_____

_____

_____

Purposefulness: the act of setting goals for yourself and visualizing them and following this up by taking whatever action necessary to achieve it. Having intent in life and being creative, committed and joyful with it. Do you set realistic goals for yourself? Does your life have purpose? Are you committed and focused? List your goals and how you'll go about reaching them. Then do it. Start today. You'll be glad you did this time next year.

_____

_____

_____

Reliability: the act of being dependable. Answering to others in a way that doesn't undermine you or your values. Selecting integrity and loyalty as opposed to untrustworthiness. Keeping your promises, appointments and commitments without falling behind. Can you be counted on? Do you keep your promises? List a few you've kept and ones you haven't—if you haven't. Then examine why you didn't and how that made the recipient of the promise feel. Can you make up for it? Be that reliable person and make no further excuses for not being him/her.

_____

_____

_____

Respect: the act of giving particular attention that is due to some-one or something. Exercising dignity and reverence as opposed to inconsideration. Do you respect others? Do you respect yourself? If you answered "no" to any of those two questions, why aren't you? What needs to change?

_____

_____

_____

Responsibility: the act of being responsible as in moral, legal and mental accountability. Being courteous, tactful and trustworthy as opposed to exercising selfishness. Taking accountability for your own actions. Do you take responsibility for yourself—for your actions? Are you a responsible individual? If not, what will you do to become more responsible?

_____

_____

_____

Self-discipline: the act of being committed and determined to reg-ulate yourself for the sake of improvement. Remaining focused and on task. Are you self-disciplined? Do you stay on task and keep your eyes and heart focused on what you want? What needs to improve in this area, if anything?

_____

_____

_____

Sincerity: the act of being free from pretence or deceit; proceeding from genuine feelings, honest and authentic. How genuine, authentic and sincere are you? And if you're not, what needs to change and how will you go about bringing this change?

_____

_____

_____

Tactfulness: the act of having a strong moral sense of what to say and do for the purpose of maintaining good relations with others and avoid offensiveness. Exercising graciousness and responsibility for the things that you say and do. How tactful are you? Do you need to improve in this area and if so, where specifically? How will you accomplish this?

_____

_____

_____

Temperate: the act of exercising a habitual moderation in your indulgences, appetites and attitude. Adhering to moderation as opposed to excessiveness. What, if anything, needs to be addressed here and how do you plan to do it?

_____

_____

_____

Thankfulness: the act of exercising a spirit of gratitude and being conscious of the benefits that you receive and have. Did you express your thankfulness today to God, the Universe or simply to life in general for the good fortunes you have? How about to others for what they have done, are doing or about to do? Take time to thank yourself for the good you do for yourself as well.

_____

_____

_____

Tolerance: the act of having capacity to endure pain or hardship. Exercising sympathy and understanding for beliefs and practices that may differ or conflict with your own. Being patient and tenacious as opposed to remaining narrow-minded. Are you a tolerant person or do you need to become more so? What areas need to be addressed here and what's keeping you?

_____

_____

_____

Trust: the act of having assured reliance on the character, ability, strength or truth of someone or something. Being loyal and respectful as opposed to being doubtful or skeptic. Having a firm belief in the reliability, truth, ability, or strength of someone or something. Are you a trusting person? Are you trustworthy? If you answered "no," what needs to be addressed here?

_____

_____

_____

Truthfulness: the act of telling and being disposed to tell it like it is; being honest and trustworthy as opposed to being corrupt and deceitful. Do you tell it like it is? Are you a person of your word? Do you say what you mean and mean what you say?

_____

_____

_____

Understanding: the act of exercising the ability to try to understand the opinion or feelings of others while making adjustments for differences you may have. Understanding that you don't have to agree, but making an effort to see and respect the opinions of others. How understanding are you? How open are you to others?

_____

_____

_____

Unity: the act of being joined to someone, a group or a purpose. Understanding that we are all part of the same universe and the same world and that you have a duty to live in harmony, love and peace as opposed to being on your own and lonely. Do you appreciate how connected we are to each other, to this world and to this universe? If not: why not? Jot a few ideas on how connected we are here ... you may be surprised just how similar and united we are.

_____

_____

_____

Wisdom: the act of being well read and knowledgeable. Seeking the advice of others who are more knowledgeable than yourself. Drawing from your past experiences and the lessons learned in order to make the right decisions today and say the right things. Do you exercise wisdom or are you quick to act, forgetting what life taught you in an earlier experience? How can the lessons of your past or that of others help you become wiser?

_____

_____

_____

This list of virtues can be used as an effective tool for self-examination to determine where your strengths and weaknesses lie and what questions you should be asking yourself to grow into the person you'd like to be. Asking yourself the right questions and examining where you are right now and what in your thinking, emotions, and behaviors is keeping you hostage, will allow you to return to reevaluate your strengths and weaknesses and come up with a plan and blueprint for change which will propel you forward to where you want to be.

EFT—The Emotional Freedom Technique

Compliments of David Gilbert, Integrative Therapist

While writing this book, my brother asked me if I had ever heard of the "Emotional Freedom Technique." I had not. He went on to tell me a bit about it; and I found it intriguing, especially since this book, *Hostage,* is about setting out the methods to free ourselves from intrusive thoughts and feelings, the very nucleus of the Emotional Freedom Technique. I'm an investigator, so I decided to visit my brother in Ottawa and to drop by to see David Gilbert, an "Emotional Freedom Technique" practitioner.

David has been a practitioner of this technique for several years and has himself experienced the benefits associated to this form of therapy. "Emotional Freedom Technique," or EFT as it is known, is a form of psychological acupressure, targeting the very same energy pathways in the body along which vital energy flows. It has been used in traditional acupuncture to treat physical and emotional ailments for over five thousand years, but without the invasiveness of needles. Instead, a simple exercise of tapping with the fingertips is used to input kinetic energy into specific areas on the head, chest and hand while focusing on the specific problem or stress you're experiencing—whether it be a traumatic event, an addiction, a pain or other such stress—AND combining your focus and tapping with the repetition of positive affirmations.

This combination of tapping the energy meridians and repeating positive affirmations has been proven to effectively clear the "short-circuit" (the emotional block) from your body's bioenergy system, thereby restoring the mind and body's balance. David reports that it has been scientifically proven to work effectively at eliminating Post Traumatic Stress Disorder in many patients as well as a vast array of ailments in others, without the use of drugs and long, lengthy psychotherapy sessions. In some cases, patients only needed one or two one-on-one sessions to effectively treat what had afflicted them. Sleep can be improved as well as attitude and countless other stresses relieved and/or eliminated.

I was so interested in this technique, I asked David if he would contribute a chapter to my book. He agreed; and, instead of retelling what David had to say, I give you his own words instead, in the following:

Coming Back from Pain

EFT otherwise known as Emotional Freedom Techniques or "Tapping" has been a powerful tool for healing mental, emotional and often physical pain for tens of thousands worldwide. Recently a team of EFT practitioners worked in the Philippines after a devastating typhoon. Thousands were relieved of the recurrent retraumatization every time the wind picked up. Emotional Freedom Techniques have been enthusiastically embraced by such well-known health proponents as Dr. Oz, Dr. Mercola, and Deepak Chopra, MD, among many others. As time goes on, more and more studies are being conducted and published in the medical literature.

What is EFT? EFT is a technique to allow the conscious and unconscious mind to communicate in a safe environment using simple acupressure points and cognitive techniques. These allow practitioners and clients to work together to remove the negative emotional burden from thoughts and memories. At the same time, the clients should be learning to use these tools on an ongoing basis on their own. EFT becomes a part of his/her daily hygiene; both when something in particular crops up, and as a daily habit to continue processing the backlog of not fully integrated negative life experiences.

Interestingly, when researchers connected EFT practitioners and their clients up to EEGs to record their brain waves, they found that once well into the session, both displayed the brain activity typical of a meditating monk who has spent most of his life honing his skills. Although both practitioner and client are wide awake, they are also in a deep meditative state. This allows for a unique and tremendously effective two-way dialogue between the subconscious and the conscious mind while the sequential use of special acupressure points "bleeds" away the emotional charge around traumatic or painful memories and associated emotions.

Why Is This Important?

No one gets through life unscathed. The slings and arrows of outrageous fate sting us all at times; and everyone has differing capabilities to bounce back unharmed. In an ideal world, we learn whatever lesson is necessary, the memory is retained, and the emotional and physical pain are let go. We're designed to remember that something hurt physically and/or emotionally. That accumulation of experiences helps us successfully navigate life and avoid repeatedly getting burned. We're not designed to remember the actual physical or emotional pain. If we did, women wouldn't have more than one child; or, once having had their heart broken, no one would try again.

A scenario everyone can relate to is stubbing your shoeless baby toe. Boom!!! go your emotions. You're shocked, mad at the furniture, mad at yourself; and, for good measure, irritated with anyone else nearby. The logical part of your brain then goes . . . "dang that hurt. Keep your baby toes away from the furniture when you're in bare feet." The energy of that surge of shock and anger is processed and dissipated while the memory remains. When those negative experiences, memories and emotions are not processed completely and are instead internalized, things start to go very wrong.

An excellent example of this is the tagging of polar bears as part of conservation efforts. Wildlife biologists have learned that when chasing down and tranquilizing a polar bear from the air, they must observe the animal as it begins to awake. If it looks as though it's having a fit—but when observed closely, you see that the legs are trying to run—the polar bear will get up, shake itself and continue to live a happy polar bear life. If this fails to happen, the animal will not continue to thrive. The fight or flight reflex has instead been internalized and creates long-term biological stress and biochemical havoc. When big "T" and little "t" traumas have not been fully processed and the emotional component released, the memories are stored in both the mind and body—often with profoundly harmful effects from that point on.

I work with clients step by step—working backward defusing troublesome memories and the emotions attached to them. It's amazing how frequently they will at some point have an often intense bodily sensation related to that memory or experience. Once these body memories appear, we're able to quickly defuse their power in very short order. Clients typically report that the unpleasant or painful sensations have lost their grip and have entirely disappeared. Then we're free to continue on our path of healing.

This can sound a little intimidating, but it's important to remember that the subconscious is working to protect us. These buried sensations and memories are not released to the conscious mind until enough of the baggage has been sorted and properly filed away that the subconscious mind feels safe to let them into the light of day.

To view videos and articles on the personal use of EFT and specific techniques for better responses, see: www.EcoSysHolisticWellnessCenter.com. I do suggest having at least a few sessions with a qualified and experienced EFT practitioner with whom you easily connect and feel safe. If you cannot locate someone you feel comfortable with locally, I work very effectively with clients by telephone, or computer cam and microphone.

For those who have never worked with a skilled EFT practitioner who is a good fit, this can seem like some bizarre hocus-pocus. How could simply tapping on your body have powerful and long-term beneficial effects on mental, emotional, and physical pain? The whole thing seems ridiculous.

I must admit I felt the same way until back in 2005 when I couldn't get past the loss of a woman I had loved with my whole heart a couple of years earlier. I'd spent far too long torn to pieces by this;

including the loss of my singing voice. Not only could I not perform, it was as though all desire and skill had been surgically removed without a trace. Although intellectually I found it odd that a lifetime of performance pleasure could just disappear, emotionally, that part of me which had been so intimately connected with this woman was just gone.

I was at that time already working in holistic health and so had heard rumors and had seen a few articles about this EFT technique in the literature. I hadn't paid much attention to it until then and was highly skeptical, but also sick and tired of suffering. I did remember listening to a lecture many years earlier in which a researcher had become curious about acupuncture and decided to determine, once and for all, whether there were areas of the human body with different intensities of electrical fields. Low and behold, it turned out there were numerous nexi which matched up with the five thousand year-old acupuncture charts. Who knew?

Armed with this very basic information and having had more than enough of feeling heartsick, I arranged for an EFT session with a trauma specialist skilled in these techniques. Although a single one-hour session did not entirely eradicate my emotional distress, the degree of relief was profound. I quickly realized it was important that I become trained and skilled in these techniques; both for my own sake and for the well-being of my clients. And so, I became certified for EFT in 2006; and the more I learn through the years of experience and continuing education, the more I stand in awe of its power and potential to heal.

The funny thing is that for many clients, after a successful session, the troublesome memory or experience we've worked on has lost its grip so completely that they literally cannot find the pain anymore. They have a hard time believing it had really been such an issue until experiencing EFT. We're not using talk therapy to drag memories out kicking and screaming. We're simply taking the issue at the top of the pile and removing its power so the subconscious feels safe in offering up the next piece.

Those clients I've worked with using EFT have consistently observed how powerful and notably painless this technique has been for them. One example is a mental health professional who, having come to me with anxiety, stress, and hyper-irritability, made a wonderful comment. At the end of her second session she said, "I was afraid to come to see you. I've been in therapy for much of my life and it's been so painful. But this didn't hurt. It just gently lifted off the pieces one by one and took away their power."

Our view of the world, our place in it, and our sense of safety are always colored by what the subconscious mind believes to be true. Remember, the subconscious wants to keep us safe. The problem is that from birth to the present, people are continuously writing on the interior walls of our heads. These form the subconscious programming which influences every aspect of our thoughts and actions.

Unfortunately, the more recent knowledge and opinions formed by our big prefrontal cortex, the logical part of our brain, are often seriously at odds with the subconscious beliefs; and the subconscious always wins. Sadly, might doesn't make right. Often our subconscious beliefs are either entirely erroneous or no longer fit our current reality. As Samuel Clemens is reported to have said: "It's not what you don't know that'll kill you. It's what you do know that 'taint necessarily so."

Clients are often curious as to why we keep concentrating on the negative. The answer is that positive affirmations are a bit like putting latex paint on an oil-based wall. If you don't prepare the wall first, the paint doesn't stick very well. If your conscious mind is saying, "I'm thin, I'm happy, I'm successful, attractive . . . " or any of a thousand affirmations, but your subconscious is saying, "I don't think so . . . "—guess who wins?

Once that negative, faulty, or no longer relevant subconscious programming has been safely disarmed by removing all the negative charge, then, and only then, can we accept affirmations and positive feedback from our big forebrains as the healthy well-integrated beings we were meant to be.

I strongly encourage those dealing with anxiety, phobias, guilt, stress, repeated self-sabotage, burn-out, or PTSD, etc. to find a qualified and experienced EFT practitioner to work with. Remember, not every client and practitioner is a good fit. If you find you're not able to feel safe and secure with one practitioner, discuss it with him/her. If that's not successful, try another on for size.

Those with questions may contact David Gilbert directly at david@david-gilbert.com with EFT questions in the subject line.

Do It Yourself EFT

Although EFT therapists have spent years honing their craft and continuing education to maintain their qualifications, basic EFT can often be done at home on your own to good effect. It may not be as efficient or quick but you can do it any time anywhere at no cost.

Find a quiet place and can get comfortable with a lined pad of paper. Relax, take a deep breath in and out; then ask yourself what is the issue, feeling or memory that is at the top of the pile. Be as specific as possible and write it down along with a number from 0–10 to represent how powerful the "emotional charge" on that thought, feeling, or memory is. If you're feeling silly, nervous or are experiencing resistance to getting started, use that as the issue on the top of the pile.

Basic setup: Using the tips of your pointer and middle fingers, begin to tap on the karate chop point on the side of the opposite hand while repeating three times: "Even though I have this issue _____ I'm learning to deeply and completely love and accept myself." Remember to be specific.

Once this is done, pick one or two words which represent the particular specific issue or part of the issue and continue to repeat it as you go through the tapping points. Tap 8–10 times on each of the following points:

The crown of your head. Think of a line running across the top of your head between your ears and tap on the midpoint of that line.

1. The inside end of your eyebrows.

2. The outside edge of your eyebrows.

3. On the midpoint on the crest of the ridge of bone under your eyes.

4. Upper lip under your nose.

5. In the midpoint just below your lower lip.

6. Where your neck joins with your chest, you will feel two knobs of bone. Tap just below these on the flat breast bones.

7. If dealing with feelings of guilt or self-recrimination use this point. For men it is about two inches directly below the nipples. For women it is the same point, but just below where the breast rises from the chest wall (lower bra line). This is not part of the basic recipe but is useful for this specific issue. If there are no feelings of guilt etc. this point can be skipped.

8. The side of the chest wall about the same height as the nipples or for women, on the side of the chest in the middle of the bra strap area.

9. Tap the side of the thumb on the palm side between the knuckle and the end of the thumb.

10. Holding the hand with the thumb pointing up, tap on the same point between the knuckle and end of the pointer, middle and baby fingers. This is the upper side of each finger. The ring finger is skipped because there is no effective acupressure point there.

This all seems complicated but in reality it quickly becomes automatic. Where there's room on the points you can use both hands at once.

Once that round is finished, take a deep breath in and out. Notice if there are any particular sensations arising in your body and again write down the number which now represents the intensity of the emotional charge attached to that specific issue. If the emotional charge is not yet down to "0," record the new number which may be lower, higher or the same. There is no right or wrong about what happens. Then go back to the karate chop point repeating: "Even though I have this remaining _____, I'm learning to deeply and completely love and accept myself." Continue rounds until the charge is near or at "0."

As the first thought or memory loses its power, in most cases another thought, memory, or emotion will arise to take its place. This is normal and exactly what you're looking for. Continue the process, recording your issues and their accompanying intensity numbers as you go. Ideally you're making the statements aloud; but if you're in a situation where that's not practical, making the statements forcefully in your head is the next best thing and also works well.

Memories are stored in the body as well as in the mind. If you reach the point where body memories or sensations are becoming uncomfortable or intrusive, then address them as—"Even though I have this body memory/pain/sensation—I'm learning to deeply and completely love and accept myself," etc. Again remember to document your intensity numbers and the issues to which they're attached.

Negative memories and/or emotions can have many aspects. If EFT has been effective, but when viewed from a different situation or perspective, some symptoms return, simply use the same technique on this aspect. Sometimes there is no need for repeating the process; other experiences may require revisiting from time to time. This does not in any way indicate that EFT has not actually been effective earlier; it's just different aspects.

Now, to respond to a few questions which may arise:

Q: What if I've done everything you've said but I'm not getting anywhere?

A: The following neurological exercises will often open the door to progress and can be done at any time.

Start tapping in the hollow in the back of your hand between the tendons of the baby and ring finger just below the fingers. While continuing to tap, do the following: eyes closed, eyes wide open, while keeping your head still, roll your eyes in a big circle to the right, then the left, hum a line of a simple song such as Happy Birthday (if it has no negative connotations), count to five, then sing another line of a song. Once you've done this, return to the previous program.

Q: What if the feelings or memories become too intense?

A: Just continue through rounds of tapping without concentrating on any particular issues or memories until you feel comfortably able to continue with specifics again.

Q: How long should I do this each time?

A: I give one hour sessions; but you can easily fit quite brief sessions into your schedule as often as you have time for. I wouldn't normally go for more than an hour or so at a time as fatigue will set in and you'll just be spinning your wheels.

Q: I can't find a local EFT therapist I feel comfortable with. Can I work with you?

A: Yes. I can work effectively either over the phone or ideally with computer cams and microphones so we can see each other as well.

Q: What if I don't know what's bothering me?

A: Try: "Even though I don't yet understand what's bothering me, I'm learning to deeply and completely love and accept myself."

A Different Approach

Another tool I've found to be very powerful for anxiety, depression, PTSD, and insomnia is the Equilib Nutrient/enzyme Protocol; a sophisticated compilation of amino acids, amino acid chelated minerals, metabolic support plant nutrients and vitamins in highly bioavailable forms and appropriate ratios and volumes. It's highly synergistic with EFT and almost always compatible with prescription medication.

For those who participate in the free symptom and monitoring program, they may be able to access a 100% return of material costs if compliant participants don't show substantial improvements over and above any current medications and/or other programs. Make certain you specifically ask to be included in the response warranty program if you contact them. It was designed for physicians to be able to use at their discretion; but if requested, I expect they'll allow participation. (www.EvinceNaturals.com)

It seems that when the body drops below a critical point of any of the building blocks to the neurotransmitters, metalo-enzymes, hormones and all the rest of the chemicals which control our functioning, a whole lot of things start to go wrong physically, mentally and emotionally—including depression and anxiety.

American and Canadian military personnel and veterans with anxiety disorders or PTSD may be able to enroll in their program for at least eight weeks at no cost.

In my own case, the Equilib Nutrient/enzyme Protocol was highly effective for anxiety and insomnia triggered by some very challenging life events. Interestingly, a number of other seemingly unrelated troublesome health issues also cleared up within a month or two of starting. These included chronic heartburn, painful pelvic cramps, IBS, constipation, and perhaps most surprisingly, severe carbohydrate and sweets cravings. Prior to this program they were totally out of control. Once I started, I couldn't stop.

I continue to use both EFT and the Equilib Nutrient/enzyme Protocol because between them I get to remain a highly productive and happy member of society regardless of what life throws at me from time to time.

I wish you all joy in your journeying.

~ David Gilbert ~
September 2015

www.ecosysholisticwellnesscenter.com/
wellness@david-gilbert.com

Index

About the Author

For over three decades, **J Paul Nadeau** has studied the dynamics of achievement and self-worth. As a decorated former police detective and Hostage Negotiator with more than 30 years of policing experience, he amassed considerable expertise in hostage and crisis negotiations, international peacekeeping and homicide, and sexual assault/child abuse investigations.

He has received several noteworthy awards, including recognition by the United Nation's International Peacekeeping Branch. In 2005, he successfully negotiated the peaceful arrest of a suspected terrorist who had made threats aboard an Air France 747.

Today, he is an admired international instructor, major news consultant, lecturer and motivational speaker. He was a featured TEDx Toronto speaker in 2015 and received a standing ovation for his talk on "finding humanity in terrorism." His lectures on domestic violence and the correlation between Stockholm syndrome and emotional and physical abuse in relationships has helped police services and women's groups alike better understand "domestic relationship terrorism." Paul is a thought leader. *Hostage to Myself* is his first book.

Made in the USA
Charleston, SC
11 January 2016